FROM THE COUNTER
to the
BOTTOM LINE

FROM THE COUNTER
to the
BOTTOM LINE

Carl Warren
and
Merl K. Miller

dilithium Press
Portland, Oregon

ISBN: 0-918398-11-8

Library of Congress catalog card number: 79-52263

Printed in the United States of America.

dilithium Press
P.O. Box 92
Forest Grove, Oregon 97116

For

My Dad

And

A Wonderful Character Called Ace

CDW

For

My Dad

And

Another Character Named Ace

MKM

ACKNOWLEDGMENTS

This book would never have been started or completed without the help of my wife Anne and the understanding of my daughter Tami. A great deal of thanks also goes to Bob Jones, the publisher of *Interface Age* magazine and my boss, who shared his knowledge of small business with me and allowed me the use of his now-famous survey questions for small businessmen.

Besides these apparent helpers, much credit goes to John Solensten and John Mignot, who gave me encouragement and who are responsible for shaping my writing ability.

Finally, it is important to thank the many businessmen around the country who took the time to answer my many questions, as well as Tom Bailey and several other accountants, who helped with the hard questions. Of course, the Torrance Public Library, which provided the resources necessary to finish the work, must be included in the list.

CDW

Sometimes the people behind the scenes never receive credit for what they do. I would like to thank my partner, Richard Abel, for his help and encouragement and my assistant, Carol Jendresen, for help, especially in typing the manuscript. Both Carl and I would like to extend a special thanks to David Heath for his excellent copy editing. Last but most important, I would like to thank my wife Patti. Words cannot adequately describe her selfless contribution. As production manager for dilithium Press, she is responsible for all the books we publish, including this one.

MKM

PREFACE

This book is designed to show business men how to implement the microcomputer in the work-a-day world. It also demonstrates what is needed in an accounting package and what each system within the package does. Whether you are starting out on a new venture or you are an established businessman anxious to automate your business, we will guide you through the web of accounting techniques as they apply to the small computer system.

Even if you are on a small budget and can afford only the least expensive system on the market, we will provide useful accounting techniques and programs that can be used to your benefit. For the businessman who is able to afford a complete, integrated system, this book is a must since it presents a complete package that covers every area from the counter transaction to figuring the bottom line profit margin.

For manufacturers and sellers of small systems concerned with educating intended users, this book is an invaluable tool; it presents valuable information regarding system requirements and operations.

Chapter One opens with a discussion of the purpose and scope of the book. It includes a discussion of what a computerized business system is and provides an overview of the flow of data and how the various aspects of the system relate.

In this chapter, the intended user of the book is identified and the exact benefits of computerized accounting, from the ability to plan to the ease of preparation of financial statements, are discussed. Finally, we show you how the computer allows you to develop procedures, gauge performance and identify potential problem areas in time to initiate corrective action.

Chapter Two is provided to help you understand the accounting package and automation in general. In this chapter a scenario of a typical small business is presented, based on a survey of needs and problems associated with running a business.

Chapter Three introduces the accounting package. A block diagram of the entire system is presented, along with a description of the purpose of each subsystem and its interaction with the general ledger package. We also discuss how the inputs and outputs are handled. The subsystems and general ledger are discussed in general from an accounting point of view. We present the ancillary packages, planning and deposit, in the same detail, with descriptions of their functional purpose and types of data required to use them.

Chapter Four deals with application implementation. We discuss how to convert from a manual to an automated system and the document flow for system input.

The introduction of the accounting package follows in Chapter Five. The format for the procedure chapters is discussed, and the purpose of the SYSTEM MENU is shown.

Chapter Six covers the inventory and purchasing aspect of automated accounting. Logic flow, program makeup and sections of the program are presented. We also discuss how management can make use of the data generated by this program.

Billing, probably the most time-consuming task involved in running a small business, is presented in Chapter Seven. The same method of presentation used for inventory is employed in presenting this aspect of automation.

Chapter Eight ties directly into billing, showing the method used for keeping track of accounts receivable. The chapter concludes with a brief discussion of how management can use the information available.

Chapter Nine is one of the major subsystems of the accounting package, Accounts Payable. This chapter covers the method of keeping track of what is owed to whom, along with a discussion of how management can make use of the information.

The last key system is the general ledger. This is discussed in Chapter Ten in much the same manner as the subsystems, but with a discussion of how the subsystems and general ledger integrate. In fact, we show how the bottom line is generated. Also, we give the user the ability to format financial statements.

Chapter Eleven presents two of the more exciting programs: planning and deposit. We present these programs in the same

general format as that used for the subsystems. We also discuss
the useful applications of the planning program and how
management can make the best use of it.

The deposit program is what we refer to as an ancillary
routine, meaning that we feel that if you can use what it does,
fantastic; if not, its omission does not affect the rest of the accounting package. We do, however, feel that if a small
businessman automates the bookkeeping, the cash drawer
should be included.

Chapters Five through Eleven are intended to be used as a
procedure manual for the accounting system. These chapters
are set up to guide you through each "step" of the application.
At the end of each chapter, we have provided a comprehensive
guide to error responses. The error response guide also points
out the necessary procedure for recovering from the error.

The programs presented in this book were written in the
BASIC language, since it is popular and easy to understand. We
make no claim that our system will solve all of your problems.
Our main concern is that we have made available an accounting
package that is easily understood and can be implemented with
minimal effort.

At the end of the book, we have included a glossary of terms
that are either used in the book or necessary to understanding
some concept in the book. Throughout the book we have
marked new terms with an asterisk (*) as they are introduced.
Appendix A presents some of the general flowcharts used in the
CTBL package along with a discussion on tape techniques and
special MECA tape handling functions.

The CTBL account package described in this book is currently being developed for the MECA tape system and Radio
Shack TRS-80. Both will be available from dilithium Press.

TABLE OF CONTENTS

Contents

Contents   xvii

INTRODUCTION

The commercial availability of the minicomputer since 1961 and the microprocessor some 12 years later has had profound effects on the course of computer technology in general and of data processing in particular. The growth of personal computer technology has changed the computer market entirely. No longer is the computer restricted to large companies; it has found its way into thousands of eager hobbyists' homes and, recently, into the small business environment.

However, the most significant aspect of this growth of the personal computer is the lack of application-oriented software. Little time has been spent by hardware and software designers to fill this gap. Software for the so-called personal computer has, until now, consisted primarily of games, mathematics, and text editing routines. This is not to say that the application problem has been ignored. As you will see from reading this book, useful accounting applications have been developed using the material at hand.

Applications program design for the personal computer must be viewed from a systematic, top-down approach. That is, emphasis is on the broad aspects of an application, rather than on the restrictions of the language being used. Even though we have chosen the BASIC language for the applications presented in this book, we have investigated every aspect of small business accounting. As a result, we have written programs within the scope of both small business accounting and the restrictions of the BASIC language.

A small system approach to computerized accounting offers an important benefit for the personal computer user. Now the small computer is no longer a toy, but a useful tool. For a relatively small outlay, the small businessman can use this type of system to perform the mundane tasks of inventory control, billing and general accounting.

As you progress through this book, we hope that you will discover some of the important facets of automated accounting. We hope, too, that you will be able to employ our applications so as to increase profitability and avoid cash flow pitfalls.

Therefore, to all the owner-operator stores and young entrepreneurs, we dedicate our work.

Chapter One

SHOULD YOU AUTOMATE?

In this chapter, business computer systems are described, along with what they do. Also, accounting is explained in general, and automated accounting is described in specific terms. The hardware is presented in terms of what is generally required. The user is defined in terms of need. To help you better understand your needs, several guidelines are provided in the form of questionnaires. The concept of planning is presented as a summary to the chapter.

1.1 A COMPUTER BUSINESS SYSTEM

Computer systems are designed to do time-consuming tasks with speed and accuracy. Basically, a computer is task-oriented. It can perform one job at a time, with each job being made up of several, integral parts or small tasks. To be more general, computers can be, and are, used in all forms of business applications. We are exposed to computer business applications several times a day, from buying breakfast at the local restaurant to purchasing airplane tickets.

The logical question to ask is, "What is a computer business system?" A simple answer is that it is an automated method of handling inventory, billing, accounts receivable, accounts payable and payroll. Business systems also provide for a logical flow of bookkeeping and record updating.

Figure 1-1 is an example of the general makeup and flow of an automated system. However, in order to fully understand the concept of an automated system, some terms must be defined.

Accounting is the measurement of business activity. All functions that make up a business environment are tracked. An *ac-*

counting package is a collection of subsystems that are designed to provide meaningful measurement of each area of a general business activity. The accounting package detailed in this book contains the following subsystems designed to work with the general ledger:

- Inventory Control
- Accounts Receivable/Billing
- Accounts Payable
- Payroll

A *subsystem*, in automated accounting, represents a detailed list with a total that stands alone. The subsystem is, in fact, a stand-alone system that is designed to interact with other members of the overall system.

As shown in Figure 1-1, the accounting package is both a horizontal and a vertical system. Each major subsystem supplies data to feed the general ledger, while, at the same time, affecting other subsystems. For example, the inventory control subsystem horizontally affects the assets picture of the general ledger and, at the same time, affects the accounts payable subsystem. This, in turn, generates figures for the general ledger, under liabilities and equity, and produces the bottom line, or profit/loss picture. Thus, an accounting package is interactive—each part depending upon the other.

A *computerized business system* is defined as a collection of several small subsystems designated by task, working in such a manner as to provide stand-alone and integrated totals, representing business activity.

In Figure 1-1, the makeup of each of the subsystems as separate entities and how they interact can be seen. The first subsystem is inventory control. This system is really made of two smaller systems: purchasing and inventory. Together, they make up the *inventory control package*. From the diagram, it can be seen that inventory must be purchased, thus creating expenses that can be grouped under the heading, *Cost of Sales*. At the same time, the assumption is made that inventory is purchased to sell. This logically moves us into the accounts receivable/billing package.

The *accounts receivable/billing package* is a direct result of sales. Non-cash sales create a billing situation and generate accounts receivable. *Inventory* and *accounts receivables* grouped

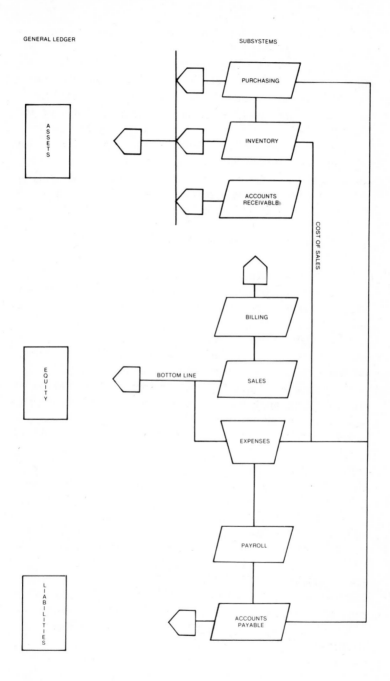

Figure 1-1 An automated accounting system

together become a major portion of current assets. Assets are shown on the general ledger.

The inventory was purchased and received, assets were acquired. You now owe somebody something and have *accounts payable*. Together, expenses, borrowing and the purchase of assets create *liabilities*, which is another major area of the general ledger.

When the amount of revenue coming in and the amount of expenses going out are calculated and set off against each other, the *bottom line* is created, which becomes a part of the equity of the company (either plus or minus). Admittedly, this is an oversimplification of an accounting package.

1.2   EVALUATING THE HARDWARE

When you evaluate a system, first determine the job to be performed and the scope of the need. Figure 1-2 is a representation of a typical microcomputer-based system, showing different system options. The bus* structure of existing microcomputers will allow you to use any or all of these devices. The available read/write memory* can be from 4K to 48K.* This range provides workspace for a variety of applications, large or small.

The microcomputer will give you a great deal of flexibility in structuring an application to meet your specific needs. The microcomputer allows greater mobility for the user, since the system is small enough to be moved around as needed and requires no special facilities. You can even continue to use existing forms. Easily interpreted outputs are available as either CRT* status or hardcopy* reports, again depending on your specific needs.

The accounting system in this book stays within the restrictions of the hardware and uses the programming language, BASIC. In a sense, the much larger minicomputer is emulated. The data is handled in a method that will give you the most meaningful information. Also, error messages,* sort routines* and save routines* are handled in a manner that can be incorporated on most microcomputer systems. The microcomputer is really restricted only by the amount of available peripherals and memory.

*Throughout this book, asterisks will be used to refer you to the Glossary.

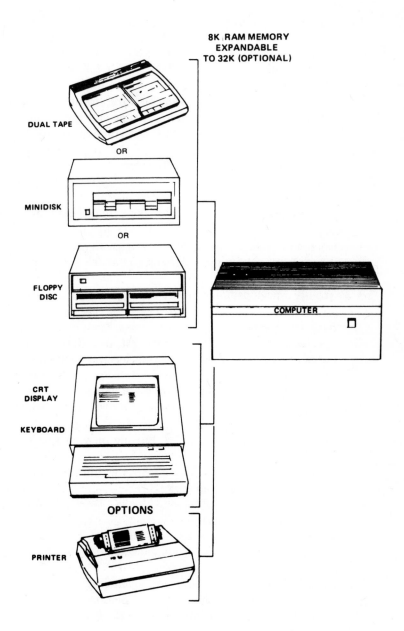

Figure 1-2 A typical microcomputer system

1.3   THE USER

In previous sections we briefly discussed the intended user of a small system accounting package. We are assuming that you are a businessman who is having trouble keeping track of inventory and determining what sells, what doesn't sell and why. Also, you are probably the type of person who has to spend a lot of time, after hours, bringing your books up to date.

You have decided that bookkeeping is time-consuming and you would like to consider automation. But you don't know if you can afford it. You might look for the following conditions when considering whether you should automate:

- Inventory is large or varied.
- Receivables consist of both over-the-counter cash and billing.
- Accounts payable are frequent or numerous.
- The general bookkeeping is difficult to handle within normal hours.
- Payroll is time-consuming and records updated manually.

Based on a review of your general business situation you can make a decision about automating. However, the decision can be somewhat difficult if the analysis of your business situation is not handled correctly. To assist you in this decision-making process we are providing the following questionnaires. These are designed to enhance the above guidelines and will allow for a systematic approach to automation.

1.4   INVENTORY

1. What are your product categories?
2. Are your products packaged individually? Bulk? If bulk, are they sold individually?
3. Are there pricing considerations for quantity?
4. How many new items are added or deleted per month?
   Average?   Maximum?
5. How many finished products are in inventory?
   Average?   Maximum?   Seasonal?
6. Do you have minimum/maximum levels maintained by item?
7. How is their cost tracked?

8. What percentage of damage occurs?
   Average?   Maximum?
9. How is this damage, with respect to inventory control, reconciled?
10. Are there any raw materials involved in your inventory?
11. Do you carry or sell any nonstandard products?
12. Do you ship substitutions?
13. In what mathematical form is inventory kept?
    Fractions?   Decimal?   Other?
14. Is inventory maintained by lot?
15. Do you have inventory transfers?
16. Are weight or volume measurements maintained in your inventory control?
17. Do you have a priority system in inventory to be moved?
18. How do you control the receipt of new material and incoming inspection?
19. How does the pricing structure change when price increases are passed on by manufacturers?
20. What reports are required?
    A. Price List
    B. Stock List
    C. Inventory Shortage Report
    D. Inventory Turnover Report
    E. Receipts and Adjustment Report
    F. Order Report
    G. Stock Depletion Report
    H. Back Order Fulfillment Report
    I. Other

1.5 ORDER ENTRY

1. What is your average number of orders per day?
2. What is the highest number you expect to ever enter per day?
3. How many "bill to" customers?   Active?   Inactive?
4. How many "ship to" addresses?   Active?   Inactive?
5. Average ratio "bill to"/"ship to"?
6. What is largest number of "ship to's" to any one "bill to"?
   Active?   Inactive?
7. How many line items per order?
8. Do you extend the orders?

9. How many types of customers do you service?
   A. Over-the-counter cash   retail
   B. Over-the-counter credit   retail
   C. Wholesale broker
   D. Wholesale distributor
   E. Special trade discount
   F. Consignment
   G. Commission sales
   H. Service sales
   I. Other
10. How are back orders processed?
    Priority   Amount   Cancelled
11. Do any accounts receive special treatment?
    Discounts   Prices   Shipping priority
12. How are your accounts tracked? Alphabetically? Numerically?
13. Do you check your accounts' credit?
14. Do you assign credit limits?
15. How are credit delinquencies treated?
16. How many prices established per item?
    Cost   Burdened   Wholesale   Retail
17. Should computer provide price information?
18. Should computer provide invoicing?
19. Should computer provide bill of lading?
20. Should computer provide shipping labels?
21. What is average number of shipping labels per order?
22. What is highest number of shipping labels required per order?   Active   Inactive
23. Are partial shipments allowed?
24. Do you ship direct or drop ship from other points?
25. How do you control cost/sell relationship?
26. What reports do you required?
    A. Daily/Weekly Sales
    B. Daily/Weekly Invoice
    C. Daily/Weekly Credit Hold
    D. Daily/Weekly Order Acknowledgment
    E. Cash Flow (Cash *vs.* Credit)
    F. Back Order Report
    G. Account Order Status
    H. Other

1.6 SALES ANALYSIS AND COMMISSIONS

1. How many salesmen?
2. Do you require a sales history?
3. Number of individual sales by salesman?
4. How is commission rate determined?
5. Are split commissions allowed?
6. How do you pay your commissions?
   A. Orders booked
   B. Shipment
   C. Receipt of customer payment
   D. Other
7. Does your sales analysis report show:
   A. Selling prices
   B. Costs
   C. Profit
   D. Other
8. What reports do you require?
   A. Salesman by Product Category
   B. Salesman by Territory
   C. Product by Customer
   D. Territory Sales by District, Area, Region
   E. Sales *vs.* Returns
   F. Commission Report by Salesman by Customer
   G. Other

1.7 ACCOUNTS PAYABLE

1. What are your average accounts payable by day?
   Week?   Month?
2. Number of vendors?   Average?   Maximum?
3. Do you use purchase orders?
4. Do you take advantage of fast payment discounts?
5. Number of purchase orders (if used)?
   Average?   Maximum?
6. How many lines per purchase order?
   Average?   Maximum?
7. Do you extend purchase order prices?
8. What is the average length of time from placing a purchase order to the time of delivery?

9. Are vendors' invoices checked against original purchase orders?
10. How are disbursements made? Daily? Weekly? Monthly? Other?
11. What other discounts are taken?
12. Are discounts taken on purchases or payments?
13. How do you select a priority of invoice payment?
14. How many checks do you disburse per month?
15. What reports do you require?
   A. Purchase Journal
   B. Purchase Order Priority
   C. Discount Priority
   D. Cash Requirements Report
   E. Vendor Activity Report
   F. Vendor List
   G. Check Register
   H. Prepayment Report
   I. Other

1.8 GENERAL LEDGER

1. How often do you require a financial report?
2. How many accounts do you have in your Chart of Accounts?
3. What is the frequency of updating your General Ledger?
4. What is your general ledger account number structure?
   A. Number of digits
   B. Major and subcode
   C. Other
5. What is the average number of transactions used to update the General Ledger in posting period?
6. Do you set income and expense amounts to zero (0) at the end of the year?
7. What is your fiscal year?
8. What reports are required?
   A. General Journal
   B. Detail Trial Balance
   C. Summary Trial Balance
   D. Supporting Schedules
   E. Profit and Loss Statements
   F. Balance Sheets

G. Special Reports
H. Year-End Journal
I. Chart of Accounts Listing
J. Capital Statement
K. Consolidated Statements
L. Other

1.9 PAYROLL

1. How many employees?
2. How many employees do you expect to hire or lay off in the next 12 months?
3. What is the average employee turnover time?
4. Are your employees salaried or hourly or both?
5. Do you have a profit-sharing plan?
6. Do you offer incentive programs?
7. Do you pay daily? Weekly? Bi-monthly? Monthly?
8. Do you offer overtime, vacation or sick pay?
9. Do your salesmen work on straight, draw or a combination of salary/commission?
10. Do you take deductions from commissions?
11. Do you offer loans or advances?
12. Do you offer a stock purchase plan, pension or long-term savings programs?
13. How do you handle federal, state and local withholding taxes?
14. What reports do you require?
    A. Paychecks
    B. Payroll Register
    C. Deduction Reports
    D. W-2 Forms
    E. Form 941A
    F. Quarterly Earnings Report
    G. Employee Master List
    I. Other

The worst thing that the small business owner can do is purchase a computer and the necessary software packages thinking it will automatically solve every problem. *It will not.* It will, however, help you pinpoint the areas that need to be watched and help you manage these problems.

1.10   BENEFITS OF SMALL SYSTEM AUTOMATION

A microcomputer system can provide the small business with the benefits of a computerized accounting system and allow it to use many of the high-level business techniques normally affordable only by large companies in handling day-to-day business.

Let's look at exactly what the benefits are. First, by using an automated system you can process information fast enough to make projections and plans that are necessary to the well-being of your business. In addition, a small system will make billing a lot easier. Billing is usually one of the more tiresome functions. It takes a great deal of time to produce the bill, book the receivables and hand age the account. The automated system is designed to provide a data base for billing, calculate dates for receivable aging and reduce the work load.

After automating billing and receivables, the next item is updating the receivables ledger and keeping track of these necessary items. All of this is done by the computer with speed and accuracy.

Another important aspect of the automated system is that it provides ease in preparing financial statements. The statement can be formatted in any row/column structure required.

To review, the benefits of an automated system are:

- Ability to plan
- Automated billing/accounts receivable
- Automated accounts receivable ledger
- Automated payroll*
- Speed and accuracy
- Ease in preparation of financial statements

One last word on accuracy—the computer is dumb. It will respond only to what is put into it. The old saying, "Garbage in, garbage out," holds very true. Error messages are provided in all computer systems to help guide the user, but you must be willing to take the time to learn the capabilities and needs of the system if you want to achieve the greatest benefits.

There is still another major benefit obtained from using the automated system: it will help minimize small business failures. Many small businesses fail due to lack of understanding of what is happening and why it's happening. They lack sufficient information to analyze and prevent problems. This is not to say that the computer is going to analyze volumes of data and make the necessary decisions, nor that it will create some wonderful idea that will save an already dying company, but it will help you manage better.

Let's look at what the automated system will do—or, more correctly, what it will provide—to help prevent financial disaster. The automated system will provide information regarding such areas as inventory—reorder points indicated, slow and fast movers pinpointed—and accounts receivable aged to show who is late. The system provides reports that identify a profit or loss mode and what is causing either mode.

Automation means an overall improvement in the handling of business bookkeeping. The use of the microcomputer means flexibility, cost effectiveness and the ability to use large-scale methods on small-scale machines.

The information available from an automated accounting system will provide you with an opportunity to measure the performance of your company based on whatever factors you feel are important. Variance analysis can be used to determine how your planned performance compares with your actual performance.

As stated earlier, many businesses fail because management had no idea the companies were in trouble until it was too late. The automated system will help you identify potential problem areas in time to initiate corrective action. For instance, let's look at *cash flow*. This is, in the simplest terms, the timing of cash going out compared to the timing of cash coming in. For a new business, this can be a major problem until a clientele is established and setup costs are paid off. Therefore, it is extremely important to analyze cash flow and prevent cash shortage situations.

Inventory maintenance is another area where a small company can get into trouble. By establishing which items are the better sellers and which are the most profitable, inventory levels can be maintained that provide the greatest yield.

If you watch cash flow and inventory trends and make wise decisions based on this information, you can have a very positive effect on the profit margin of your company. The computer doesn't do this—your management decisions will.

An important point is that the computer is not a savior; it is a tool and must be viewed as such. If the computer makes more work for management, it is not valuable. If it causes a major cash flow problem, it isn't needed. An automated system is only as good as you want it to be.

For several years, the cost of electronic data processing has made it untouchable for the small businessman. With the use of the techniques briefly described in this chapter (and fully explored later on) you should be able to see total EDP benefits in a microcomputer environment.

Chapter Two

SCENARIO OF A TYPICAL SMALL BUSINESS

This chapter ties the entire book together by presenting the story of the Jack Wilhoite Hardware Company—a mythical business created for this chapter. Some typical problems faced by a small owner/operator-type store are discussed, as well as the solutions provided by automation. The chapter is meant as a guideline for businessmen who are considering the possibility of automation.

2.1 INTRODUCTION

The following story is about the Jack Wilhoite Hardware Company in River Falls, Iowa. The story is fictitious and is based on the authors' study of several types of small businesses over the past two years.

This scenario is meant to be informative to those readers planning to go into business and instructive to those businessmen who plan to automate at some point in the future. Any resemblance of any character in this story to any person, living or dead, is purely coincidental. Only the scope of the scenario is meant to be of a factual nature.

2.2 BACKGROUND

River Falls was a quiet little town nestled somewhere between Des Moines and Cedar Falls, Iowa. The town was medium-size, about 30,000 inhabitants. It was generally a good place to do business and raise a family. Nothing much had changed in all the years Jack Wilhoite had lived in River Falls. Oh sure, a few more people had moved in since his childhood and some shopping centers had gone in, but the town was the same old town—clean and moderately paced.

Jack and his family had lived in River Falls all of his 35 years. His father and mother had moved to River Falls from the grime of the big cities some 40 years before and found a place to go into business and raise their family. Yes, 40 years earlier they had started the Wilhoite Farm and Garden Supply.

During Jack's childhood he had spent many afternoons after school working with his mom and dad, waiting on customers, cleaning the place up and helping stock inventory. Jack really had never thought of doing anything differently. He loved that old store and the hustle and bustle of the patrons as they came in for sacks of manure and bales of barbed wire.

Although Jack was no different from any other young boy on a summer day, he looked forward to working in the store during the sultry days. Jack's dad would have to scoot him out the door and force him to go swimming with his friends. Everyone used to joke that Jack was a born merchant and would someday be a millionaire.

Well, that wasn't really Jack's dream. He enjoyed the store and looked forward to the day he would be a full partner with his father. Jack had an eye for business and enjoyed the small-town living and day-to-day hustle of the store.

Eventually, Jack graduated from high school and went off to college, where he studied general business and accounting. As he attended school, he became more and more excited about the possibilities that were open to him in the business world, particularly for the family company.

The spring of 1966 brought graduation, and the entire family was on hand to see Jack, in his collegiate gown, accept the hard won degree. Jack had other things on his mind that day for, while in college, he had met a pert brunette named Denise Santorie, whose family owned a major hardware chain. Jack was head-over-heels in love with the girl and, in short order, they were married.

In a few years, Jack's parents retired and the company became his. As with every type of business, things needed to be changed. River Falls was no longer a farming community, but was made up of commuting businessmen and writers. Jack decided to change the nature of the store and call it the Jack Wilhoite Hardware Company Ltd.

While in the changeover, Jack found it necessary to carry different types of inventory, such as coffee pots, drills and, of course, general hardware. After a great deal of investigation, he decided to contact the Santorie Hardware Company and make arrangements to become one of their limited distributors. In this way, he was able to maintain sole ownership and, at the same time, increase his product line without raising his costs.

Within a very short time, Jack found business was booming. Now it was necessary to make some decisions as to where he wanted to go with the business. It was important to take into account all things currently affecting the business and all things that would do so in the future.

This brings us to the present. The Jack Wilhoite Hardware Company is now the largest store in River Falls, Iowa. It employs 15 people, ten of whom work full-time. During the Christmas and summer periods as many as 20 employees are carried on the payroll. Jack does, on the average, $1.5 million in receivables yearly and is growing.

2.3 PLANNING TO AUTOMATE

Since his decision to change the scope of the company, the business has experienced a growth rate of about 15 percent a year in receivables and a corresponding amount in payables.

Jack has found some important problems have cropped up, specifically in the area of cash flow. During the early years of the company, and even up until 1975, when the company was reorganized, it had never been necessary to take out a loan. Now, due to slowness in receivables and the higher cost of inventory items, Jack has found it necessary to take out a loan occasionally to cover immediate inventory changes or to add additional space to the company.

In early 1977, Jack borrowed $30,000 to cover the cost of an additional building to handle the sport clothing division he'd added. The plan was to pay the original loan off in ten years, plus show at least a 6 percent annual growth rate on that portion of the business. Jack's main concern was that his average monthly receivables were about $175,000. His payables consisted mainly of inventory items and fixed bills, such as the loan for the new building. Jack found that keeping track of the cash flow, even though he had instituted good accounting procedures originally, was becoming burdensome and required more time to keep track of. As a result, Jack found it necessary to employ two bookkeepers, rather than only one. He also had to pay the accounting firm more so he could have immediate projections of what was happening.

Even with this, Jack was not satisfied with the information he was getting and felt it was becoming necessary now to automate his business, particularly the inventory function. The inventory had grown from just a few hundred items to over 3,000 different items. Jack had to hire a special accounting team, from the bank, to help figure out the inventory at audit times.

What could really be done? Jack was unsure, but he had been reading several articles in accounting magazines and general interest magazines about automated accounting. He had read several articles covering the art of automation and the possibility of using microcomputers in the business environment.

While in college, Jack had been introduced to some computer techniques as part of his normal training but had never seriously thought of putting a system into his business. He thought computers cost too much. As Jack read, and as his hair turned greyer as a result of his accounting difficulties, his interest in automated systems grew. This interest created another problem—what did he want and, more importantly, what did he need?

Jack was a businessman, not a computer expert. He knew that he could do business in a much more efficient manner if all or part of it were computerized. He was in a dilemma, since had had no idea where to begin in the automation process.

2.4 TIMESHARING

Jack knew that the bank could automate his business. They already took care of his payroll and receivables. This was fairly expensive, but he didn't have to worry about it. He was more concerned about the inventory problem and how to automate that function. The bank in his town could not handle that function but recommended an outside firm to do it on a timesharing basis. Jack was interested and gave the company a call. Within a few days the salesman appeared and sat down with Jack to discuss what could be done.

"Well, Mr. Wilhoite, from what I can see of your operation it will be no problem to get you started. We have two possible plans. The first is to provide you with a terminal and an acoustic coupler that will connect you to our computer system in Des Moines. Or we can use the card method, which you will send in once a month. We will provide you with an updated inventory report a few days later. I would like to recommend the terminal since it makes it possible for you to immediately update your inventory records and get instant reports. Of course, the cost is slightly higher."

"How much is 'higher'?" Jack asked.

"Approximately 25 percent higher. This is because we are renting you a terminal and you are paying for the amount of space you take up in the computer as well as the amount of time it takes you to talk to the computer. Regardless of the method, the terminal or the card, you will still save money over what you are presently spending.

"By choosing either system, you will need only one bookkeeper. Your inventory record is perpetual now and will be perpetual in our system, plus we will give you a worksheet to do a physical inventory for special input to the computer.

"You will also get other benefits, Mr. Wilhoite. Should you start carrying dated inventory items—let's say milk—our inventory system can handle that, also. You have already been shown that reorder dates and points are available. This is a 'must destroy' date or 'return date,' which would be important to you. Other features include total cost of inventory data on items returned, back-order information and vendor information. In fact, we can even generate the purchase orders for you and provide a complete order entry system.

"The beauty of all this is that you take inventory now and later add your receivables, payables, payroll and any other features you want added. Of course, as you add, the cost goes up. But we do provide you with the most up-to-date equipment and highest-quality software on the market."

Of course, Jack was interested and began comparing costs of the system to what it was costing him already. He quickly came to the realization that, even though he would be able to let some manpower go, the cost remained the same because of the cost of the system. What he would gain would be accuracy and immediate reports—both very important.

2.5 MINICOMPUTER SYSTEMS

Jack, being a good businessman, knew there were other alternatives and he wanted to check all of them before making his decision. He then contacted one of the larger minicomputer makers. A salesman came by. Jack found from this company that a system could be installed and the functions brought online. All essential personnel would be trained and a maintenance contract worked out. It would be necessary to have a special contract with another vendor to maintain software and immediate maintenance problems. Also, the system would cost about $50,000, which could be amortized over a 20-year period. This brought the monthly and yearly costs down considerably and made it actually lower than the timesharing system. What bothered Jack was what would happen when new equipment was wanted or needed. The answer was to buy it, with a certain amount of credit being given for the other equipment.

This alternative did not particularly excite Jack, since he felt he would be going into the data processing business and wasn't ready for that. There was still one more alternative and it related directly to what he had been reading about microcomputers.

Jack found he could purchase a microcomputer system to handle all payroll records and inventory reports, all for about $12,000. At the same time, upgrade would be as low as just a few hundred dollars. There was no problem obtaining the hardware. It was readily available. But problems existed in setting up maintenance contracts and finding the programs to meet his specific needs. That was the key; Jack decided to set forth what his specific needs were and what he could legitimately spend for data processing, based on current and projected business.

2.6 DEFINING THE NEEDS

Before he made his decision on what type of computer system to buy, Jack decided that he would sit down and write out exactly what his current costs were and what he could expect to save. This way, he felt that he could better communicate his wants and needs to the so-called DP professionals.

After writing this information down in the form of two tables, Jack again talked to the computer system vendors. Now he was able to find only two, the timesharing company and the

Table 2-1
Current Costs Per Month

Manpower:	Sales: 5 sales persons, avg. $650/mo.	$ 3,250.00
	Bookkeepers: 2 at $850/mo.	1,700.00
	Inventory Clerks: 6 at $500/mo.	3,000.00
Over-Inventory Cost, Estimated		2,500.00
Lost Sales Acct., Under-Stock, Estimated		6,000.00
Jack's Hours Spent on Projections and Other		
Account Chores at $20/hr., avg. 60 hr./mo.		1,200.00
Cost of Bank DP Services		2,100.00
	Average Costs	$19,750.00

Table 2-2
Special Needs of Business

Fluctuating Payroll—goes from 10 to 20 employees, based on seasons.

Seasonal Inventory—only certain items are carried during specific seasons of the year; lead times and stock quantities are very important on these items.

Diverse Inventory—inventory cost of everything from nails sold by the pound to golf balls sold by the dozen. Also, a certain amount of aged items are carried—important to keep track of "must sell" dates.

Backorders—a problem both from vendors and to customers; important to keep track of both ends of the problem.

Payables—in excess of $100,000 per month and over 300 checks are written each month.

Receivables—consist of over 400 invoices a month with the average payment made 60 days from invoice date; 19 percent of the invoiced customers are in the 90- or 120-day payment range. The company experiences an 11.5 percent bad debt write-off per month.

minicomputer manufacturer, that could meet all of his current and projected needs.

Microcomputers, Jack learned, could meet the need in the form of available hardware and initial costs but could not offer needed maintenance or software reliability, at least at the outset. Jack was enticed by the microcomputer idea, however, since it meant the best cost and possible return for the invested dollar.

Finding a vendor that could deliver the goods and maintain them was the problem. Jack was able to find a company that offered a unique situation in that he was not able to buy the computer but could rent it for a reasonable amount and the rent would be based on the functions and amount of hardware needed. Even though this was similar to what the timesharing company was offering, in the long run it was still cheaper.

2.7 THE SOLUTION

For the initial startup, Jack found he was able to rent a system consisting of a microcomputer with sufficient memory to handle his inventory functions along with the required memory, mass memory storage system and printer for creating reports. Jack also had a group of routines included in his package that allowed him to send information on receivables, payables and payroll to the timesharing computer for analysis and report generation. This reduced his timesharing costs.

Using this system, Jack was able to keep online and inhouse his primary problem area of inventory control. He was also able to keep the necessary receivable, payable and payroll records on local memory devices. These records were used by the larger timesharing computer for creating bills and setting up reports. Jack's only cost to the timesharing house was for the time needed to connect to perform the billing and record updating functions. All primary information was kept on his system.

From the microcomputer rental company Jack learned that, at a later date, the entire company could be put on the system inhouse with additional expansion of the basic system. It was suggested to him that an additional unit be placed in the warehouse to keep track of all inventory items with daily updates performed from the sales function to keep the inventory at correct levels. Later, it was planned to integrate the system by using a primary system with added terminals to use the same data base.

Working with the systems designer from the microcomputer company, it was decided that Jack would be fully automated with microcomputer systems inhouse within 24 months. The system would be updated as necessary by the company and Jack would not have to worry about becoming a data processing professional.

2.8 DESIGNING THE SPECIFICATIONS

Once the money considerations and plans were laid out and agreed upon, the systems designer spent time in Jack's company finding out exactly how Jack ran his business. It was important that the installed computer work for and not against Jack's company. This meant that the programs would have to work in a manner very similar to what Jack and his employees were used to.

After the systems designer had spent time with Jack and found out what was needed and how it should look, a set of specifications, geared specifically to the Jack Wilhoite Hardware Company, was written. This set of specifications covered everything from initial installation to what the system would be doing in five years. Everything was gone over with Jack and his employees; changes were made and a final specification agreed upon.

With the final specification signed, the systems designer was able to provide exactly the system Jack needed, along with established, yet flexible, times for additions and upgrades. One thing Jack insisted on was that he didn't want "computer" people running around his business fixing computers.

During regular maintenance or fix times the system would need to be removed and a replacement unit installed. This, the microcomputer company felt, was easy to do since the unit was a rental, which meant they could take longer on preventive maintenance.

Because Jack was smart enough to do a great deal of investigation before getting involved with a computer system, its introduction to the company was fairly easy. The employees did not experience the normal fear of computers, since they had been involved in the process of designing what was needed.

2.9   EFFECTS OF AUTOMATION

With the system up and running, Jack has found it possible to know, in minutes, the state of his inventory, the status of any account and the condition of cash flow. As a result, Jack has been able to establish better vendor lead times and lower inventory taxes by not carrying slow-moving inventory above the amount that will sell. The cash flow has increased and the one remaining bookkeeper can spend time making sure that slow-paying accounts are paying.

With the automated system, only 6 percent of the invoiced companies are in the 90- to 120-day pay period, but bad debts still remain about the same, mainly due to the amount of business Jack does. Also, Jack is seeing his cost of payables going down because of better tracking and greater cash flow. He is also able to take advantage of all possible discounts which, in his case, represent a fair amount of actual cash over a year. Jack has also received a side benefit from automating the system—instead of writing several checks to the same vendor, he is able to write one or, at most, two; thus, the number of checks written per month is going down. Jack has established, through the bank, a method of keeping cash in savings accounts until Fridays. Then, based on information from the computer, the necessary amounts are placed in the correct checking accounts.

Jack estimates that, with the help of the computer, within a 12-month period he will have saved enough capital to add other goods and services to his operation without adding to his current loan.

Jack Wilhoite was always known as the kid who would make a million. Well, maybe he never will, but Jack has learned how to control costs and make his business profitable. Maybe next year he can consider opening another business.

2.10   SUMMARY

This scenario has been provided as a brief look at the important considerations and processes in deciding to automate a business.

The most important point to consider in analyzing your own business is to find out what it is you do. Next, work closely with the systems designers, either from timesharing houses or from computer companies. Let them know exactly what you need and what you can afford. In more cases than not, it will be found that the microcomputer will not meet your needs and a larger system will be necessary.

Most accounting-related problems can be handled in a computerized environment—the mundane tasks find the easiest solutions. Quite possibly, for businessmen reading this book, only a mailing list will need to be automated; for others, it may be necessary to get the entire business on computer. If this is the case, you may want to do what Jack did.

It is hoped that accounting students and computer science students reading this book will make use of this scenario to draw up a guideline.

From the cynic's point of view, the whole scenario can be summed up this way: know what you are talking about and then ask to be shown, and shown again. A great deal of benefit can be achieved from automation, and costs can be lowered. But the reverse is also true if you don't take care in choosing the system and the design.

Chapter Three

INTRODUCTION TO CONCEPTS IN AUTOMATION

This chapter presents the idea of automation from general concepts to an overview of input statements and data bases. Each function of an automated accounting system is presented, providing a foundation for understanding the complexity of accounting systems.

3.1 GENERAL CONCEPTS

To get the greatest benefit from an accounting system you must be able to understand it. Up to this point, our discussion of the accounting package has been very general. It is now important to look at two key items: how the data is handled in an automated system and what to expect. This is done to help you interact with an automated package so that as each system within the accounting package is introduced the idea of automation is foremost in your mind.

To fully understand the makeup of the accounting package you must understand the concept of interactivity. Figure 3-1 shows the general ledger in the center with the four major subsystems (inventory control, accounts receivable/billing, accounts payable and payroll) surrounding it. Each subsystem generates specific data that can, as stated before, be used alone and with the general ledger.

Each of the blocks making up the subsystems and general ledger represent a specific function to be performed within the entire package. The importance of each block is defined in this

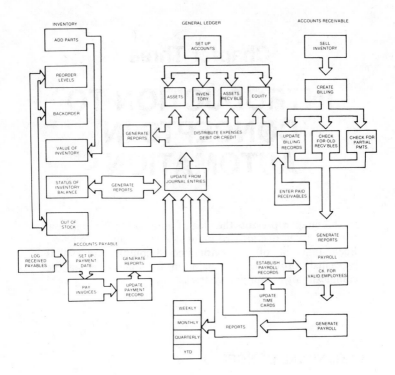

Figure 3-1 Interactivity of an accounting package

chapter. Each subsystem is covered procedurally in Chapters Five through Eleven.

Since this accounting package is designed for automation it is important that you understand how this computer communicates with the user.

3.2 INPUT FIELDS

Let's begin with the handling of input data fields. An input data field is the area in which you tell the computer, through some input device,* what data is to be used for a specific operation. The usual misconception is that the computer is inherently ready to respond. Actually, the computer must be programmed with instructions telling it what to ask for and what to expect. There are several ways a program does this but, since the goal of this book is to spare you unneeded technical details while making the system easy to understand, we will use the prompt technique. The input prompt is designed into the BASIC language, which is used in the CTBL package.

The applications presented in this book make extensive use of the prompt technique. The prompts will always be in this format: **prompt name?**   . The response is entered directly after the question mark. In some cases, to avoid errors, the prompt will include a brief example—which, incidentally, can be removed. This type of prompt will take the form shown in Example 3-1. Throughout the book all *program*-related examples will be shown exactly as they appear on the CRT screen of a computer. If you have purchased the accounting package that accompanies the book, you should enter the program on your computer. This will give you an opportunity to learn the package while you read the book. If you have not obtained the package, the examples shown in the book should suffice. The examples parallel the package exactly. (The package can be purchased from either dilithium Press or MECA, 7026 O.W.S. Road, Yucca Valley, California 92284.)

Notice that the response follows the question mark. In this example, as in most examples in the book, both the prompt and the response are shown. In some cases, you will be asked to do this; the format shown in Example 3-1 will be used. Notice that the inputs are separated by commas (,). This tells the program that there is really more than one data input being entered. If the commas are left out, the response for display will be a double question mark (??) indicating that more data is to be entered. It should be mentioned at this point that, in order for the BASIC interpreter to know that you have typed a response to an input, the return key must be pressed. This generates a carriage return and line feed and tells the program to progress to the next program item. See Figure 3-2 for an example of a keyboard.

Another type of input statement used in this package is the "yes" or "no" type response. In some cases, the actual response expected will be yes or no and, in some cases, a zero or a number code. When this occurs, the program will present the input statement in a manner that indicates what is expected for the given situation.

The BASIC interpreter does supply certain error responses to indicate program errors. However, definitive error responses are in the program to guide you through the application. This

technique of error response is needed to ensure the integrity of
the data.

```
PROMPT NAME  (EXAMPLE) ?
NAME:  (DOE, JOHN) ?
```

Example 3-1

Figure 3-2 A terminal keyboard

3.3   DATA AND DATA BASES

The types of data the system will be asking for will consist of inventory numbers, quantity descriptions, cost per package, invoice numbers, check numbers and other items that are important to track in an accounting package. However, it will be found that not all the data can be handled in this manner; some must be handled in the form of data statements.* This type of data is implanted within actual program statements and will be pointed out in the chapters covering use of the programs.

The basic purpose of entering data into the computer is to have the machine use it in calculations, sorts or other operations. Within this particular system the input and implanted data will be used to set specific inventory boundaries—that is, minimum and maximum reorder points. Also, it will be used to test for the inventory level desired and direct the program to inform you of status, either when it goes below the desired level, or on request. Also, the application manipulates the data to provide outputs that indicate the status of the activity being questioned. The most important computation that can be performed, and one of the most exhaustive, is the sorting of data. Since most accounting information has meaning only if it is in some order, all data is sorted by date, customer or quantity. Within the programs, sort routines exist that will sort the data in the sequence necessary to give the greatest benefit and flexibility.

The concept of collecting data, either through input statements or by creating data statements, is not as complex as it appears. The data statement is possibly the most frequent method of creating a data base. Figure 3-3 is an example of how the data statement is used in BASIC.

In data statements, the line numbers (a) are present as in all BASIC statements. The actual data is preceded by the word

```
          c            e    d              d
10 DATA "HARDWARE ", "104 A". 1000. "MIN"
 a    b
```

Figure 3-3 Format of a DATA system

DATA (b). This word tells BASIC that the information following is unique to the entire program. The quote ("), item (c), is used in the data statements to indicate a string* value. The data, item (d), can be either numeric or composed of both alpha and numeric characters. When alphanumeric information is in the data statement, the quotes (" ") are used to indicate that a string is in the data base. The comma, item (e), is used as a data item separator and indicates to BASIC that a data item is ended. BASIC makes use of the data statements by looking at the first data line and the first item within that line. BASIC continues through each data line until it "sees" the last item in the last line. Certain programs within this accounting package make use of data statements. These programs are covered in detail in the procedure chapters.

The other method of creating a data base is by use of the previously mentioned input statement and a matrix method of manipulating the data. The matrix method can be compared to a pigeonhole filing system (see Figure 3-4). The information and data are arranged in a row/column format, with specific information residing at a given index or address point. The index, or address, is the point where a row and a column intersect. Using this method of data handling, information can be retrieved,

Figure 3-4 Pigeon-hole filing system

added, deleted or rearranged to suit the specific requirements of an application need.

The data base concept is not only involved with how the information is represented inside the computer, but also with how it is arranged on the mass storage device.* This discussion, however, is merely an overview to provide insight into data manipulation.

With this basic understanding of how data is input and of the interaction involved within the system, each part of the package and what it does can now be presented.

3.4 INVENTORY CONTROL OVERVIEW

In Chapter One, inventory control was discussed as it relates to other subsystems and the general ledger. The inventory control package is important because it gives better control over items sold by a company. With this control, a manager can regulate the other portions of his business.

The inventory control package is designed to provide the capability to determine the status of inventory balances. This means that for each item a business handles, the current inventory level and items held can be determined at a glance. For example, suppose the owner of a small paint store carrying 20 different colors of paint wants to know exactly how many gallons, quarts and pints he has on hand in each color. More importantly, he probably would like to know which colors are selling the best and which ones are not—in other words, a ranking of fast- to slow-movers. An inventory control package gives this capability.

The inventory control package can also help you determine which items bring the greatest profit based on costs, overhead, etc. Suppose a stationery store sells two types of calculators. The profit margin is 30 percent on one and 35 percent on the other. This is where an inventory control system is particularly helpful. By using the information from the inventory balances and the fast-to-slow ranking, it is possible to determine which calculator should be carried with the greater inventory level. It may not be the higher-profit-margin item.

An inventory control package is used to make decisions regarding inventory levels based on what is selling, what is not and which item returns the best profit margin.

By maintaining proper inventory balances, capital investment and inventory taxes can be reduced. An inventory package is set up in such a way that it monitors the minimum number of stock quantities needed and flags items below this point. Also, it indicates which items are at maximum levels. Items out of stock are flagged* and monitored so that they are not forgotten. Back-ordered parts are monitored and flags set so that a tight rein can be kept on the supplier.

To review, an inventory control package can do the following for a small business:

- Give the status of inventory balances.
- Differentiate fast movers from slow movers.
- Help reduce stock levels by keeping track of minimum and maximum order points.
- Flag out-of-stock items and keep track of back-ordered items.

But that's not all an inventory control package does. If manual, it helps the bookkeeper or inventory control clerk generate reports. On an automated system reports are generated by the computer. A list of inventory, in order of total value or by item number, is generated. The report is formatted as shown in Figure 3-5.

INVENTORY VALUE

PART #	DESC	OHD	TTL $
100111	ROOTS	20	400.00
100112	COUNTER	20	200.00
100113	JAWS	15	150.00
	TTL VALUE		750.00

Figure 3-5 Inventory control report

3.5   ACCOUNTS RECEIVABLE/BILLING OVERVIEW

Once the inventory is established and the items begin to sell, another situation is created. When a customer purchases your company's goods and/or services on account, an account receivable is created. The accounts receivable/billing package is constructed to give control over customer billing, keeping track of when a payment is received and what bills are old—aged receivables and partial payments.

The accounts receivable/billing package requires that certain information regarding the customer transaction be input. First, the transaction date is entered. The computer uses this information to age the receivable and set flags regarding the status of the account. Next, the customer number, name and address are required. Finally, the goods and services purchased are listed as line items with costing. The package uses this information to create a billing. The subtotals, applicable taxes and grand totals are calculated from this information, which you supply.

Unfortunately, not all customers are willing to stay current, so they have previous balances which must be carried forward and any service or late charges added. This requires that a new grand total be generated. In some cases, the customer may have several invoices outstanding and the billing portion must reflect the invoice number and detail again, generating the appropriate totals, based on age.

The accounts receivable/billing application presented in this book ages each of the receivables based on the original entry or creation date related to the current date, which is entered at the start of each billing cycle. Flags are set to provide the necessary reminders to customers regarding their account status and also to let the manager decide whether or not the company wishes to continue doing business with a particular customer.

Another important area of this system is the tracking of payments received. The important figures needed are the date and amount paid. It may not be paid in full and, consequently, a paid-in-full flag is *not* set; this causes the account to enter the status of a partially paid account. This is a frequent occurrence since many customers are willing to stay current only within the extreme limits of the payment terms. For example, Customer A has six open invoices and has chosen to pay only the two oldest, leaving four open and creating a partially paid account.

To help you maintain control of accounts receivable, reports are generated that provide specific information regarding account status. This is extremely important information since, without it, it is impossble for you to know current and projected cash flow and, quite possibly, you will be unable to function on a current basis. The package provides for three types of reports to help you make decisions and plan an operating profile.

The first report is Aged Receivables, based on the last billing date compared to the current status date.* The information is sorted by customer name with the receivables aged within five categories:

- 0 to 30 days
- 31 to 60 days
- 61 to 90 days
- 91 to 120 days
- 120 days and over

This report is important since customers may have more than one bill due. The report groups open receivables according to customer name and lists each receivable by age category. Figure 3-6 is an example of the format of this type of report.

This report gives you the ability to check customer status and decide what steps to take, depending on the age of the receivables, the number outstanding for a given customer and the amount of money involved.

The next report generated is similar to the first, except that Outstanding Receivables (any receivable past the chosen cut-off date) are reported by the oldest date first. The report is important because it helps establish priorities regarding collection of receivables and, again, gives totals that help you project cash flow. Figure 3-6 is also an example of the format of this type of report. As previously indicated, a customer may choose not to

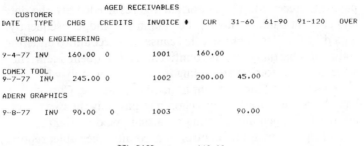

```
                          AGED RECEIVABLES
      CUSTOMER
DATE   TYPE   CHGS   CREDITS   INVOICE #   CUR    31-60   61-90   91-120   OVER

     VERNON ENGINEERING

9-4-77 INV   160.00   0          1001    160.00

COMEX TOOL
9-7-77   INV  245.00  0          1002    200.00   45.00

ADERN GRAPHICS

9-8-77   INV   90.00   0         1003             90.00


                          TTL PAID      160.00

                          TTL PARPAID   200.00

                          TTL UNPAID    135.00
```

Figure 3-6 Aged receivables report

pay an entire bill for one reason or another. This creates partial payments and the files must reflect this. It is important, for planning purposes, to know which customers are in this partial payment status. This report gives the customer name, date paid, amount paid and amount still owed. The report is sorted by customer name to give the same type of information as the first report.

The final report generated by this system is the Month-End, giving a closeout list of all paid invoices, listed by customer name. This report, when generated, removes that specific customer item from the file.

As revenue is received it must be distributed over the income accounts. The system is designed to allow for distribution into specific account types and to flag invalid or incorrect account entries. The final report by the system is a complete listing of the journal entries by account number, description and amount, with the total amount distributed given at the end. This is for all the invoices received. However, when an invoice is being distributed, the amount distributed must equal the invoice amount; otherwise, the system will consider it invalid and re-cycle it for the correct entries.

As shown in Figure 3-6, three totals are generated for comparison purposes: first, the total of all paid invoices; second, the total of all outstanding unpaid invoices; and, finally, the total, showing the sum of partially paid invoices.

3.6   ACCOUNTS PAYABLE OVERVIEW

Running a business would be wonderful if all there was to contend with was establishing an inventory, selling it and having receivables as a result. But when inventory is purchased, the building rented and the business set up, accounts payable are created. These are the vendors and suppliers of services that now are invoicing your company for goods and services rendered. Consequently, these invoices as well as when and how they are paid must be tracked.

The accounts payable package discussed procedurally in Chapter Nine is a system designed to handle the important items associated with accounts payable. First, as bills are received, a decision may be made to pay them at future dates. The system allows for entering the invoice with the desired date of payment.

This date becomes a reminder that a bill is due on a specific date.

Most invoices specify terms, such as "2% 10 net 30," meaning that if the bill is paid in full within 10 days of the billing date a 2 percent discount may be deducted. This is a very desirable feature since it is important to take advantage of any revenue-saving technique possible. The invoice entry system asks for any discount information and automatically calculates the saving. The system presents the status of your payables, as shown in Figure 3-7. As the invoices are paid, additional information is requested: date paid, amount paid and the number of the check issued. This provides management with a complete report of what is still active and what has been paid.

```
STATUS OF PAYABLES - OPEN INVOICE LISTING

VENDER #      VENDER        INVOICE #      AMT      TERMS      DDPD
1414          XTRAN         12034B         47.22    2/10/30    9/5
1716          UNINTED       26721A        184.00    ----       10/1
2222          MECA          37122V        277.06    ----       10/1
```

Figure 3-7 Status of payables and open listing reports

Since payments must be distributed among the debit and credit accounts, the system asks for the specific account number and the amount to be distributed. This is done for each invoice, and the amount distributed must equal the invoice total. If it does not, the accounts payable system gives an error response, clears all of the indicated fields and recycles for the correct input. Also, only certain account numbers can be debited and credited. The system looks for these by account number and sends an error message if an incorrect or invalid account is entered.

Like the inventory and accounts receivable packages, the accounts payable system generates reports designed to help in the effective management of your business. The accounts payable package generates, on request, three types of reports. First is the Open Invoice Listing. This report was shown previously in Figure 3-7. Notice that this is a list of all invoices owed at the time the report is requested. The invoices are sorted in desired payment date order, establishing a schedule of payment. As the indicated dates come by, each invoice is cleared for payment. Also, the capability of sorting this list by vendor name or number exists. Vendor sorts allow examination of vendor activity and open invoice, by vendor.

The second report is the Discounts Not Taken, sorted by vendor name. In some cases, due to a company's operating capital profile, the manager may decide to hold onto an invoice for as long as possible before payment, thereby losing the benefit of any offered discount. There are some situations in which the vendor does not offer terms, and it may be desirable to hold these invoices for payment on the latest possible date. These must be flagged to indicate that no discount was involved in the first place and to keep them off the Discounts Not Taken report. This report, shown in Figure 3-8, is used to help in planning. If you use this report, you will be able to take advantage of these discounts and increase both cash flow and profits. At times, it may even make sense to borrow the money from the bank.

```
                      DISCOUNTS NOT TAKEN

VENDER #      VENDER       INVOICE#     AMT       TERMS      DATE PAID
1010          KENWOOD      16058A       70.00     5/10/30    11/15
1090          VENDROM        473C       16.88     2/10/30    10/2

2117          WICKS        88516        99.20     2/10/30    11/15
2150          CDW CO       11180       485.00     1/5/30     11/15

                                      TTL PAID     ****       671.00
                                      TTL DISCOUNT  $
                                      LOST         ****         5.48
```

Figure 3-8 Discounts not taken

The last report is Invoices Paid in Full. This report is in the same format as previous reports and is sorted by vendor name. The entire record of what, who and when paid is reflected. Also, the total account distribution for the paid invoices is generated in the format shown in Figure 3-6.

Before proceeding to the payroll package, let's review the benefits this accounting package is providing so far:

- The inventory is tracked and controlled.
- Definitive reports that help manage the inventory are generated.
- The billing is generated and accounts receivables tracked, giving you full control over current and projected cash flow.

- Accounts payable are handled in a manner that allows you to keep track of all invoices. This means you can take the best advantage of offered terms.
- Definitive reports from the accounts receivable and accounts payable packages help you make necessary decisions regarding the day-to-day operation of your business.
- Journal reports are generated, giving the account distribution for both accounts receivable and payable, allowing for quick updating of the general ledger.

Naturally, these reports are meaningful only if correct information was entered in the first place. Even though error routines are included to look for bad data, nothing can be done to handle carelessness.

3.7 SMALL BUSINESS PAYROLL OVERVIEW

Because the primary design of this accounting package is for owner-operated type stores, it is important to address payroll for smaller companies. Therefore, a minimal payroll package can be developed that keeps track of wages earned and generates the necessary quarterly and yearly reports. A check calculator should be built in to assist in record keeping.

The payroll package is made up of one type of daily input record: the time card. This time card gives the basic information necessary for tracking an employee's wages; one must be maintained for each employee. It is completed by filling in hours, or by a time clock card arrangement.

The system is designed to handle current employees with provisions for addition of new employees. The information required is the employee's name, number, Social Security number, rate of pay, marital status, exemptions, sex and address. This information is used to generate reports and mailing lists for the W-2s and other employee information. Flagging of terminated employees is possible. It will help you avoid generating incorrect payroll information while retaining the file for W-2 and 941A preparation. This is done by asking for the specific employee record, entering final pay information and setting a termination flag.*

In order to calculate an employee's pay correctly, the program should request tax data from manual tables and from the employee data statements. The computer calculates the correct pay, based on the base pay, exemptions and other deduction information (Figure 3-9). The program then displays the correct paycheck data, so that a manual check can be written, and saves the data for quarterly and yearly reports.

```
101MPT    PAUL T. MONCKTON              TYPE=S     RATE= 760.000

    ---HOURS---   --EARNINGS-   --------DEDUCTIONS--------   ---TOTALS---
    REG=  0.000   REG=   0.00   FIC=   0.00   INS=   0.00   EARN=   0.00
    OT =  0.000   OT =   0.00   FED=   0.00   MI1=   0.00   DEDU=   0.00
    OH =  0.000   OH =   0.00   STA=   0.00   MI2=   0.00
                  COM=   0.00   CIT=   0.00                 *NET=    0.00
                  MIS=   0.00                               CHECK NO.

101SSC    SUZI C. SAVOY                 TYPE=S     RATE= 350.000

    ---HOURS---   --EARNINGS-   --------DEDUCTIONS--------   ---TOTALS---
    REG=  0.000   REG=   0.00   FIC=   0.00   INS=   0.00   EARN=   0.00
    OT =  0.000   OT =   0.00   FED=   0.00   MI1=   0.00   DEDU=   0.00
    OH =  0.000   OH =   0.00   STA=   0.00   MI2=   0.00
                  CCM=   0.00   CIT=   0.00                 *NET=    0.00
                  MIS=   0.00                               CHECK NO.

*** TOTALS - DEPARTMENT 101

---EARNINCS---   ----------DEDUCTIONS----------   ----TOTALS-----
REG    0.00   FIC    0.00   INS    0.00   EARN    0.00
OT     0.00   FED    0.00   MI1    0.00   DEDU    0.00
OH     0.00   STA    0.00   MI2    0.00
COM    0.00   CIT    0.00                 *NET    0.00
MIS    0.00
```

Figure 3-9 Payroll register

The payroll package generates two payroll registers—quarterly and year-to-date. For system simplification, both reports are in the same format. Figure 3-10 is an example of the format of the quarterly and year-to-date reports.

The payroll calculator is used for writing the paychecks. The other reports are used for the information required by state and federal governments, for planning uses of current revenue and for planning future operations.

The last report generated by the system is the Journal Entries. These entries use the same format as the accounts receivable and payable. Here, the system is designed to pick up the required information from the register information and either debit or credit it to the proper account number. This report is generated on request and is used for journal entry posting to the general ledger.

AMW ENTERPRISES

RUN DATE: 01 - JAN - 80   PAGE 001

FOR THE PERIOD 12/01/79 TO 12/31/79

CHECK NO	DATE	GROSS WAGES	TAXES					INSURE	DEDUCTIONS			NET PAY
			FICA	FWT	SWT	SDI	CWT		UNION	SAV-BND	MISC	
EMPLOYEE: 1000 WARREN, CARL D												
113579	12/03/79	1,000.00	.00	188.93	50.55	15.21	.00	17.50	.00	10.00	.00	717.81
115790	12/17/79	1,000.00	.00	188.93	50.55	15.21	.00	17.50	.00	10.00	10.00	707.81
123456	12/31/79	1,000.00	.00	188.93	50.55	15.21	.00	17.50	.00	10.00	10.00	707.81
3 CHECKS	EMPLOYEE TOTALS:	3,000.00	.00	566.79	151.65	45.63	.00	52.50	.00	30.00	20.00	2,133.43

SAME DETAIL FOR ALL EMPLOYEES WITH GRAND TOTALS AT END

Figure 3-10 Quarterly and year-to-date reports

3.8 GENERAL LEDGER OVERVIEW

The General Ledger, as seen in Figure 1-1, is constructed of a Chart of Accounts. These are the asset accounts, account receivables, inventory accounts, plant and equipment and miscellaneous accounts. Each of these account types can have several accounts within it. Consequently, each account must be numbered in such a manner that its account type is easily identifiable. For an automated system, this numbering is used by the computer to determine whether the correct information is being entered into an account. The normal convention of numbering accounts is as follows:

- Asset accounts 10
- Liabilities   20
- Income   30
- Expenses   40

The liability portion of the general ledger is made up of items such as accounts payable (all vendors and suppliers of services to whom a company owes money as a result of doing business), notes payable (any loans incurred for purchasing inventory, rolling stock or any other money that has to be paid back with interest).

The equity portion of the ledger is made up of those accounts that reflect the net worth of the business as it applies to the total capital available. The following types of accounts can be found in the equity portion of the general ledger: *retained earnings*, either plus or minus, is the difference between income and expenses for all prior periods; *net income*, the difference between income and expenses for the current period. The net income is usually based on week-to-date, month-to-date and year-to-date balances. The equity accounts are designed to give the status of a company's income at any point within the fiscal year.

The income portion of the general ledger is made up of two types of accounts—those that track revenue generated from normal sales of inventory and from capital gains. The sale of plant equipment represents income under the heading of capital gains—for example, the sale of a fixed asset such as a sewing machine no longer being used and no longer representing an asset.

Expense accounts track the amount of expense incurred as a result of doing business. They are grouped under the heading of operation expenses. The expenses are normally rent, utilities, maintenance and inventory.

The whole purpose of the general ledger is to keep track of the accounts mentioned. Therefore, journal entries must be made that show the account debited or credited, description of the entry and the amount of the entry. For accounts receivable and payable packages, journal entries are generated for entry into the general ledger. For an interactive system, this ledger entry must be done manually. For a totally integrated package running on a large system, the hand-off to the general ledger is automatic. As stated, when the journal entries are made, regardless of whether the system is automated, debits must equal credits and the distribution must equal the amount of the item being distributed.

The accounting system presented in this book is based on the premise that the books will be closed every month. Therefore, when posting data to the accounts, your first entry will always be the beginning balance for the current month. The final entry will be the ending balance. Within the system network, the account posting to the general ledger will be handled automatically as the journal entries are made.

Before discussing the types of reports the general ledger provides, it is important to talk about how financial statements are formatted. It is important for you to have the financial statement in a form that is easy to read and gives you the most information. For manual systems, the statement can be done in just about any format. This flexibility is carried through in an automated system by providing a structuring routine that allows you to specify types of accounts, row and column structure and heading types for the statements. Chapter Eight gives a complete description of how this works and several examples of formatted statements.

The general ledger provides information for the creation of four types of reports necessary for effective management of a business. The automated system provides these reports as either CRT status* or hardcopy* reports. These reports consist of the Trial Balance, General Ledger, Balance Sheet and Income Statement. The Trial Balance is just that—an indicator of what is happening within all of the accounts without specific detail. It lists all accounts in numerical order with a zero-balance or out-of-balance condition. The next report is the General Ledger Account Detail record. It lists all the accounts in numerical order with the entire detail of activity listed for the current period. If the report is taken in the middle of the month, the information will reflect month-to-date activity. The next report is the Balance Sheet, which gives the total detail of each account activity. The account balances used in this report are taken from month-end figures. Consequently, the Balance Sheet has meaning only at the month-end close of books. The automated system presented in this book generates this report automatically, as the books are closed each month.

The final report is the current month's Income Statement. The Income Statement shows the activity of income and expense accounts. The beginning balance is subtracted from the current balance. The result is either plus or minus, depending on how well the business has done in the period in question.

3.9 AUTOMATED PLANNING

The Financial Statements are a summation of all the activities of the business. They reflect totals generated from all subsystems and provide a central area for analyzing business activity and developing workable, effective management decisions. However, sometimes you will need additional help in the decision-making process. There is a method of comparing actual activity with planned activity, giving information that can be used in planning the future operation of the business. This can be done by using the planning package to handle the necessary data manipulation to create a model of the business.

The planning package described in this book is an ancillary package. This means that, even though it depends upon the information contained within the main system, it is not necessary for the complete functioning of the system.

The planning package compares monthly values for the accounts coded as income and expense accounts, and calculates percentage and amount increases. For example, a company plans sales to rise by 1.5 percent per month, or $200.00, based on past and current activity. The planning package allows a manager to decide whether static amounts are to be used in the calculation for the current period or whether separate variables are to be entered. Based on the type of information entered and the current activity of the business, comparisons of planned values to actual ones are made on a monthly and year-to-date basis. Amount and percentage variances are flagged for inspection. Figure 3-12 is an example of the format for this report. The planning package compares sales, cost of goods sold, gross profit and operating expenses, based on current and planned data.

The planning package represents the end of the accounting package. Therefore, it is imperative to review the capabilities the package offers:

- The decision to go into business is made, plant and equipment are rented or purchased and inventory is purchased. Expenses are incurred which may become accounts payable.
- Sales are generated and customers owe you money; bills and accounts receivable now exist.
- Business grows, employees are hired, payroll must be created and tracked and another account is created—payroll.
- The totality of business activity is tracked; the general ledger is now in use, generating Financial Statements.
- Planning becomes important to ensure profitability; the planning package is now used.

3.10 DEPOSIT

Even though the items presented in this chapter are the basics of a complete accounting package, there is still one last item included in this book—a deposit program.

The deposit program gives you the opportunity, if desired, to automate the cash drawer and provide information to the general ledger. The deposit program also provides for automatic reconciliation of the drawer at the end of each business day.

The deposit program is designed to provide for totalling, on a daily basis, all the over-the-counter transactions that take place and to provide a detailed deposit memorandum listing checks and money orders by make and amount, as well as total currency and coin. The screen status report gives the total amount of checks and cash that must be deposited and the amount needed to return the drawer to its starting balance. Chapter Ten covers this deposit sequence in detail.

PLANNING REPORT FOR 09/02/78   BASED ON 9% GROWTH RATE

	JAN	FEB	MAR	APR	MAY	JUN	JUL	AUG	SEP	OCT	NOV	DEC	JAN
SALES REPORTS													
GROSS SALES	10000	10900	11881	12950	14115	15386	16771	18280	19925	21718	23673	25804	28126
SALES RTN	1100	1199	1306	1424	1552	1692	1844	2010	2191	2389	2604	2838	3093
NET SALES	8900	9701	10575	11526	12563	13694	14927	16270	17734	19329	21069	22966	25033
INCOME ACCTS													
ACCTS RECV	25000	27250	29702	32375	35289	38465	41927	45700	49814	54297	59184	64510	70316
RENTALS	200	218	237	259	282	307	335	365	398	434	473	516	562
REV/EXP ACCT													
INTEREST	4000	4360	4752	5180	5646	6154	6708	7312	7970	8687	9459	10321	11250
DIVIDENDS	200	218	237	259	282	307	335	365	398	434	473	516	562
GEN EXPENSES	1000	10900	11881	12950	14115	15386	16771	18280	19925	21218	23673	25804	28126

From this example report, you can see that the percentage option calculates a straight growth pattern and does not take in account your innate abilities to second guess what will happen over a given period of time. This option report is useful however for establishing goals and should be used as such.

Figure 3-11 Planning report

Once you have decided to purchase a computer and to use it in your business, it becomes necessary to work out the procedure needed to convert to the automated system. In any system's conversion, a little pre-planning goes a long way. Document flow and employee training are important aspects of converting to an automated system. Chapter Four is a discussion of what is required to convert from a manual to an automated computer account system.

Chapter Four

CONVERTING FROM A MANUAL TO A COMPUTERIZED SYSTEM

Conversion from one type of accounting system to another is not an easy task. This chapter describes the steps that must be followed to ensure an easy and efficient conversion.

4.1   INTRODUCTION

If you are a small businessman you probably maintain a manual set of books. They are a general journal, a general ledger, a cash receipts journal and a cash disbursements journal. Depending on the type of business, various subsidiary ledgers may also be maintained, of which accounts receivable ledger cards are the most common. This chapter discusses the sequence of events you will go through to convert the manual system to an automated system that uses a microcomputer.

4.2   GENERAL LEDGER AND GENERAL JOURNAL

The first step is to initialize the general ledger in the system. This is done by establishing the specific chart of accounts for your business in the general ledger application. Each account number is entered with an account description and an account code indicating whether it is an asset, a liability or an equity account, a revenue or an expense account. The account code is

used as part of the edit routine; it helps prevent posting to improper accounts, and it generates financial statements. To input
beginning balances into the chart of accounts, a journal entry is
made debiting the various asset accounts and crediting the
liability and equity accounts.

The general journal, instead of being entries on a set of ledger
sheets, becomes a notebook arrangement with a journal entry
sheet for each transaction entered in the computer (see Figure
4-1). For each journal entry, a number is assigned, along with a
description of the entry and the date of the entry. This entry is
carried on the transaction line for each account affected by the
entry. Therefore, the first journal entry used would establish
beginning balances for all the newly established accounts. This
would be journal entry number 001. Its description would be
something like "Beginning Balance Forward" and the date of
the entry. For each account in the general ledger, this line item
would be shown:

Acct #	Date	Journal Entry #	Description	Amount
XXXXXX	XXXXXX	001	Beginning Balance Forward	XXXXX.XX

Generally, non-cash transactions are the only items which will
require individual journal entry postings. Cash transactions oc-
curring in the accounts payable, accounts receivable, and
payroll applications will be summarized and posted in total by a
summary journal entry. The detail is maintained in the corresponding application based on this summary, generally at the
close of each business day for accounts receivable and accounts
payable and on paydays for payroll.

In the general ledger application, a separate file is established
to allow custom designing of financial statement formats. This
allows each business to structure its statements in the format
most useful in measuring operational performance. There may
be several cash accounts maintained by a business: one for paying operating expenses and purchases, another for payroll and
possibly a third for savings accounts. For financial reporting
purposes, these balances may be combined and shown as one
total on a single cash line. The financial format file allows a
business to design statements with line titles, subtotals, and
totals that fit its individual requirements. A separate section of
the general ledger chapter discusses the details of how this is
done.

JOURNAL ENTRY SHEET

Journal Entry No. __051__   Prepared by:_____TRB_____

Effective Date __9/29/77__   Date Prepared __9/29/77__

Acct. No.	Acct. Distribution	Dr. Amt.	Cr. Amt.	Comments
100	Cash	100.00		sales of 9/29/77
400	Sales		100.00	
	TOTAL	100.00	100.00	

Entered by: _____TRB_____

Date Entered __9/30/77__

Figure 4-1 General journal entry sheet

4.3 ACCOUNTS RECEIVABLE

To initialize accounts receivable, the various customer records that make up the beginning accounts receivable balance are entered into the accounts receivable detail file. Each customer becomes a record and is assigned a customer number which is controlled by a customer number log. The log is a numerical listing beginning with 1 or 100 or any other reasonable starting point. The log is pre-numbered sequentially with the name of each additional customer corresponding to the next number available on the log. This insures that no numbers are used more than once and that the numbers are used sequentially.

For each customer record established, the outstanding invoices for that customer must be entered. Each invoice will be entered as though it were a current billing, but for the initialization phase only, the printing of the invoice will be suppressed, since an invoice has already been sent under the manual system. All outstanding invoices are entered for each customer. The resulting total must agree with the general ledger control account for accounts receivable.

The type of accounts receivable customers in the file will depend on the type of business. For example, many clothing stores finance their own credit and accept credit cards. If the customer has a store account, it will be entered on the file. As payments become due, they are entered into the accounts receivable system. For those items purchased with a credit card, a receivable account is set up for each card type accepted by the store. Each purchase for a specific card type is entered with the customer name in the description portion. These items are cleared when the funds are received from that specific credit card institution. The various revenue and tax accounts to be credited are entered for each item and are accumulated to facilitate one journal entry to the general ledger at the close of each business day.

4.4   ACCOUNTS PAYABLE

To initialize accounts payable, a vendor record is established for each vendor, regardless of whether the vendor has any invoices outstanding. The outstanding invoices are entered under the appropriate vendors. The total invoices outstanding for all these vendors must agree with the accounts payable control total in the general ledger.

The system has the flexibility to allow a desired payment date to be included with the entry of each invoice. Thus, if you pay bills weekly or twice a month or at any other fixed interval, the date is entered for the desired normal pay date in the future. It may be the next scheduled bill payment date or three payment periods ahead. An inquiry can then be made to print out or list on the CRT those invoices which have been scheduled for payment on a specific payment date.

An inquiry should be made daily to pick up entries scheduled for payment on a day not normally scheduled for bill payment. The entry may have been made in error or it may be a special pay item entered to take a discount offered for early payment. This also helps in cash flow planning. It will show what your cash requirements for various days during a given month or months will be.

4.5 INVENTORY

To initialize the inventory application, you must assign an inventory number to all items to be tracked individually. Many companies will be able to use existing part numbers; however, the part number field is limited to a six-digit number. This may require modification of existing systems using alpha-numeric codes or part number greater than six digits. The part number description and cost are then input on the file with zero quantity balances.

To initialize the inventory file with accurate balances, you must take a physical inventory. This will establish beginning quantities on hand.

Several methods of costing can be used. These include standard cost, average cost and actual cost. For the standard cost method, purchase price variances are recorded at the time of acquisition of new inventory items. Favorable or unfavorable variances are recorded for a purchase price below or above the standard price, as indicated on the file.

Standards are determined by examining previous costs for each item, allowing for market trends, inflation and other known forces affecting the price. The methods of using average cost, actual cost, and standard cost are discussed in the inventory chapter.

For each sale, a separate entry is made decrementing inventory and crediting the appropriate cost of sale expense account. Special adjustments of inventory quantities, for such situations as physical inventory adjustments or damaged or obsolete inventory items to be written off, are also handled by the software package. The total inventory value calculated by the inventory application must, of course, agree with the general ledger inventory control account on the balance sheet.

There are fields within each inventory part record for minimum/maximum order information. By examining past sales of individual items, a monthly, weekly or quarterly turnover can be determined. Then, by considering the lead time (time from ordering the item to receipt of the item), a minimum stock level for reordering can be calculated. In addition, a maximum order quantity can be calculated to prevent over-stocking of an item. This minimum/maximum order quantity feature can help you manage inventory by automatically generating a list of those items requiring reorder. It includes the projected cost required to purchase the minimum order quantity for each item. This eliminates the tedious manual evaluation of inventory to determine what should be reordered. The minimum and maximum parameters can be changed whenever necessary to reflect a change in demand or supply of an item. This feature becomes a powerful, flexible tool for the small businessman.

A back-order field is also maintained on the inventory application. If a particular item is out of stock and orders for it have been received, it can be tracked on the item records. When a receipt is posted for a back-ordered item, a message to that effect is printed or displayed. This indicator will remind you to check the back-order cards to see which customers make up the back-order total. As an item with a back order is sold, a message is printed or displayed asking if the back orders should be decreased by this sale, since a particular sale may or may not be made in fulfillment of a back order. The back-order feature allows you to use a single inquiry to determine how many units of a particular item are reserved for back-order commitments.

When initializing the inventory file with beginning balances and minimum and maximum quantities, the back-ordered items are also entered for each applicable part number.

4.6 PAYROLL[1]

The first step in the payroll application is to establish special tables for federal, state, and possibly county and city taxes. These rates vary widely from state to state and in counties and cities within the various states.

Even a business with only a few employees will benefit from taking the time to set up these tables and records. This is because a high turnover of employees is common in small businesses, especially where several part-time employees are used to support the operation. A payroll application keeps track of all these employees and the quarter-to-date and year-to-date totals of the various payroll items. These are required for city, county, state and federal government reporting and for preparation of forms W-2 and 941A at year-end for all persons employed during the year.

---

[1]Because of the intended audience of this book, students and small businessmen, payroll is only discussed in terms of the ideal. We have made no provisions for a payroll package in the current CTBL packages.

A record is established for each current employee and for any individual no longer employed but who worked for a period of time in the current fiscal year. The total earnings to date at the time the payroll application is initialized is entered, rather than each of the past payroll periods individually. The manual records must be saved to provide the detail support of the year-to-date totals.

For subsequent payrolls, the detail of a current payroll cycle is printed on a report with the various quarter and year-to-date total fields updated. Once the detail is printed, it is no longer stored in the payroll application. These reports are saved for referencing payroll detail for any specific payroll cycle.

As each new employee is hired, a new record is established with the employee's pay rate, deductions and other pertinent information. As employees are terminated, their status code is changed to inactive. This prevents unauthorized generation of a pay check.

4.7 FORMS

In almost all areas except billing, existing forms can continue to be used. They are collected at intervals during the day for input into the system. The store copies of currently used sales slips are batched in groups of 20 to 50 for input into accounts receivables, revenue, cost of sales, and inventory accounts. A batch header is made for each batch, indicating the dollar total of the batch. As each sales slip is entered in the computer, the total is accumulated. At the end of the batch this total is compared to the batch header total. This ensures the input was correct and in balance. If individual sales slip detail is not required, a summary of the revenue accounts and part numbers affected can be made and only the summary posted to the accounts receivable application. These summaries can be made at the end of each day's business.

This method of summarizing at the end of each day is very reasonable for most small retailers. However, making several batches during the day streamlines the summary process at the end of the day, allowing a quicker getaway after the close of the business day.

The billing portion of the accounts receivable application restricts the user to the limitations of the printer used in the system. Many microcomputer systems use electrostatic printers which require special electrosensitive paper. If the more expensive pin-feed line printer is used an almost unlimited variety of paper forms or stock can be used. The printing flexibility will depend on which printer you buy when you select the microcomputer system configuration. In most cases, existing billing forms must be written off and thrown away upon conversion to the computer billing process.

Modification of existing forms or of the information recorded on the forms is generally necessary to ensure information is recorded in a consistent manner. This aids data entry into the computer. At the point of sale, the part number and quantity sold should be recorded at a consistent place or column on the sales slip. This facilitiates updating of inventory records.

In each of the application chapters, Five through Eleven, the data required for the various types of entries is shown. These chapters should be reveiewed when you determine how existing forms can be used to record the necessary data for each sale. A sample form should be prepared and posted in an accessible place such as next to the cash register.

Chapter Five

INTRODUCTION TO THE PACKAGE

This chapter provides you with a first glimpse of what is provided in the automated accounting package. An introduction to the tape system and some of the most important terms are presented. The menu concept is discussed and the executive menu is presented.

5.1 INTRODUCTION

The previous chapters presented a general overview of what you will establish in an automated accounting package. Some items, such as payroll, were mentioned in terms of the ideal. But this must be further investigated.

For most small businesses (those that gross around $150,000 per year and have fewer than ten employees), automating the payroll can be more burdensome than helpful. However, certain payroll information must be tracked and used in the general ledger. The task of keeping updated computer records and generating checks finds its best usage in much larger businesses. This is not to say that the capability doesn't exist, but considering the amoung of time involved and the number of employees, the process may not be cost-effective for a small business.

5.2 THE FUNCTIONS WITHIN THIS ACCOUNTING PACKAGE

To make this book useful to the small businessman, the functions of inventory control, billing, accounts receivable, accounts payable and an automated general ledger have been provided. We feel these areas are the most time-consuming and error-prone aspects of a manual system.

The applications we present are written for use in the minimal system environment and have been adapted to a variety of machines. Each program, or application, is divided into program segments. Each segment is designed to handle a specific task, thus taking advantage of the memory available in the minimal system. In addition, the applications are designed for use in a digital tape environment, and will work with systems using controlled cassettes—either the ordinary audio units or the MECA Alpha I tape system.

The BASICs used are: Microsoft Extended BASIC, XITAN Extended BASIC and Northstar BASIC. The purpose of incorporating all these variations is to provide versions of the package that are suitable for most users. With the exception of the version written expressly for TRS-80, the Microsoft and XITAN versions are designed specifically for tape systems.

The goal of this book is to provide the new entrant into the field of microcomputing with a feeling of what is involved in the use of a computer and the accounting packages. Also, it is hoped that, through this book, you will be able to determine exactly what you need to automate your business.

5.3 WHAT THE USER NEEDS TO KNOW

You will need to be familiar with the chosen system and be aware of changes that may be necessary to allow the system to run on the hardware you choose. Appendix A has been provided to assist you with this.

Also, it is extremely important that you read this book in its entirety. This will ensure that you have a complete understanding of what is involved.

5.4 STRUCTURE OF THE PROCEDURE CHAPTERS

Chapters Six through Eleven are arranged to make it possible for you to achieve the greatest benefit from the accounting package. Each chapter begins with a general overview of the topic at hand and a block diagram of the general flow.

Each function is identified by both subject and item name. Next, you will learn the purpose of each item and its relationship to the system. This will be followed by a section explaining the subject. Flow charts for the function are presented in the explanatory section. The last section details the actual procedures involved.

Since errors do happen, even in the best systems, error routines are built into each function of the accounting package and comprehensive tables of error responses and recovery are provided. Each chapter ends with a summary section describing the benefits that you should derive from using the function described.

5.5 PREPARING TO USE THE SYSTEM

Once you have an understanding of the hardware, you will be prepared to use the accounting package. To do this you must first ready the system in the manner specified by the user's manual and, second, you must load BASIC. Once BASIC is loaded and the machine readied you can enter the program. Open your system manual and begin typing in each line of the program for the listing marked SYSTEM. When this program segment is completely typed in, verify each line against the listing in the system manual. Next, to ensure that the program is correct, type in RUN and depress the RETURN key. Example 5-1 shows what should appear on the screen.

This is the date portion of the program. It establishes the date parameter used to age records. Any other response will indicate that there is an error in the program; it will then be necessary to check the listing again and make the necessary corrections.[1]

If all lines of the program are correctly entered, the system will respond with the date request. Further check the program by entering the date in the manner shown by the display in Example 5-2.

Once the date is entered, depress RETURN. The system should respond with the SYSTEM MENU, as shown in Exam-

---

[1]Most BASICs indicate the line number on which an error has occurred. This makes it easier to correct the problem—a process called debugging. However, should the system respond with an error, such as the next program element or a system error, defined by the BASIC user's manual, the problem is more subtle and can mean more time spent in the debugging process. It may indicate a problem with the hardware or even require that BASIC be reloaded into the system.

Example 5-1

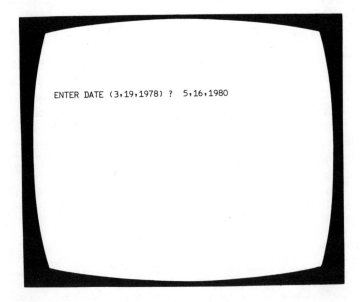

Example 5-2

ple 5-3. Any other response is an error and will require that the debugging process be gone through once more.

When it is established that the program has been entered correctly, save the program on a mass storage device. For disk-based systems it is suggested that this record be called "EXEC," since it is the routine that directs the calling of the different functions within the accounting package.

```
ENTER SELECTION AND DEPRESS RETURN

    INVENTORY CONTROL            (1)
    BILLING/ACCOUNTS RECEIVABLE  (2)
    ACCOUNTS PAYABLE             (3)
    GENERAL LEDGER               (4)

ENTER SELECTION ?
```

Example 5-3

Tape-oriented systems, the type this package is primarily written for, call for a different saving technique. Most BASICs have a feature called CSAVE or TSAVE, meaning to save the record on tape and identify it by a key letter or word. For systems that use the key letter, call the program "E"; for tape systems that allow for a word identifier, call the program "EXEC," the same as for a disk system.

When this program segment is verified and saved,[2] move on to the next segment in your system manual. Each time a segment is entered it must be verified and tested to make absolutely sure it is correct.

---

[2]When you save programs on a mass storage device, it is good practice to save the program at least twice. This is done to ensure that a working version is always available.

In the process of entering the programs in the computer, you should be able to get an understanding of program structure and design. Also, you can add any feature desired if it is predesigned to be compatible with the total system. It is recommended that the lines beginning with REM, for remark, not be entered. These lines are provided in the listing to help you understand the program. They don't perform an actual function in the program. REMark lines are numbered concurrently, while functional program lines are numbered by tens (see Example 5-4).

To assist you in verifying the programs, each program segment specifies the location in the book where displays can be found. The ideal procedure is to enter the program, check it against the listing and then turn to the chapter covering the function and follow the procedures; any errors will be pointed out immediately and corrections can be made.

```
1 REM:  SYSTEM MENU
2 REM: BY CARL WARREN
3 REM: THIS PROGRAM IS THE EXECUTIVE CALLING
4 REM: PROGRAM FOR THE ACCOUNTING PACKAGE
5 REM: CLEAR SCREEN BY PRINTING 24 BLANK LINES
10 FOR A= 0 TO 24 : PRINT : NEXT :
```

Example 5-4

5.6 SYSTEM MENU

The SYSTEM MENU, briefly mentioned in Section 5.5, is the key to the entire accounting package. It is this program that calls the other functions out, sets the date the system will use and provides a degree of flexibility and interactivity to the system.

This menu is the link to the program functions available and, consequently, can be written in several ways, depending on how the hardware is configured. The SYSTEM MENU in this book is written with the minimal system in mind—specifically, a 16K machine using one audio cassette recorder as the main storage device. As a result, the calling functions (those functions that request the other programs) are written to reflect this type of system. However, notes explaining other alternatives are provided with the listing.[3]

5.7   SUPPORT PACKAGES

The support packages, PLANNING and DEPOSIT, are presented in the same manner as the other functions of the accounting package. These features are provided to give yet another dimension to automated accounting. Although these packages are not noted on the SYSTEM MENU, they can be included by adding another two lines of code and subroutines. This will call them from the mass storage device.

The routines are designed to be used outside of the normal accounting package but use information generated from it. The PLANNING package uses information taken directly from totals generated from the general ledger. DEPOSIT can be used as an automated cash register and will help speed up the process of making the daily report.

5.8   REVIEW OF THE SYSTEM

The accounting package is made up of four distinct subsystems, as shown in the display in Example 5-3. Each subsystem is designed to perform a specific function in the maintenance of the books of a small business.

To achieve the greatest benefit from this system you should follow these guidelines:

---

[3]This applies only to the general CTBL systems package. The MECA and TRS-80 versions are for larger systems.

- Read this book in its entirety.
- Read Appendix A to fully understand the system structure.
- Prepare the system as specified in the user's manual.
- Load and verify each program segment as covered in the CTBL systems book.
- Before entering any real data, prepare dummy data to familiarize yourself with the system. Use the examples provided in the procedure chapters.
- When preparing to use the system on a day-to-day basis, begin with inventory control and create the entire data base before moving on to the next function.
- Establish the practice of making duplicates of all programs and data records. This will avoid the loss of any vital information.

Important: This system is a report keeper and a data analyzer. You should not expect the same level of operation from this system as that achieved with much larger systems.

Chapter Six

FIRST KEY SYSTEM: INVENTORY AND PURCHASING

This, the first procedure chapter, begins with an explanation of the subject of inventory control and purchasing. The procedures are presented in a point-by-point format. The chapter ends with a discussion of management's use of the information.

6.1 INTRODUCTION

When you set up a business that involves selling something other than a service, stock must be obtained to sell. Obtaining this stock is called purchasing: the stock is purchased from one or more vendors. Once the stock is on hand, it becomes inventory, which is then resold to the customer.

Purchasing and inventory control are extremely complicated aspects of the small business environment. We will discuss them separately, but though they may appear to be separate and distinct, they actually work together in a total system.

For purposes of this book, purchasing and inventory will be discussed in terms of a retail store, rather than a manufacturer. This is necessary since these functions have very unique requirements in a manufacturing environment.

Figure 6-1 represents the general flow of the events that take place when stock is purchased and set up as part of a retail inventory. It is easy to see that several problems must be considered. First, you will need to add the parts to your stock while keeping track of each item and determining whether its inventory level is near the necessary order points.

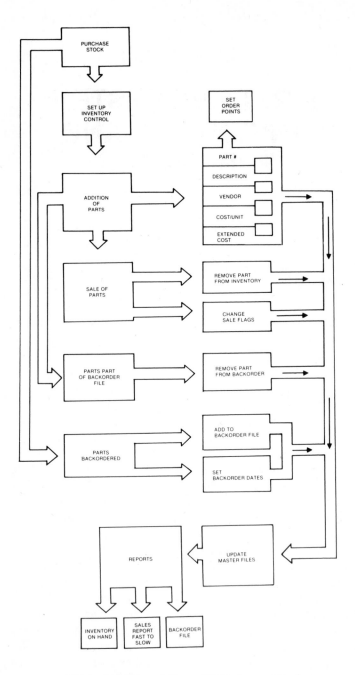

Figure 6-1 General flow of inventory control

Along with adding parts, the ability to remove parts as a result of sales is important, as is establishing some form of tracking for back orders. To make the inventory/purchasing system meaningful, records must be updated and reports of some form generated to the manager or order clerk. Whether the inventory/purchasing system used is manual or automated, all of these points must be considered. These areas are all primary but, like all information systems, they can be expanded upon. For example, it may be important to establish in the inventory file exactly where a specific item can be found, or there may be several small items that make up a unit, so that some link between them must be established.

Before we get into a full explanation of inventory control, let's look at the idea of purchasing and the method of tracking purchases.

6.2 PURCHASING

Purchasing is the process of procuring the necessary items of commerce. For small businesses, this process is usually carried out by the owner, but regardless of whose responsibility it is, purchasing represents about half the money spent for the operation of the business. Taking this into consideration, it can be seen that keeping a close eye on purchasing can mean the difference between profit and loss. This phrase, the difference between profit and loss, will be used several times in this chapter since it applies equally to both purchasing and inventory.

6.3 DETERMINING WHAT IS PURCHASED

The determination of what should be purchased is a difficult problem for a new company. It becomes even more difficult when the owner or manager of the business has no prior knowledge of what will sell and what will not. Consequently, before you set up your business, it is extremely important that you be familiar with the market being entered.

Besides the inventory to be purchased for stock, other items for the business must also be purchased. These items may include desks, sales cases, decorations, sales books, ledger sheets, bathroom supplies and computer supplies, if needed. Everything that is bought for use in the business must be purchased and, as a result, must be tracked. For the most part, purchases are tracked in the accounts payable records and general ledger records, but records must be kept of authorization information, such as purchase orders and order records. Some formal flow must be established when you set up the purchasing scheme.

6.4 PURCHASING PROCEDURE

The procedure in most small businesses is that when an item is needed, either the supplier is called and the order put in, or, if it's small enough, the owner runs next door to the drug store and picks it up. This is fine in some situations, but it offers the chance that the business will lose track of what was bought. This will be a serious problem when you want to deduct these expenses from your taxes. Of course, the situation can be worse. You may not be able to prove all the credits taken, due to inadequate tracking of purchasing records.

For example, suppose your business uses sales receipts to write up each sale of the day. Normally, a box of fifty pads is purchased from the stationery supply company along with other paper goods, and is more than likely placed under one heading, such as office or sales supplies, in the ledger. When the pads are used up and there is not sufficient time to get them from the supplier, the normal tendency is to run to the nearest store and purchase a few out of pocket or petty cash to get you through. The problem is that no authorization was given for the purchase and no record kept of the purchase. A few instances of this haphazard procedure can have a severe impact on the cash position of the company and, as stated before, can upset the tax credit situation.

Regardless of what is needed—supplies or inventory goods— a specific procedure must be established to ensure that good audit trails are set up, if for no other reason than to help keep track of cash. The following information is all that is required in most environments:

- A purchase order authorizing the purchase of goods or services (more on that later).
- The amount to be purchased, description, and an indicator of form of payment, i.e., credit, check, cash, or petty cash.
- Where the items are to be purchased.
- For heavy expenditure items, what the bid or quoted price was.

This procedure is only the beginning. Once the purchase order (PO) is issued, it must also be followed to see that the items are, in fact, purchased and delivered and that the correct check was issued or credit authorization given. Items paid for with petty cash must be returned with the sales slip attached. Items such as inventory become crucial and the PO gives the vehicle to follow up on the delivery of the goods. As will be discussed under inventory control, inventory items may be delivered damaged, short or back ordered, all of which must be tracked. The PO is the link to following these situations.

When we were discussing procedures, we used the term services. Services can be anything from a repairman coming in to fix the plumbing in your office to hiring outside labor to install an item you bought or sold. The purchase order becomes the audit trail to define exactly what service was purchased, who performed it, and what it cost.

As with most accounting situations, rules of thumb exist for purchasing. The simplest is the best. The rule is: before you buy it, put it on paper.

6.5 PURCHASING INVENTORY

Up to this point, inventory purchasing has only been mentioned. There has been very little discussion of what to do about it. The important point brought out so far has been the purchasing procedure; the same rules apply to purchasing inventory.

The problem most people will cite is creating a PO for each item of inventory needed. For inventory purchasing a PO is handled differently. The PO becomes a blanket PO to cover all items needed. The purchase order should list the stock number description, vendor order number, vendor, cost per unit, extended cost, the date the PO was issued, and who issued it. From the PO, the individual orders are made and the order slips attached to the PO. This way a double audit trail is kept, giving you a record of when each item was ordered and by whom.

For the most part, once a method of controlling the inventory is established, setting up the purchasing system becomes relatively easy.

6.6 SUMMARY OF PURCHASING

Once the purchase order is sent out for inventory items, the order must be followed up. This will ensure that items ordered are received in good order. The follow-up procedure takes this format:

- Check to see that the vendor received the order.
- Check the date of delivery—this is very important for critical items or items that are traditionally hard to get.
- Set up a follow-up-by-day system to see if items are delivered on time.

Even if the order is called in to the vendor, it is an excellent practice to send them a confirming purchase order with a return copy for them to sign with the promised delivery date. This sets up a contract between you and the vendor.

As each PO is filled, the accounts payable ledger must be brought up to date. If the PO was for items paid for in cash, the cash disbursements ledger must be updated.

6.7 INVENTORY CONTROL

Once stock is purchased and is on hand or coming, some method of controlling inventory must be established. There are several methods of setting up inventory control or maintenance.

For the simplest case, the mark on the wall will work. In this model, only a few items are carried and the total stock is bought once a month. Each month, the last item is sold on the last day of the month. This is very simple and easy to follow, but in order for you to know how many of each item are left, sold items must be marked off. At the beginning of each month the wall behind the sales counter is repainted and the ten items the store sells are written down with 100 lines indicating the number of items on hand. As each item is sold, a mark is drawn through one of the lines to indicate that it has been sold.

What happens when more than ten items are carried, or more are added during the month, or more or less than 100 are sold in any given month? Chaos!

Since inventory represents the single greatest investment a company has, it is very important to keep track of each item from the time it is ordered to the time it is sold. Figure 6-1, discussed earlier, presents all the items necessary to incorporate an inventory control package.

6.8   THE INVENTORY RECORD

In the example of the wall inventory, the system was a month-to-month inventory that made some assumptions based on past history. There was little need to maintain inventory in a perpetual manner or worry about costing information, since the items always cost the same and sold for the same. However, in real-life situations, a perpetual inventory record must be maintained that keeps track of the number in stock, on order, required, and sold. The perpetual inventory record makes it possible to tell at a glance the actual status of the inventory and guide you in making reasonably wise decisions. Remember, with the largest investment being inventory, the way it is handled can make the difference between profit and loss.

The inventory record for either a manual or an automated system has, as shown by Figure 6-1, the following information:

- Stock number—this number can be related to the vendor number or a unique inhouse number.
- Item description—what the item is, e.g., "wrench ¾ hex."
- Total on hand—the actual number of items, per stock number, on the shelves.
- Cost/unit—what the unit costs.
- Extended cost—this is stock on hand multiplied by cost/unit.
- Vendor—this can be the name of the vendor or a vendor number that translates to a vendor description.

Once the inventory record is set up, consideration must be given to how it will be stored, if manual, how easy it is to retrieve information from it, and how easy it is to determine what the information is: minimum number, back orders, order dates, quantity ordered, location of the item, etc.

6.9   INVENTORY PRICING

Because inventory items cost something, the cost of each item must be reflected in the inventory record. It is this cost that determines the final cost of the item, the retail price. There are several methods used for costing unit items: weighted average, simple average, moving average, first in first out (FIFO) and last in first out (LIFO). Each of these pricing methods has its advantages and purposes. The easiest method to use is simple average. It is the pricing system used in this inventory program. The following information is entered for each item: the cost/unit price; the total on hand; items being updated; and the new cost/unit. The new totals on hand will change the data base cost/unit. The system removes the existing cost/unit and adds the new cost/unit. The new cost per unit is then established.

6.10　THE PHYSICAL INVENTORY

When you establish a new method of inventory control, you will have to take a physical inventory. This is the process of actually counting the items on the shelf and checking them against the booked records. For rotating inventories, closed and reopened at the end of each month, a physical inventory is taken each month. Perpetual inventories, if handled correctly, need to be physically checked less often—quarterly or at the fiscal year's end.

The physical inventory worksheet should look exactly like the inventory record. This makes it easy to compare records quickly and to make sure that only legitimate information exists. Once the inventory is set up on an automated system, the computer will generate a list of inventory items or worksheets to be used in the physical inventory. When converting from a manual to an automated system, the physical inventory is a must to ensure accuracy of the data base being created.

The physical inventory worksheet should look like Figure 6-2. This sheet asks for all the information necessary for the inventory program used in this book but can be expanded to meet your specific needs.

6.11　THE IMPORTANT ITEMS IN INVENTORY CONTROL

This chapter began with purchasing and what was needed to control that function of the business. The purchasing information is really related to the accounts payable portion of the package but was discussed because it is directly related to inventory.

As you will remember, when purchase orders were discussed, the vendor of the items was mentioned. Vendors are important

DATE: 05/28/77   PAGE ____ of ____

Stock #	Vendor #	Description	Onhand	Remarks
------	------	----------- ----------	----	_____
------	------	----------- ----------	----	_____
------	------	----------- ----------	----	_____
------	------	----------- ----------	----	_____
------	------	----------- ----------	----	_____
------	------	----------- ----------	----	_____

Fill in each blank with only the number of characters indicated.

Stock #—6 characters	Vendor #—6 characters
Description—21 characters	Onhand—4 characters

Remarks is freeform and is used for indicating information such as damaged items.

Figure 6-2 Inventory worksheet

people, and accurate records must be kept on them. The inventory record must have some link to the vendor so that purchasing can be handled in a relatively easy manner. Basically, there are two methods of handling the vendor in the inventory record.

The first method is to build a record within the inventory record that describes the vendor, including the contact, company name, address, phone and track record—how fast they deliver and the terms they offer. For the manual system, this can be done by using a large enough card or attaching another card. In the automated system, this becomes even more cumbersome and cuts down the storage space that can be used for the inventory function.

The second method is to assign a number to the vendor. This number can be any unique number that works or contains information that quickly describes the vendor. A descriptive number might contain a code such as 01, meaning that this vendor supplies only paint. The next number in the sequence would indicate whether the vendor is local or out of state. Thus, a four-digit number now exists that would appear as 0102, pointing to a paint vendor in the second state, named on a separate list. This is purely arbitrary, but it will serve well. We have two numbers left to fill since our inventory record calls for a six-digit vendor number. The last two digits can be used to indicate how fast the vendor delivers. Now the number appears as 010209, the 09 meaning that this vendor is very slow in delivering. Analyzing this numbering system, you have probably realized that the six digits will not work in all cases, since if you use this type of system, it is possible for two different vendors to have the same number. What is needed in this type of coding scheme is an additional three digits at either the start or the end to identify the vendor as a unique entity.

The importance of the vendor number is that it is used to establish a vendor file that gives complete vendor history. This system is used in both manual and automated systems, since in both cases it saves space and is used only when necessary. Of course, in the manual system, this means that two or more files will be open at the same time. The same thing happens in the automated system, but it becomes reasonably transparent.

There is another number that becomes important in handling inventory—the stock or part number. This system uses a six-digit number for identification of the part. As with the vendor number, the stock number can be used to pinpoint the location of the item in the stock room. The system used here starts the stock number at 000001.

The next important item is the part description. This describes each item in the most concise manner. For example, a hardware store may carry 20 different types of hammers. The hammers may have different handle lengths and serve different purposes. So the description of a hammer might look like this: HAMMER SL½, meaning a half-pound sledge hammer. The description should tell what the item is in order to make retrieval from the stock room easy. In some inventory systems, classes of inventory are set up so that a class of items, such as hammers, might come under a unique classifier, say 3. Therefore, the inventory record would contain an extra field indicator that would hold the classifier. This makes the description easier. For the example previously used, the first entry would be a 3, indicating hammers; all other entries would be assumed to be hammers until changed. The description fields then would be ½ pd sledge or 12 in claw, and so on. The hammer identifier is set up once. Obviously, this is the ideal and it can be found in some commercial inventory packages. For the package portrayed here, a 21-character description field is allowed.

The next fields are of utmost importance: the total on hand, cost/unit, minimum reorder point, and maximum on hand. Information for these fields is taken from purchasing and receiving records. Sales information is entered in the form of inventory items removed as a result of the sales process. From this data, a sales analysis can be generated that is similar to that of Figure 6-3.

INVENTORY ANALYSIS 112778

STOCK # VENDOR #	DESCRIPTION ONHAND	COST	a CUR MTH b LT MTH	c 2ND PREV d YTD	LT ORD ON ORD	REC ORD #
000001 176345	HEX WRENCHES 0100	5.10	10 11	21 150	102278 0025	9 110674
000002 176346	C CLAMPS 0256	11.23	23 34	11 200	092378 0010	31 113467
000003 176347	PHILLIPS SD 1000	00.25	150 254	333 9389	110178 0500	1000 112374

Figure 6-3 Inventory analysis

6.12 INVENTORY RECORDS

For any inventory system to be worthwhile, some form of report must be generated. In Chapter Three, this was discussed briefly in terms of what to look for. Figure 6-3 is the sales analysis report. The essential information—stock number, vendor number and description—is given. The important points of this report are: the number of items sold during the current month, the number of items sold last month, the number of items sold the second previous month, and the total number sold year-to-date. This information is used to determine if an item should be kept as part of the inventory. The next items are the last order date for the item, total on order, total received, and the last issued order number. All this is very important information that must be used by the company's management to keep track of cash flow in relation to inventory flow. This knowledge can determine the difference between profit and loss.

6.13 PROCEDURES

The following examples will show how to use the inventory system. All displays and outputs to the hardcopy device are assumed to be 64 columns and are formatted as such.

Since it is almost impossible to address specific hardware types, it is assumed that you know how to use the computer at hand. Therefore, in this chapter and in all subsequent chapters, the procedures begin as if the computer is ready to go. Regardless of the system type and whatever modification is made by the user, the basic procedures will remain the same.

6.14 SYSTEM MENU

Example 6-1 is the SYSTEM MENU. It guides the application to the option desired. For this chapter, inventory control is wanted, so item number 1 is entered. The computer will, upon entry of item number 1, check to see if 1 is valid and if 1 directs the program to go somewhere else. Should an error be made, either zero (0) or a number greater than 7 be entered, the program will then recycle and redisplay the SYSTEM MENU.

Although there is no option built in to terminate the program, the entry of **CTRL C** will cause the program to revert to the command mode, and it will usually respond with: **READY:**
However, it is suggested that you do not do this unless you have a full understanding of the system.

As stated, when option number 1 is entered, the computer makes its error checks, then checks to see what option number 1 is supposed to do. In this case the program is directed to load a program called inventory control.

Since it takes time for the program to load, the computer will appear to be doing nothing. The only activity noticed will be in

```
            SYSTEM MENU

      ENTER SELECTION AND DEPRESS RETURN

          INVENTORY CONTROL            (1)
          BILLING/ACCOUNTS RECEIVABLE  (2)
          ACCOUNTS PAYABLE             (3)
          GENERAL LEDGER               (4)
          PLANNING                     (5)
          DEPOSIT                      (6)
          UTILITY                      (7)

      SELECTION ? 1
```

Example 6-1

the cassette storage system as the computer looks for the program.

Once the program called inventory control is located and loaded into memory, a special function in the program will cause the program to immediately go into the run mode.

6.15 INVENTORY CONTROL MENU

Since all software for the inventory program is written in a modular fashion, the next item displayed is the INVENTORY CONTROL MENU. This menu offers options that pertain directly to using the automated inventory system. Example 6-2 shows the INVENTORY CONTROL MENU with the selection to update the inventory.

6.16 UPDATE INVENTORY MENU

This selection gives us the display shown in Example 6-3. Our selection (1) puts the system in the ADD ITEM mode.

```
        INVENTORY CONTROL

   ENTER SELECTION AND DEPRESS RETURN

      UPDATE INVENTORY        (1)
      LIST INVENTORY          (2)
      ANALYZE INVENTORY       (3)
      MINIMUM QUANTITY LIST   (4)

   TYPE MENU TO RETURN TO SYSTEM MENU

   SELECTION ?   1
```

Example 6-2

```
   TYPE @ TO EXIT AND RETURN TO INVENTORY CONTROL MENU
   TYPE MENU TO RETURN TO SYSTEM MENU

      ADD ITEM     (1)
      REMOVE ITEM  (2)
      CHANGE ITEM  (3)

   SELECTION ?   1
```

Example 6-3

6.17   ADD ITEM

While in the ADD ITEM mode, the system is working with the data base—the area containing all information about the inventory. The question in Example 6-4, HOW MANY ITEMS TO ADD ?, is used by the program to set up a loop. For example, if 3 is entered, the program will cycle through the input phase three times and on the last entry will print the message: MORE TO ENTER (Y/N) ?. Should the answer be Y, or yes, the question HOW MANY ITEMS TO ADD ? will be displayed again. If the answer is N, or no, the program will then assume you are finished and redisplay the INVENTORY CONTROL MENU.

If you enter the word MENU, the computer will immediately direct the program to return to the SYSTEM MENU. The entry of @ will direct the program to return to the update selection. These inputs work with the HOW MANY ITEMS TO ADD and MORE TO ENTER (Y/N) questions. The idea is to provide as many alternatives as possible until you make up your mind.

The program is set up to allow only six numerics (all numbers) to be entered for a stock number. Some error checking is done on this input statement. The first check is to see if the entry was three nines (999). This entry signals the software that, for some reason, you want out of the routine and want to return to the INVENTORY CONTROL MENU.

Should fewer than six numbers be entered, the program will respond with the error message: ENTRY TOO SMALL ENTER 6 NUMERIC CHARACTERS. For entries greater than six characters, the system will display the error message: ENTRY TOO BIG ENTER ONLY 6 NUMERIC CHARACTERS. If alpha characters are entered in error, the system will respond with the error message associated with the version of BASIC being used. For most BASICs the response will be similar to: INVALID INPUT, and it will then redisplay the input prompt question.

Once a correct or valid entry is made and RETURN depressed, the program will accept the information and display the next question. The number in the upper left-hand corner of the display is the count. For the vendor number, the same rules of error checking and entry apply. In our example, for instance, 000 must be entered. Once a valid number is entered, the system will respond with the next input question.

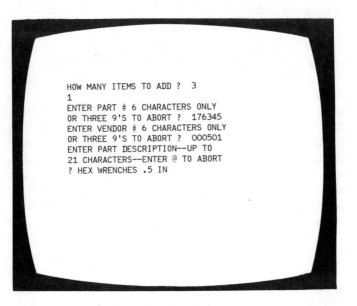

```
HOW MANY ITEMS TO ADD ?   3
1
ENTER PART # 6 CHARACTERS ONLY
OR THREE 9'S TO ABORT ?   176345
ENTER VENDOR # 6 CHARACTERS ONLY
OR THREE 9'S TO ABORT ?   000501
ENTER PART DESCRIPTION--UP TO
21 CHARACTERS--ENTER @ TO ABORT
? HEX WRENCHES .5 IN
```

Example 6-4

The description field is an alphanumeric field (containing both letters and numbers) that can be up to 21 characters in length, including spaces. If more than 21 characters are entered, the system responds with the error message: ENTRY TOO BIG ENTER ONLY 21 CHARACTERS. When an error such as this is encountered, the system recycles and redisplays the input message.

Once a valid entry is made, the system responds with the next input question. There is one problem you should be aware of. As any entry of 21 characters or less is valid, it is possible to enter garbage. At this point the screen is cleared.

Our display is now shown in Example 6-5. The on hand field will accept only numeric characters, up to four. Should more than four characters be entered, the system responds with the error message: ENTRY TOO BIG ENTER ONLY 4 NUMERIC CHARACTERS. The input message will then be redisplayed. If anything other than numerics is entered in this field, BASIC will respond with the message: INVALID INPUT and redisplay the input prompt question.

As with other inputs, once a valid input is received the system then responds with the next question. In this case the question

```
1
ENTER TOTAL ON HAND
UP TO 4 DIGITS ?   26
INPUT MIN, MAX, COST/UNIT, CUR # SOLD,
SOLD LST MTH, SOLD 2ND MTH PRIOR,
SOLD YTD ?   50, 100, 5.50, 0, 0, 0, 0
```

Example 6-5

requires several inputs to be satisfied: the minimum/maximum reorder points, cost/unit, number sold this period, number sold last month, number sold second month prior and number sold year-to-date.

In a multiple-entry situation such as this, if all fields are not satisfied when RETURN is depressed the system will respond with a double question mark (??) indicating that some value was not filled, and will continue doing so until all values are filled.

If an incorrect or invalid input is made for any one of the fields, the system will abort the entry and will display the error message: INPUT INCORRECT PLEASE REENTER and redisplay the input prompt question.

Other error responses are directly related to the error checking done for each variable. For the minimum/maximum reorder points, the entries must be all numeric and no greater than four characters. If the system detects an error specifically related to this field it will respond with the error message: M/M INPUT GREATER THAN 4 CHARACTERS. The system will then redisplay the entire input question and all fields will have to be reentered. If an alpha character is entered in any one of the numeric fields, the system will abort the input and display the error message: INPUT INCORRECT PLEASE REENTER and redisplay the entire input message.

To help understand what happens for each input in this multiple input statement, Table 6-1 is provided to show what is allowed.

The inputs into this or any multi-input prompt must be separated by a comma (,). The comma is used as a field delimiter or divider that advises the program that one entry is finished and another is starting.

Once this question is answered with valid inputs and no error is encountered, the system will do one of two things: if the items-to-add response was more than 1, it will recycle to the start; if you have finished with the session and you have answered the add question with a 1, the system will recycle to the INVENTORY CONTROL MENU.

Table 6-1
Valid Inputs for Multiple Input Statement

Field	Type	Size	Error
MIN	Numeric	4 char	MIN TOO BIG
MAX	Numeric	4 char	MAX TOO BIG
COST/UNIT	Numeric*	8 char	C/U TOO BIG
CUR # SOLD	Numeric	4 char	CUR TOO BIG
SOLD LST MTH	Numeric	4 char	SLM TOO BIG
SOLD 2ND MTH	Numeric	4 char	S2M TOO BIG
SOLD YTD	Numeric	4 char	SYTD TOO BIG

*In this numeric input decimal points (.) are allowed. Each encountered error causes the system to reprompt and request reentry of all the information from the start of this input question.

6.18   REMOVING AN ITEM

Occasionally it becomes necessary to remove an item of inventory from the data base. In manual systems this is a fairly easy operation; you scratch the item off the inventory card. For automated systems, essentially the same thing happens. You tell the computer that the item is no longer needed and it is scratched from the data base, but the tape system is still active until the utility program is run. The utility program will pick up all deleted items and repack the tape; that is, it will tighten up all the information on the tape so that no blank spots exist. This will be covered in more detail under UTILITY.

Removing an item from this system is relatively straightforward. The UPDATE option is chosen from the INVENTORY CONTROL MENU and the REMOVE AN ITEM option chosen from the UPDATE MENU. Example 6-2 shows your first selection. Example 6-6 shows your second.

The system then responds with the question: ENTER STOCK # TO BE REMOVED ? (see Example 6-7). Once the number is entered and RETURN depressed, the system will search the data base for the correct item. Once the item is found it will be displayed on the CRT screen and the question asked whether it is the correct item with the question: ITEM CORRECT (Y/N) ?. If a Y(es) response is given the system will then ask: OK TO REMOVE (Y/N) ?. A Y(es) response will cause the system to set a deletion flag on the item and rewrite it to update the data base tape (see Example 6-8).

In cases where N(o) is entered to ITEM CORRECT (Y/N) ? the system will respond with ENTER STOCK # TO BE REMOVED. It will do this only three times. If you are still not sure of the number of the item to be deleted, it will automatically print the entire list of inventory items on the system hard-copy device (the printer).

If N(o) is entered for OK TO REMOVE (Y/N) ?, the system assumes that you didn't want to be there in the first place and cycles back to the UPDATE MENU.

The entry of the at (@) symbol at any time in the dialogue will abort the dialogue and recycle back to the INVENTORY CONTROL MENU.

If a stock number greater than six characters is entered, the system will respond with the error response: STOCK # TOO BIG REENTER and redisplay the input question. If an alpha character is entered, the system will print the error message: INVALID INPUT and redisplay the input prompt question.

Should you enter a nonexistent stock number, the system will try to find it and, being unable to do so, will print the message: UNABLE TO LOCATE STOCK # PLEASE REENTER. It will then redisplay the input prompt question. This will take place only three times. If you try a fourth time, the entire inventory list will be printed.

```
TYPE @ TO EXIT AND RETURN TO INVENTORY CONTROL MENU
TYPE MENU TO RETURN TO SYSTEM MENU

  ADD ITEM     (1)
  REMOVE ITEM  (2)
  CHANGE ITEM  (3)

SELECTION ?  2
```

Example 6-6

```
ENTER STOCK # TO BE REMOVED ?   176345

**** SEARCHING ****
```

Example 6-7

```
STOCK #  176345
VENDOR #  000501
DESC HEX WRENCHES .5 IN
TTL OHD  26
MIN  50
MAX  100
COST/UNIT  5.50
CUR # SOLD  0
SOLD LAST MTH  0
SOLD 2ND MTH PRIOR  0
SOLD YTD  0
ITEM CORRECT (Y/N) ?  Y
OK TO REMOVE (Y/N) ?  Y
****REMOVING ITEM****
```

Example 6-8

6.19 CHANGING AN ITEM

Since all things are subject to change, it is necessary to be able to change an item in the inventory data base. The process is similar to that used for removing an item. The UPDATE MENU is requested and the CHANGE AN ITEM option is chosen. The system will respond with: ENTER STOCK # TO BE CHANGED ?. This display is shown in Example 6-9. All error responses in the REMOVE option are used in this routine.

When a valid stock number is entered and found, the system responds by displaying the record with item numbers and the question: WHICH LINE(S) TO BE CHANGED ?. This display is shown in Example 6-10. This entry will accept any number from 1 to 11 or the word ALL. If ALL is used, the system will prompt you through each entry, item by item, by displaying the input prompt and the old information. If a selective change is done, the system will respond with the input prompt and the old information. This display is shown in Example 6-11.

Once all the information to be changed is reentered, the system will redisplay the record and the message: RECORD OK (Y/N) ?. An entry of Y(es) will cause the system to update the

```
TYPE @ TO EXIT AND RETURN TO INVENTORY CONTROL MENU
TYPE MENU TO RETURN TO SYSTEM MENU

   ADD ITEM     (1)
   REMOVE ITEM  (2)
   CHANGE ITEM  (3)

SELECTION ?  3
ENTER STOCK # TO BE CHANGED ?  176345
```

Example 6-9

```
  1  STOCK #   176345
  2  VENDOR #  000501
  3  DESC HEX WRENCHES .5 IN
  4  TTL OHD   26
  5  MIN  50
  6  MAX  100
  7  COST/UNIT  5.50
  8  CUR # SOLD  0
  9  SOLD LST MTH  0
 10  SOLD 2ND MTH PRIOR  0
 11  SOLD YTD  0

ITEM CORRECT (Y/N) ?  Y
WHICH LINE(S) TO BE CHANGED ?  4, 7
```

Example 6-10

```
TTL OHD   26
INPUT NEW OHD OR ENTER - AND # TO
BE REMOVED ?   -6

COST/UNIT  5.50
INPUT NEW COST/UNIT ?   6.00
```

Example 6-11

data base and display the message: **WRITING UPDATED RECORD** (see Example 6-12). When it is finished, the system responds with the INVENTORY CONTROL MENU.

If the response was N(o), the system will ask which items are to be changed and start over.

One important point should be mentioned. When you are removing or changing data base items, all items should be removed or changed at one time rather than switching back and forth. Also, the change item function is used in this system for updating inventory by adding items newly arrived or subtracting for items sold, and, of course, updating the sales items. The utility program will take care of updating the last month, second month prior and year-to-date totals, although they can be done manually.

If you change **TTL OHD** (total items on hand) by entering an unsigned number such as **10**, the system will assume items are being added and will update the total. If the entry is preceded by − , a minus sign, the system will then remove that many items from the **TTL OHD** and update the **CUR # SOLD** field by that number.

```
1    STOCK #  176345
2    VENDOR #  00501
3    DESC HEX WRENCHES .5 IN
4    TTL OHD  20
5    MIN  50
6    MAX  100
7    COST/UNIT  6.00
8    CUR #·SOLD  6
9    SOLD LST MTH  O
10   SOLD 2ND MTH PRIOR  O
11   SOLD YTD  O
RECORD OK (Y/N) ?  Y

****WRITING UPDATED RECORD****
```

Example 6-12

When the cost/unit field is updated or changed, the system will do an automatic average and the field will reflect that average. For example, assume you have ten items currently on hand that cost $1.00 apiece and you add ten that cost $1.25 each; the cost/unit will show the average of the two, or $1.13 per unit.

During the change operation, the vendor field can be changed to include up to three additional vendors. You can do this by entering the vendors, beginning with the current one and separating each vendor number by a comma.

6.20 INVENTORY REPORTS

In the UPDATE section of inventory control, the system has allowed you to add items to the data base, remove them and change them. You can see from the INVENTORY CONTROL MENU (see Example 6-2) that there are three other functions: list inventory, analyze inventory and minimum quantity list. All of these are reports generated to the hardcopy printer device. All that is required is that the data tape be in the reader device.

The data tape used must be the most current and must have passed through the UTILITY portion.

6.21   INVENTORY LIST

To obtain these reports, request the INVENTORY CONTROL MENU and type in the desired selection. If 2 is chosen, the system will respond with:

INVENTORY LIST

STOCK #	VENDOR #	DESCRIPTION	OHD	COST/UNIT
176345	000501	HEX WRENCHES	20	6.00

The same detail is given for each item in the current inventory.

6.22   INVENTORY ANALYSIS

If item 3 is chosen, the system will respond with:

INVENTORY ANALYSIS 112779

STOCK # VENDOR #	DESCRIPTION ON HAND	COST	a CUR MTH b LT MTH	c 2ND PREV d YTD
000001 176345	HEX WRENCHES 0100	5.10	10 11	21 150
000002 176346	C CLAMPS 0256	11.23	23 34	11 200
000003 176347	PHILLIPS SD 1000	00.25	150 254	333 9389

The number 112779 represents the date the report is requested. This is taken from the system startup sequence. You will notice that this report does not have the order information shown on the analysis report (Figure 6-3). This is because the system as written did not incorporate that feature. It can be added in the code if you need it. Remember that this is basically a bare bones system designed to be expanded upon by the user.

6.23   MINIMUM QUANTITY LIST

The final report available, the minimum quantity list, is accessed by entering the number 4 for the option selection in the INVENTORY CONTROL MENU. The system responds with:

MINIMUM QUANTITY LIST

STOCK #	VENDOR #	DESCRIPTION	MIN	OHD
176345	000501	HEX WRENCHES	50	20

This report will list any and all items that are at or below the established minimum quantity. The main purpose of this report is to provide information on what should be ordered, so that adequate stocks can be kept on hand.

6.24   UTILITY

The utility function for the inventory package is accessed directly from the SYSTEM MENU. Option number 7 provides this function not only for inventory, but for all records and files associated with the accounting package. This display is shown in Example 6-1.

As shown in Example 6-13, when UTILITY is asked for, the system responds by displaying a UTILITY MENU. This menu simply asks which data base you are working with. UTILITY also displays the question or message: IS DATA BASE TAPE ON DRIVE ZERO WHEN READY DEPRESS RETURN. An E entered will cause UTILITY to update as of the end of the month. A Y entered will cause UTILITY to update as of the end of the year. If you depress RETURN without entering either E or Y, there is no updating.

When RETURN is depressed, the screen will clear and the message: UTILITY IS RUNNING will be displayed. When this happens, the system is loading the data base item by item and checking to see if it exists more than once. Each record is examined and then written out to the new tape on drive number one. Once the update has taken place, UTILITY will display the message: READY TO SORT PLACE NEW TAPE ON DRIVE 0 AND A BLANK TAPE ON DRIVE #1 DEPRESS RETURN WHEN READY ? (see Example 6-14). Now UTILITY will read the tapes one more time and begin the sorting process. Since the sort process is limited to the amount of memory, the total number of records that can be in memory at any one time is restricted. The process is relatively slow and, depending upon the number of records, may require a great deal of time when tape systems that cannot back up are used. This will necessitate swapping the tapes several times to get a complete sort. For MECA or other controlled digital tape systems and, of course,

```
        UTILITY MENU

        INV UT  (1)
        A/R UT  (2)
        A/P UT  (3)
        G/L UT  (4)

     SELECTION ?  1

     IS DATA BASE TAPE ON DRIVE O
     DEPRESS RETURN ?

     ****UTILITY IS RUNNING****
```

Example 6-13

```
     READY TO SORT PLACE NEW TAPE ON DRIVE O
     AND A BLANK TAPE ON DRIVE #1 DEPRESS
     RETURN WHEN READY ?
```

Example 6-14

disk systems, no swapping of the tapes is necessary. What the system does is look for the lowest stock number on tape. This means that the records are sorted by stock number only.

To get around swapping tapes on a non-controlled tape system, do the following: once the end is found on a pass, the UTILITY Program will display the message: REWIND THE TAPE. The system will then start looking for the next stock number in sequence. When the memory contains 25 sorted records, they will be written to the new data base tape, and the function will continue until the last record is sorted.

If you have a MECA system, you will find that the UTILITY function will be much more transparent and will not require using the extra tape or swapping. The MECA system UTILITY updates, then sorts from old tape to new. Then it goes back one more time and writes the sorted data to the end of the old tape, so that it can be stored as an archive tape.

The other functions UTILITY takes care of are updating the LST MTH, 2ND MTH PRIOR and YTD figures. But this only happens when the letter E is entered on the opening UTILITY question. This signals UTILITY to update these fields and set the current month field to zero in all records. Y is entered to inform the system that it is the end of the year, and all these fields are set to zero, with the archive tape containing the last figures.

A good practice to get into when using this inventory package is to set up a specific day of the week to run the UTILITY. This way all current transactions are updated and the reports will reflect this information. The UTILITY function must be run at the close of each month so the records are updated and the next month starts correctly.

To further facilitate the use of UTILITY in the inventory control environment, Table 6-2 is provided as a guide to what must be done on a step-by-step basis.

6.25   ERROR MESSAGES

The error messages provided in this application are designed to help lead you through its use. Unfortunately, it is almost impossible to provide error routines that check for everything. Consequently, care must be taken during the data entry portion to ensure correct information.

Appendix A contains not only the flowchart of this application, but also a table of variables used, as well as each of

Table 6-2
Guide to Using Utility

1. Select the UTILITY function from the SYSTEM MENU.
2. Select INVUT from the UTILITY MENU.
3. Remove system tape from drive 0 and replace with data base tape.
4. Put blank tape on drive number 1.
5. For manual cassettes, put new data base tape from drive number 1 to drive number 0 and a blank tape on number 1.

---

the error responses and recovery procedures. However, when a system error occurs—an error directly related to BASIC—it may be necessary to start from the beginning.

6.26 SYSTEM SUMMARY

The inventory package presented in this chapter is by no means complete, nor is it meant to be. This package is bare bones and is designed to be added to and changed to meet your needs. The system does provide a method that will greatly enhance your inventory handling.

The three reports provided can be used to ascertain quickly what is on hand, what is to be ordered and how sales are fluctuating. Purchase order entry and order tracking were mentioned, but not implemented in this version. However, plans are being made continually to update this package and to make it available in a full-blown form on cassette tape.

The inventory control function is only one-sixth of the total accounting package but, if used by itself, it will surely increase profits.

Chapter Seven

SECOND KEY SYSTEM: BILLING

This chapter describes the first part of the accounts receivable package. It presents the necessary procedures for building a data base for billing and for mailing labels. The chapter provides a discussion of the importance of the system.

7.1 INTRODUCTION

One of the most difficult tasks a company has is billing. The purposes of billing are, first, to collect money due by preparing invoices to customers and, second, to provide correct credit and debit information to keep the books in balance.

Billing is the beginning of the accounts receivable function and, as such, is treated as a separate entity. The billing operation is the result of sales—credit sales, in this case—which create accounts receivable. Figure 7-1 is a functional representation of the flow of the billing process.

The bill or issue invoice is the vehicle used to create information to update an accounts receivable record for a customer. In an efficient operation, bills are issued promptly. The purpose is to notify a customer of his obligation and thereby speed up collection.

However, most small businessmen suffer from lack of time and personnel. The owner is usually the store manager, head salesman, repairman and chief accountant all rolled into one. The result is that not all functions of the business are taken care

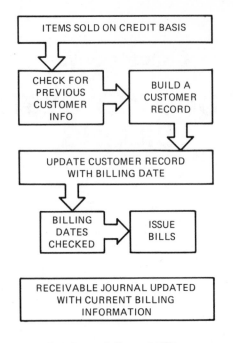

Figure 7-1 General flow of billing process

of at the most appropriate time. When the billing function is neglected a cash flow problem can result, which can cause a company with great potential to wither on the vine.

7.2   THE BILLING PROCESS

Billing is, as stated before, the method used by a company to collect money for any goods or services sold. Billing is also used to keep the accounts updated, showing who has paid what and how much they still owe. The bill also serves as a reminder of the legal contract the buyer has made with the company. The bill, or invoice, is the formal, written promissory note with payment requested.

The bill also serves to let the customer know what kind of benefits, in terms of discounts, she can get by honoring the bill quickly. The bill has another side benefit—it establishes a customer base for future advertising or special sale offerings.

The billing process begins logically with the customer ordering goods or services. Her contract begins with that order, whether it is made by phone, in person or by issuance of a purchase order. Once the goods or services are delivered or provided, you can bill the customer for the agreed payment.

The bill is written to reflect all the essential information, including:

- Date ordered
- Purchase order number
- Ordered by
- Description of goods or services
- Date delivered
- Cost

These items make up the basic information that must be included in each bill created. Along with this information must go the "deliver to" and "bill to" data—often they differ. Also included are any terms, standard or special, designed to keep the customer's business. This information can be taken from the purchase order or the sales receipt written at the time of purchase. Once all the correct information is available, the bill is ready to be sent. The bill is sent to the customer and a copy is kept for inhouse records. Also, the accounts receivable ledgers are updated for that customer.

The next step is for the customer to pay the bill. When this is done, the bill is marked "paid" and the accounts receivable ledger cards are updated to show that a specific invoice number has been cleared. In some cases, the bill is not paid in its entirety and, as a result, another bill is generated in the normal billing cycle. This bill reflects the previous balance, credits and new purchases.

7.3 TERMS

One method used to accelerate collection of money in the billing process is to offer terms. Terms mean that, if the bill is paid within a certain amount of time, the customer is entitled to deduct a percentage from the bill. For example, *2% net 10* means that if the bill is paid within ten days of the invoice date the customer can deduct 2 percent of the total bill. The usual terms are *net 30*, meaning that the entire amount of the bill must be paid within 30 days of the invoice date with no discounts. In the case of net 30 bills, there is usually some penalty added if the bill begins to age in the 31- to 60-day category, and so on. This penalty, or late charge, introduces another item that must be included on the next bill.

7.4 BILLING AND CASH FLOW

The bill represents money—but only on paper. It can't be spent in the normal sense. There are ways of turning bills, or receivables, into cash through factoring, or borrowing, on the dollar amount of the receivables, but such practices should be avoided in every way possible.

Since the bill represents cash, it determines what a company can do in any given time frame, depending on how fast the receivables clear. The bill is cash and must always be viewed as such because cash is what keeps the company in business.

The major problem many small businesses have is maintaining cash flow. When this problem becomes acute, the company cannot afford to buy material or keep current with payables. As a result, it can be forced out of business. The billing process, if handled properly, can help avoid cash flow problems. Inadequate performance in the billing process has created more cash flow problems for more companies than any other aspect of doing business.

By quickly processing orders and creating bills, the amount of cash a company has coming in can be kept reasonably steady. By maintaining billing records (keeping them up to date), cash being used by debtors (customers) can be tracked and, one hopes, collected.

7.5 SOLVING THE BILLING PROBLEM

Billing can be brought into line to achieve the greatest benefits by several means. One possibility is hiring outside services to maintain all billing records and to keep track of debtors. This does have an advantage for the small businessman, since it relieves him of considerable drudgery. The problem with this is that it is relatively easy to lose control and not know, until days or months later, the actual status of receivables.

Another possibility is to keep the standard ledger cards and billing logs and then let an outside data processing service update all records once a month. This is not a bad option and is used by many small businesses satisfactorily. However, the cost of this type of service is high.

The other possibility is to handle the whole process inhouse. For a manual system, this means staying after hours to update records and to generate bills. If it is possible to hire an inhouse bookkeeper, it can be a daily process.

However, the most exciting possibility is doing the job inhouse on a computer. By using microcomputer systems, the entire billing process can be done easily. The information is entered on a regular basis and, at the normal billing cycle, bills are created and all accounts updated with the required information.

7.6   AUTOMATED BILLING

Automated billing follows the same process as manual billing. The customer makes the purchase, the bill is created and the accounts are updated. On receipt of payment, the bill is marked "paid" and the accounts are again updated. No big deal, except that the time it takes to perform the tasks is less.

In automated systems, the billing information is entered as the purchase order is received or the sale made. This can be done in batches or as they occur, depending upon how the computer system is configured. At the billing date the computer generates all current bills with the information that has been added to the relevant accounts.

7.7   THE BILLING PACKAGE

The billing package described in this book ties in directly to the accounts receivable system and, as will be seen in the procedure portion, is a part of that package. This package, like the inventory package, is bare bones, meaning that it provides certain functions and is meant to be expanded and modified for specific purposes.

Essentially, this package provides the following functions:

- Add a customer—all the necessary data from "ship to" and "bill to" data to purchases and contact information.
- Delete a customer—the customer no longer buys from you or has been inactive for a period of time.

- Change a customer record—this makes it possible to update a customer record.
- Print the bills—create a bill based on information in the data base.
- Print mailing labels—create labels for all addresses in the data base.
- Print customer list—this lists all the customers currently in the billing data base file.

All other types of reports normally associated with billing and accounts receivable are covered in the next chapter. The functions of sorting and updating the billing file are part of the utility function found on the main SYSTEM MENU. This function will be discussed in the procedures under UTILITY.

7.8 PROCEDURES

The procedures for using the billing portion of this accounting system are relatively straightforward. The billing procedures are separate from the accounts receivable package. All functions within this portion of the package work off the SYSTEM MENU. Within the billing/accounts receivable portion are other menus used to pick specific options.

7.9 SYSTEM MENU

The SYSTEM MENU, as mentioned in Chapter Six, is the executive monitor for the whole accounting package. All functions for the package are called from this menu. When the computer is running and the program is loaded, the SYSTEM MENU should be displayed on the CRT screen. At this point, we are looking for option number 2, BILLING/ACCOUNTS RECEIVABLE. Enter the number 2 and depress RETURN (see Example 7-1).

7.10 BILLING/ACCOUNTS RECEIVABLE MENU

The BILLING/ACCOUNTS RECEIVABLE MENU contains only two items: BILLING SYSTEM and ACCOUNTS RECEIVABLE system. This is done to maximize the amount of memory being used by the program and to break the functions into two distinct segments (see Example 7-2).

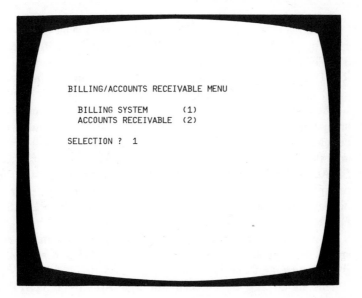

```
    SYSTEM MENU

ENTER SELECTION AND DEPRESS RETURN

    INVENTORY CONTROL            (1)
    BILLING/ACCOUNTS RECEIVABLE  (2)
    ACCOUNTS PAYABLE             (3)
    GENERAL LEDGER               (4)
    PLANNING                     (5)
    DEPOSIT                      (6)
    UTILITY                      (7)

SELECTION ?   2
```

Example 7-1

```
BILLING/ACCOUNTS RECEIVABLE MENU

    BILLING SYSTEM        (1)
    ACCOUNTS RECEIVABLE   (2)

SELECTION ?   1
```

Example 7-2

When the BILLING SYSTEM is requested, only those functions inherent to the customer data base are called. The accounts receivable package discussed in Chapter Eight will make use of this data. This menu can be escaped by typing in the word MENU. This will cause a default to the SYSTEM MENU and will display all functions.

Within this package an additional function called HELP has been added. If HELP is typed in for any selection entry the system will respond with the last known menu. For example, typing in the word HELP to the BILLING/ACCOUNTS RECEIVABLE MENU selection will redisplay the menu. Also, typing in a number greater than 2 or less than 1 will cause the same response. The entry of words other than HELP or MENU will cause a redisplay of the same menu.

An entry of HELP three times in a row to the same selection will cause the following message to be displayed: PLEASE REREAD CHAPTER SEVEN?. The entry of the letter R, for ready to continue in the application, is required. This particular error response has been added primarily as an example of error trapping and error response.

7.11   ADD A CUSTOMER

Adding a customer to the billing data base is achieved by requesting the ADD A CUSTOMER option from the BILLING SYSTEM MENU. By entering the number 1 and depressing RETURN, the system responds with the beginning of the input loop. This display is shown in Example 7-3.

The customer account number is the first item to be entered and requires a six-digit input (see Example 7-4). This input must be made up of at least six numeric figures or an error will occur and the system will print the message: ACCOUNT # TOO SMALL PLEASE REENTER. The input question will be redisplayed. If the input is greater than six digits the system will display the error message: ACCOUNT # TOO BIG PLEASE REENTER. The input question will be redisplayed. If the input is something other than a numeric character the system will respond with the error message: INVALID INPUT and redisplay the input prompt question.

This mode can be escaped and the BILLING SYSTEM MENU returned to by entering the number 999 and depressing RETURN. The system uses the number 999 as a terminator for

```
BILLING SYSTEM MENU

ADD A CUSTOMER            (1)
DELETE A CUSTOMER         (2)
CHANGE A CUSTOMER RECORD  (3)
PRINT BILLS              (4)
PRINT LABELS             (5)
PRINT CUST LIST          (6)

SELECTION ?  1
```

Example 7-3

```
ENTER 6 DIGIT ACCOUNT # ?  187643
ENTER CO NAME ?  AMW ENTERPRISES
STREET ?  1128 VERDUN AVE
CITY, STATE, ZIP ?  ELK GROVE VIL, IL  60619
PHONE ?  312-553-8383
```

Example 7-4

numeric entries and will assume that you no longer want the ADD A CUSTOMER input loop.

Once a valid input is received the system will respond with the next input question: ENTER CO. NAME ?. This input field can have no more than 15 characters; any input over that will cause the error message: CO NAME TOO BIG PLEASE REENTER and a redisplay of the input message.

The field also requires at least three characters to be valid or the error message: CO NAME TOO SMALL PLEASE REENTER will be redisplayed. The reason for this is that if you are building a customer data base record, it will probably have a name of at least three characters.

The word HELP can also be entered at this point if you are not sure what to do. When HELP is entered at this point a short message will be displayed: FIELD REQUIRES CO. NAME NOT LESS THAN 3 AND NO GREATER THAN 15 CHARACTERS IN LENGTH — ENTER R TO CONTINUE ?. When the letter R is entered the input question for the company name is redisplayed. Once a valid input is entered for the company name the system will continue with the input cycle, displaying the next input statement: STREET ?.

The street input requires a minimum of three and a maximum of 15 characters. The system will respond with one of the following error messages, depending on the condition: STREET TOO SMALL PLEASE REENTER or STREET TOO BIG PLEASE REENTER and, of course, will redisplay the input statement. Once a valid entry is made the system will ask: CITY, STATE, ZIP ?.

If you are wondering what would have happened if you had entered HELP for the street input, go ahead and try it; you see, not every input can have help.[1]

The input of the city, state and zip code is a multi-input statement made up of three fields. The city allows up to ten characters for input, state two characters and the zip code nine characters.

The city field must have at least three characters, the state must have two and the zip code field must contain five characters. All fields in this input statement are mandatory.

The following error conditions may be displayed if an incorrect input is made and will necessitate the reentry of the entire

---

[1]See the CTBL system manuals for either the MECA system or TRS-80 to fully understand this function.

statement.:

- CITY TOO SMALL REENTER—the city field contained fewer than three characters.
- CITY TOO BIG REENTER—the city field contained more than ten characters.
- CITY FIELD SKIPPED REENTER—only RETURN was pressed and a space was entered for the city.
- STATE TOO SMALL—fewer than two characters were entered.
- STATE TOO BIG—more than two characters were entered.
- STATE SKIPPED—the field was input with a space only.
- ZIP TOO SMALL—fewer than five characters were entered.
- ZIP TOO BIG—more than nine characters were entered.
- ZIP SKIPPED—a space was entered rather than characters.
- INVALID INPUT—an attempt was made to enter alpha characters into the all-numeric zip code field.

The entry of HELP at the start of this field will direct you to reread Chapter Seven. This type of HELP statement was chosen at this point because it is not always possible to build definitive help into the computer system; it can only be built in where it does not use excessive memory.

Once valid and complete information is entered, the system cycles to the last question of the customer contact data base—the phone number.The phone field requires a mandatory 11 characters. The first three must be the area code, then the three-number prefix, a hyphen (-) and the routing numbers, four characters. Any other variation of this will cause the error message: PHONE # INCORRECT PLEASE REENTER and a redisplay of the input statement.

7.12   ADDING BILLING INFORMATION

When the customer contact information has been entered, the system asks if there is any additional information in the form of billing data. It is at this point that information directly related to accounts receivable can be entered and a separate record established (see Example 7-5).

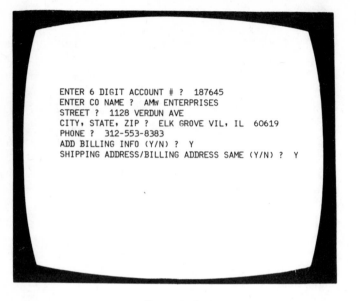

```
ENTER 6 DIGIT ACCOUNT # ?  187645
ENTER CO NAME ?  AMw ENTERPRISES
STREET ?  1128 VERDUN AVE
CITY, STATE, ZIP ?  ELK GROVE VIL, IL  60619
PHONE ?  312-553-8383
ADD BILLING INFO (Y/N) ?  Y
SHIPPING ADDRESS/BILLING ADDRESS SAME (Y/N) ?  Y
```

Example 7-5

The entry of an N to the billing information question will cause the system to respond with the BILLING SYSTEM MENU. If additional customers are to be entered, the ADD CUSTOMER option can again be chosen. However, if Y is entered to the billing information question, the system will begin another input loop that is directly associated with the customer record just built.

The first question is designed to set up the billing address. If the answer is Y, the essential information is copied over into the billing information record. If an N is entered, the system responds with an input cycle identical to that used for building the customer contact data base record. The error response used for that input loop is also used for the billing input loop.

The second question establishes the shipping address. If the answer is N, shipping information is shown as in Example 7-6.

When the billing information is established, the entry of the billing record can be made. The first question is the purchase order or order date (Example 7-7). This field has a minimum size of six characters and must be all numeric. If any one of these conditions is not met, the system responds with: INPUT INCORRECT REENTER and redisplays the input question.

```
SHIPPING ADDRESS/BILLING ADDRESS SAME (Y/N) ?  N
INPUT SHIPPING NAME, STREET, CITY, STATE, ZIP
?  AMW ENTERPRISES, 1000 VERDUN AVE, ELK GROVE VIL,
   IL, 60619
```

Example 7-6

```
PO DATE -- ORDER DATE ?  102178
INVOICE # ?  188763
SHIPPING DATE ?  102678
HOW MANY ITEMS TO ENTER ?  3
ENTER AMT ORDERED, STOCK #, DESCRIPTION, COST/UNIT
?  5, 000101, HEX WRENCHES, 5.50
```

Example 7-7

This date is part of the audit trail set up to use as a cross check when billing problems occur. The field is mandatory and, depending on the business situation, can be changed to accept both alpha and numeric characters.

When the order date information is entered, the system then requires the invoice number. That's the invoice number you will be using at billing time. This field must contain six numeric characters. Any other entry will cause the error message: INVOICE # INCORRECT REENTER and a redisplay of the input message. This field is mandatory, and if no entry is made the system will keep recycling until a valid input is received.

The shipping date follows the same constraints as the purchase order and order date. It also requires six characters and is mandatory. For incorrect entries the message: SHIPPING DATE INCORRECT is displayed along with the redisplay of the input question.

The question HOW MANY ITEMS TO ENTER ? sets up an input loop that ends only when either the first input is three nines (999) or the number entered at the beginning is reached, at which time an option for more is given.

During this input loop, the multi-input statement is used for the item information. This statement contains the amount ordered, the stock numer, the description and the cost/unit fields.

The amount ordered field can be a minimum of one character and a maximum or four. The input must be all numeric or you will get this message: INVALID ENTRY. The error responses of AMT TOO SMALL or AMT TOO BIG are used for this field. Again, an error for this field requires the reentry of all fields.

The stock number field is the same as the stock number field in the inventory package and requires six characters, all numeric, or the error response: STOCK # INCORRECT will result.

The description field can be only 15 characters long and requires a minimum of three characters. If either condition is not met, the system will respond with the error responses of: DESC TOO SMALL or DESC TOO BIG and redisplay the input question for the entire multi-entry statement.

The cost/unit field must be in the format XXXX.XX. The dollar amount can be up to four characters and the cents only two characters. The system accepts the entry and will use special formatting rules when it is called for. If an error is entered at this point, the system responds with C/U INCORRECT and the input statement is redisplayed.

When in this loop, the system makes the assumption that you may want to add additional purchase order and invoice data; if so, it displays the question: PRIMARY BILLING DATA CORRECT (Y/N) ?. If the answer is N, the system will then ask for the parts to be changed and for the additional data. If the answer is Y, the system displays the order question. This happens for each item in the loop.

When the indicated number of inputs is completed or 999 is entered for the amount ordered field, the system asks the question: FINISHED (Y/N) ?. If the answer is Y, the system recycles to the BILLING SYSTEM MENU. If not, it assumes you made an error and starts a customer contact input loop.

7.13   DELETE A CUSTOMER

Occasionally, it becomes necessary to delete a customer from the data base. Option number 2 on the BILLING SYSTEM MENU allows this (see Example 7-8).

```
BILLING SYSTEM MENU

ADD A CUSTOMER
DELETE A CUSTOMER
CHANGE A CUSTOMER RECORD
PRINT BILLS
PRINT LABELS
PRINT CUST LIST

SELECTION ?   2
INPUT DESIRED ACCOUNT # ?   187643
```

Example 7-8

When this option is chosen, the system responds with a
message requesting the account number. The entry of this
number must follow all the rules laid down for creating the
number in the data base or an error will result.

When the system locates the number, the customer contact
data is displayed on the CRT screen with a question to check
whether it is correct. If Y, the system will ask if it is okay to
delete. A positive, Y, response will cause the system to add a
delete flag to the record and write it to the data base to be
removed at file maintenance time (Example 7-9).

An N response will cause the system to ask again for the account number and will search for the new one; the cycle is
started over. If you are unable to identify the account number,
entering the word LIST to the account number question will
cause the system to list all customers, the same as option 6 on
the menu.

```
1  ACCT #  187643
2  CO NAME  CARLS EDIT
3  STREET  28 SE 82ND AVE
4  CITY, ST, ZIP  PORTLAND, OR, 97316
```

Example 7-9

7.14 CHANGING A CUSTOMER RECORD

Changing a customer record is similar to deleting it. The
system asks for the account number and, on finding it, displays

the information on the CRT. It asks whether the account number is the correct record. If not, the cycle is started over. This display is the same as Example 7-8, except: **SELECTION ?** 3.

If the record is correct, the system then asks for the line to be corrected or changed, after which the system will display the input question associated with that line and, upon input of the new information, redisplay the record with the new data. The system then asks if more is to be changed by asking for the line number to be changed. The input loop can be stopped by entering three nines (**999**), at which time the system will write out the new record to the mass storage device and will do an update at file maintenance time. This display is shown in Example 7-10.

When line 5, the billing information, is the item to be changed, the system first responds with a multi-input statement for billing information. If the billing address and shipping address are now the same, the system indicates this by allowing the use of the input S(ame), which will cause an immediate update of this data.

The data regarding purchased items cannot be changed at this level and will be discussed under accounts receivable, Chapter Eight.

```
1   ACCT #  187643
2   CO NAME   CARLS EDIT
3   STREET   28 NE 82ND AVE
4   CITY, ST, ZIP   PORTLAND, OR, 97316
5   BILLING INFO   CARLS EDIT
                   28 NE 82ND AVE
                   PORTLAND, OR  97316
ENTER LINE # TO BE CHANGED ?   5
INPUT BILLING NAME, STREET, CITY, STATE, ZIP
IF BILLING ADDRESS SAME AS SHIPPING
ADDRESS ENTER (S) SAME
?   S
```

Example 7-10

7.15   PRINT BILLS

To print the bills from the data base, the number 4 option is chosen from the BILLING SYSTEM MENU (Example 7-11). When this option is chosen the system requires that the date be entered as MM for month, DD, day, and YY, year. After the date is entered the system waits for you to adjust the billing forms in the printer. Then, when you enter the letter R for ready, it begins the generation of bills from the data base.

The requirement of the entry of the letter R before the cycle starts prevents the premature start of the billing cycle. This display is shown in Example 7-12. Table 7-1 shows the bill generated.

Table 7-1

AMW ENTERPRISES 11604 Chamniss Ave Des Moines, Iowa 50833
(515) 646-3155

INVOICE NO. 222500

SOLD TO:	SHIP TO:
176344	
WILSON'S PIPE	SAME
1968 Victory Street	
Cadillac, IA 50834	

DATE:	CUST PO:	TERMS
061978	000478	2% NET10

* *

AMT ORD	DESCRIPTION	COST/UNIT	EXTEN
5	HEX WRENCHES	5.50	27.50

	SUB TOTAL	27.50
	TAX	1.65
PLEASE PAY FROM THIS INVOICE	SHIPPING	.85
	TOTAL	30.00

```
BILLING SYSTEM MENU

ADD A CUSTOMER            (1)
DELETE A CUSTOMER         (2)
CHANGE A CUSTOMER RECORD  (3)
PRINT BILLS              (4)
PRINT LABELS             (5)
PRINT CUST LIST          (6)

SELECTION ?   4
```

Example 7-11

```
ENTER BILLING DATE (MM,DD,YY) ?   10,28,79
LINE UP BILLS IN PRINTER WHEN READY ENTER R
AND DEPRESS RETURN
?   R
```

Example 7-12

7.16 PRINT LABELS

One of the side benefits of the data base built for billing purposes is the generation of mailing labels to send promotional
material to your customers. This system generates the labels in a
single-file fashion, and only in the order of the last sort—
usually the account numbers. The possibility to sort by zip
codes does exist but was not built into this model. The data base
is constructed in such a manner as to allow for this type of sorting and for setting up random mailing labels by manipulating
the printing mechanism from the data base.

To print the labels, option number 5 is chosen from the
BILLING SYSTEM MENU and, when the labels are lined up
correctly in the printer, the entry of R for ready will begin the
printing operation. This display is shown in Example 7-11, except the following:

SELECTION ? 5
LINE UP LABELS IN PRINTER ENTER R WHEN READY
? R

Table 7-2 shows two labels.

7.17 CUSTOMER LIST

The final report generated from the billing system is a list of
all the customers in the data base. This list can be used to great
advantage when tracking the receivables or just determining
what is in the data base.

To print the customer list the system will begin with the first
item. That is, the way the list was sorted (in our case by account
number) is the way the list is printed. No receivables information is included in this list—only basic definition data. This
display is shown in Example 7-11, except: SELECTION ? 6. A
customer list is shown in Table 7-3.

7.18 UTILITY

The utility function for the billing system is tied directly into
the accounts receivable package. UTILITY is used at this point
to update all the billing records and correct any accounts
receivable data base data. Ideally, the UTILITY would be run

Table 7-2

000001
ADAMS TRUCKING CO
2377 SO. DOWNING
DENVER CO 80010

000002
BAKER INDUSTRIES
1689 FORESTER
AURORA CO 80011

Table 7-3

CUSTOMER LIST

ACCT #	CO NAME	PHONE
000100	ADAMS INC	213 587-3300
000101	AXIS HARDWARE	714 886-1100
. . .		
264001	VERNON TOOL	503 366-2787

---

primarily for the accounts receivable function. UTILITY is selection number 7 on the BILLING SYSTEM MENU. This display is shown in Example 7-1, except: SELECTION ? 7.

When UTILITY is running for the accounts receivable update, the data base tape must be on drive zero and a new tape on drive one. Selection of the accounts receivable mode is shown in Example 7-13. When UTILITY is running, the updates are run and a new sorted data base written to the new tape. The sort is performed by picking up the account numbers from each record and sorting them. Periodically, while UTILITY is running, the system will advise you to rewind the cassettes. This applies only to non-automated tape systems. MECA users will enjoy the automatic update feature, which involves little user intervention.

7.19   ERROR RESPONSES

The error responses used in the BILLING/ACCOUNTS RECEIVABLE package are designed to guide you through the

```
UTILITY MENU

INV UT   (1)
A/R UT   (2)
A/P UT   (3)
G/L UT   (4)

SELECTION ?   2
IS DATA BASE TAPE ON DRIVE 0
DEPRESS RETURN ?

****UTILITY IS RUNNING****

UTILITY IS FINISHED
PLEASE LABEL ARCHIVE AND NEW DATA BASE
TAPES WITH DATE AND TIME
REMOUNT SYSTEM TAPE AND DEPRESS RETURN ?
```

Example 7-13

use of the system. In this chapter two new error concepts were introduced: first, the HELP entry, which is designed to give a variety of messages to help you, and second, the direction error help message that directs you to a specific area in the procedure manual.

The design of error messages is one of the most important areas in application design. The trapping of errors and output of the message are important to make the application useful to you.

7.20 SYSTEM SUMMARY

The billing system presented in this chapter is designed to build a data base of customers, change or delete items in that data base and work directly with the accounts receivable portion of the accounting system.

The side benefits of the billing package are, of course, the amount of time saved and the ability to generate mailing labels, based on a sort sequence. The items within the customer contact portion of the data base are set up in such a manner that you can define specific report needs or unique sorts to best meet your needs.

One method of setting up a sort was introduced briefly—picking one item, such as the account number, then creating a file of sorted file numers to get the records. This is the system used for the total automated system of this application.

When time is taken to implement this system or a modified version and care is taken to use it correctly in a business, a fair amount of time can be saved in the billing process. It is intended to pay for itself by generating a smoother cash flow.

Chapter Eight

THIRD KEY SYSTEM: ACCOUNTS RECEIVABLE

In this chapter you will begin to use the information assembled in Chapter Six. You will study a variety of management reports. A discussion of management's use of these reports is included.

8.1 INTRODUCTION

Chapter Seven briefly discussed receivables in relation to the billing process. As stated in that chapter, sales create billing and bills are considered receivables and assets—monies to come. Accounts receivable is a simple bookkeeping procedure, but it covers more than the simple procedures of tracking what is owed to the company. Accounts receivable includes bad debts, discounts, records of indebtedness for items sold on credit and, most importantly, the formal recording of sales and flagging them as company assets.

The previous chapter discussed billing as the vehicle for collecting debts owed and for building the associated records. This chapter carries that a step further with a discussion of the interrelationship of billing and accounts receivable. Also discussed in this chapter are the necessary functions of aging and managerial reports. Accounts receivable is viewed as a management tool for handling company assets in the form of cash and promises to pay.

8.2 CONNECTION BETWEEN BILLING AND RECEIVABLES

The concept behind the generation of a bill is relatively simple—a purchase is made and a promise is made to pay in some form. The seller in this credit agreement provides the customer with an invoice that states the terms of the agreement. These terms specify what is owed and when it must be paid. You are probably familiar with a credit sale using a credit card. Your signature on the credit card sales slip is your promise to pay, not to the seller of the item, but to the credit card company, which is acting as the agent of the seller. When the bill arrives, it states several options for paying and what the costs will be if you select any option other than payment in full.

Using the above explanation, look at Figure 8-1. This figure represents the basic cycle for billing/accounts receivable. As in the credit card sale, the customer orders or makes a direct contact purchase on credit, whereupon the item is removed from the inventory and is either shipped or given directly to the customer. A bill is generated that spells out exactly what was purchased, how much it costs and any applicable terms. The seller books or marks this sale on a ledger card, considers it an

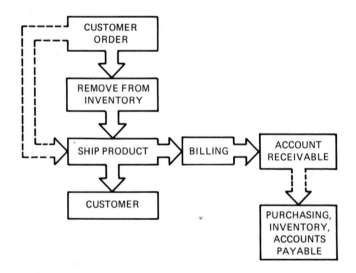

Figure 8-1 Flow of accounts receivable

asset and uses the promise of cash coming in to purchase additional inventory. This produces accounts payable, which will be discussed in the next chapter.

For now, the important part of this process is that, once the bill or invoice is created, it is logged. Every effort must be made to ensure that both the invoice and the ledger notation are correct. The inaccuracy of either of these items can cause a major bookkeeping problem and cost the company customers.

The ledger card record of the invoice is the account receivable. Companies that do a great deal of business with the same customers will find that any individual customer will have several invoices posted or written to their account. Some of these entries may be in different states and must be noted as such. Each entry represents an extension of credit by the seller to the buyer and can represent a great deal of money when carried over a period of time or on several individual accounts. The receivables record represents the detailed record of the account and establishes a payment record for the customer.

8.3 WHAT RECEIVABLES DO

Receivables show how well a company is doing and establish trends that show how well the company will do in the future. The receivables represent the amount that a company can grant in the form of credit sales and how much credit it can receive from suppliers or lending institutions. More simply, it can be said that receivables are the key to the solvency of any company.

8.4 TYPES OF ACCOUNTS

Within the business world there are different types of accounts that must be considered. Some trade accounts are informal and are established by word of mouth, purchase orders, memos, or by letters or other correspondence. There are also special trade accounts. These are accounts that cover returns or items on consignment. The consignment type of special account is considered only a memo notation on the books and not booked as a receivable until actual payment is received.

An account is established when the legal title to goods or services is passed from one party to another. In most cases this will represent an actual sale and will require booking the sale as a receivable with the expectation of payment in the foreseeable future. Special receivable accounts, such as those for replaced items, are set up at the time the contract is negotiated with the original supplier. Since some form of payment will be made either in cash or in replacement goods, this type of account must be considered a receivable. These special receivable accounts, along with consignments, can be handled by making a memo entry in the receivable ledger. This is done primarily to keep track of them.

When you set up the receivables and account types, you must classify them in some manner. This can be an alphabetical classification by customer, customer number or type of customer being served. The package described in this book classifies the accounts by customer number, as noted in Chapter Seven.

8.5   ACCOUNTS RECEIVABLE PROCESSING

Since receivables represent all monies to be paid to a company, each account must be processed and brought up to date regularly. As shown in Figure 8-1, selling, billing, and booking the receivables are all important facets of the business cycle. Each part of the cycle is a separate entity and has meaning in the accounting end of the business. The sale is made and represents cash. The sold item must be noted and steps taken to replace it. Bills must be generated that are accurate and reflect the actual transaction that took place.

Periodically, each account must be looked at and have new payments posted to it, and memos must be written to reflect any special situation. Also, the accounts must be aged to reflect their true status in relation to any payments made.

The aging process is very important since it quickly reveals who is current and who is late. This information is used to determine whether any late charges are necessary, whether collection efforts should be increased or whether it is advisable to continue doing business with that customer. Accounts are normally aged over 30-day periods broken down into: 0 to 30, 31 to 60, 61 to 90, and 90 days and over. Depending on company policy, it may be wise to remind customers in the 31- to 60-day category that they are late.

8.6   MANAGING THE CASH FLOW

The whole purpose of establishing an accounts receivable bookkeeping system is to ensure collection of bills, to provide account maintenance for accounts that have special terms, and to stay in business. With a proper system of booking receivables, the amount of promised cash, actual onhand cash, and actual expenses can be compared. Wise management decisions can be made regarding the operation of the business. On the other hand, it has been estimated by bankers and professional business consultants that 20 percent of small business failures can be directly related to the improper handling of receivables and the resulting cash flow problems.

8.7   MAINTAINING THE ACCOUNTS RECEIVABLE RECORD

Maintenance of the accounts receivable record covers a great deal of territory and can best be discussed in the form of a scenario.

A small company in Montana sells taco shell holders to taco stands around the country. All of its sales are in the form of purchase order requests. The owner of this company has a fair understanding of bookkeeping and makes every effort to keep the record straight, using the following procedures.

- For new orders, she immediately makes an entry to the company's account record reflecting the order and the invoice it will be billed on.
- She uses a running invoice system. She adds the new order to the current invoice and attaches a copy of the PO to the invoice.
- On the billing date, she sends the invoice with PO copies to the buyer, and notes the billing date on the receivable ledger.
- On return of payment, the account is immediately updated, as are the necessary journals.
- Accounts that are still unpaid or partially paid are booked as open items. These accounts provide her with an immediate understanding of what each account is doing at any given time.

From this little scenario, a basic receivables system can be established. It makes no difference whether it is automated or manual. The important point is that it exists and is maintained on a regular basis.

8.8 SETTING UP A CYCLE OF BILLING

An important aspect of the receivables system is establishing a definite cycle for sending bills and knowing when to expect payment on these bills. This is vitally important in order to bring customer indebtedness directly into focus and to help manage cash flow.

8.9 AUDIT TRAILS

Audit trails are those pieces of information that pinpoint where cash or debts came from. A receivables ledger provides this necessary service by linking an account to a specific invoice and billing date. Copies must be kept for tax purposes. The system in this book provides these trails by allowing for entry of invoice numbers and dates. It is up to you to establish a workable filing system to find the original documents when the time comes.

For an accounting system to be any good, it must generate reports. This system generates four reports, which will be discussed briefly, while format detail will be discussed in the procedures section.

The Invoice Register is a listing of all new invoice entries to the accounts receivable file. It reflects the account number, invoice number, invoice date, amount of the invoice and any discounts, along with totals for each account. This report is used as an audit trail for monitoring invoice activity and for balancing the billing activity.

The Transaction Report is a listing of all payment and invoice transactions. This report gives the account number, invoice number, invoice date, amount of invoice, date paid and amount paid, along with totals for each account.

The Aged Trial Balance Report is the report that tells management exactly what is happening with receivables by showing the status of individual accounts. This report is generated account by account. Essentially the same information is given here as in the other reports, but balances are presented under the aging periods.

The Cash Payment Report generated by this system is a replay of the transaction report except that only payments and invoice balances are presented.

All of these reports are designed to give management necessary information regarding each account's status.

8.10 PROCEDURES

The procedures for the accounts receivable portion of the accounting package are fairly simple. The accounts receivable package is designed to use the data base that was created in Chapter Seven. The primary functions of this system are, first, updating accounts and, second, generating reports. Like the systems previously presented, the receivables package works from the SYSTEM MENU and other menus built into the package.

8.11 SYSTEM MENU

The SYSTEM MENU, as previously mentioned, is the executive program that provides access to all functions within the accounting package. With receivables, we are looking for option number 2, just as in Chapter Seven. If the system is up and operating, the SYSTEM MENU should be displayed on the terminal screen (see Example 8-1).

When option number 2 is chosen from the SYSTEM MENU, the system will respond with the BILLING/ACCOUNTS RECEIVABLE MENU. This display is shown in Example 8-2.

8.12 ACCOUNTS RECEIVABLE MENU

For purposes of this chapter, option number 2 is chosen from this menu. When the number is entered, the system will respond with the ACCOUNTS RECEIVABLE MENU. This menu offers five options, each designed to work with the previously built data base (see Example 8-3).

Since this system is designed to find accounts by account number, the system will respond by asking for the appropriate number. All error responses related to the account number field

```
SYSTEM MENU

ENTER SELECTION AND DEPRESS RETURN

    INVENTORY CONTROL          (1)
    BILLING/ACCOUNTS RECEIVABLE (2)
    ACCOUNTS PAYABLE           (3)
    GENERAL LEDGER             (4)
    PLANNING DEPOSIT           (5)
    UTILITY                    (6)

SELECTION ?   2
```

Example 8-1

```
BILLING/ACCOUNTS RECEIVABLE MENU

BILLING SYSTEM        (1)
ACCOUNTS RECEIVABLE   (2)

SELECTION ?   2
```

Example 8-2

```
ACCCOUNTS RECEIVABLE MENU

UPDATE ACCOUNTS        (1)
INVOICE REGISTER       (2)
TRANSACTION REGISTER   (3)
AGED TRIAL BALANCE     (4)
CASH PAYMENT REPORT    (5)

SELECTION ?   1
```

Example 8-3

are used here. The number must consist of six numeric characters or an error will result. Entering an invalid account number will cause the system to search for it until the end of the tape, after which it will respond with: UNABLE TO LOCATE. In later cassette versions to be made available, the system will know immediately if the account is valid or not. In the case of invalid account numbers, the system will display the error message and redisplay the input question.

Once a valid number is entered, the system will display the account, with detail, up to 12 lines. Depressing the space bar will display any additional data. The system will ask if this is the correct account. If not, the account number question will be redisplayed. This display is shown in Example 8-4.

The error checking done for inputs to these fields consists of, first, checking to see if the line number exists; if not, the error message: LINE # INCQT will be displayed. Second, the system checks to see if the date is in the MMDDYY format, looking for six characters; if not, it will display the message: DATE INCQT. Finally, it will look for no more than seven characters and a

```
INPUT DESIRED # ?  187592
ACCT #  187592  DILITHIUM PRESS
  INVOICE #   INVOICE DATE  AMT      DATE PAID  BALANCE
1 001029      101678        246.18   111678     0.00
2 002063      022779        143.61   000000     143.61
3 002065      030579        183.00   032779     0.00

IS ACCOUNT CORRECT (Y/N) ?  Y
INPUT LINE TO BE UPDATED, PAYMENT DATE  MMDDYY,
AMT PAID ?  2, 032779, 143.61
```

Example 8-4

decimal point for cash, and, if an error is found, it will display the message: DOLLAR AMT INCQT.

An error in any field will require re-entry of all items, and only one line can be updated at a time. Once an update entry is made, the system will ask MORE ?; if Yes, the system will display the account number request again. If not, it will redisplay the ACCOUNTS RECEIVABLE MENU.

8.13   REPORT GENERATION

As mentioned in the beginning of this chapter, reports make up most of the accounts receivable package. Options 3 through 5 on the menu are used to call the reports and, when one is called, the system works through the data base account by account to develop the report called for. The reports are generated directly to the hardcopy printer without any screen options. The next several procedures show how to call each report and the general format of each. When you select item 2, you get this:

INVOICE REGISTER

ACCT#	INVOICE#	INVOICE DATE	AMOUNT	DISCOUNT
000000	000000	MMDDYY	0000.00	0000.00

Same detail for each invoice per account.

TOTAL *** 0000.00

When you select item 3, you get this:

TRANSACTION REGISTER

ACCT#	INVOICE#	INVOICE DATE	AMOUNT	DATE PAID	AMT PAID
000000	000000	MMDDYY	0000.00	MMDDYY	0000.00

This report provides the invoice breakdown and transactions for each account held on file. The account number is only printed once per account.

When you select item 4, you get this:

ACCT# 000000

INV#	INVDT	LSTPAY	AMTPD	CUR	31-60	91 OVER
000000	MMDDYY	MMDDYY	0000.00	0000.00	0000.00	0000.00

This report gives each account breakdown by trial balance and shows whether the payment received is for a current balance or aged over the indicated periods. INV# is the invoice number; INVDT is the invoice date; LSTPAY is the date of the last payment received; AMTPD is the dollar amount paid; and CUR, 31-60 and 90 OVER are the aging periods.

When you select item 5, you get this:

CASH PAYMENT REPORT

ACCT#	INVOICE#	INVOICE DTE	AMT	DATE PAID	BALANCE
000000	000000	MMDDYY	0000.00	MMDDYY	0000.00

Each account is listed once with all cash payments.

8.14   UTILITIES

The utilities function found on the SYSTEM MENU has a function built into it that updates the accounts receivable portion of the package. UTILITY for this package sorts by account number, updates the transaction records, and writes archive files to tape. This UTILITY is accessed by selecting option number 7 on the SYSTEM MENU. This display is shown in Example 8-1, except: SELECTION ? 7.

As shown in Example 8-5, UTILITY Prompts the user for needed functions and performs the job, all of which should be transparent to the user. In cases of non-controlled audio cassettes, messages to rewind are also built in.

```
UTILITY MENU

INV UT  (1)
A/R UT  (2)
A/P UT  (3)
G/L UT  (4)

SELECTION ?  2 -- DEPRESS RETURN
IS DATA BASE TAPE ON DRIVE 0 DEPRESS RETURN

****UTILITY IS RUNNING****

UTILITY IS FINISHED
PLEASE LABEL ARCHIVE AND NEW DATA BASE TAPES
WITH DATE AND TIME
REMOUNT SYSTEM TAPE, AND DEPRESS RETURN
```

Example 8-5

8.15   ERROR MESSAGES

For this function of the account package, there are no new error messages other than the ones mentioned. Most of the error messages used by this function are the same as those used in the billing package. However, in the systems manual, a complete list of the error messages for the accounts receivable function is provided.

8.16 SYSTEM SUMMARY

The accounts receivable package described in this chapter is like the inventory control and billing packages—bare bones and designed to be modified and enhanced by the user. It is hoped that you achieve an understanding of receivables and are enlightened regarding the possibility of automating the receivables function in your business.

It is important to point out that this package is primarily a teaching tool. This book and system should be used in conjunction with other accounting books and books on automated systems.

Chapter Nine

FOURTH KEY SYSTEM: ACCOUNTS PAYABLE

One of the most important aspects of accounting, keeping track of payables, is presented in this chapter. The chapter begins with a discussion of what a payable is and the importance of establishing payable dates. The procedure portion provides the necessary instructions to use the system. The chapter ends with a review of how management can use the data from the application.

9.1 INTRODUCTION

So far, we have discussed billing and accounts receivable, inventory, and purchasing. All three have direct ties, since one creates the next. The same is true for accounts payable. The act of purchasing items to sell or create inventory obligates you to some other company for the cost of the goods. For new companies, the original goods may have been purchased outright. However, for most companies, the purchase of goods is done on a credit basis, possibly covered by a contractual agreement.

Regardless of how the actual mechanics of the purchase were set up, the important point is that money is owed; a receivable exists for the company that you made your purchase from. The receivables you have from your customers represent an asset, and the company that holds the receivable from you because of your purchase of goods has an asset—thus, a continuous cycle.

Now that the goods have been sold and receivables set up, you must concern yourself with payables.

The concept of payables is not really very complex. What is complex is setting up a bookkeeping system that keeps it all straight and is easy to audit both by you and by outsiders. But before getting into the bookkeeping system for payables, a clear definition must be established, even though you probably have a reasonable idea already of what payables are.

9.2 WHAT ARE PAYABLES?

Payables are obligations or promises to pay for the purchase of material, finished goods, or services. Payables must be cross-checked against purchase orders before they are formally accepted by entry in the books.

9.3 WHAT PAYABLES DO

Payables serve the primary purpose of keeping track of who is owed what and when it is due. The payables system tries to take advantage of all discounts and works with the receivables system to keep cash flow steady. Payables are used to make sure the correct items were received and that they match the original invoice, that all agreed-upon discounts are given, and that the invoice reflects this information. They also make sure that, as each invoice is paid, it is distributed over the correct internal accounts so that the books reflect the most current information.

Payables, like receivables, are extremely important, since they involve company funds. The receivables represent a company's current assets and thus reveal how well it is doing, while payables reflect a company's liabilities and how it is viewed by other companies. Payables also reflect how well management handles cash flow and whether it pays attention to what is happening in the business.

9.4 THE GENERAL FLOW OF PAYABLES

Figure 9-1 represents the general flow and structure of the payables within an average company. From this you can see that the cycle is very similar to that of inventory control. The final item is paying the bills, which will in turn mean staying in business for a period of time.

One of the most important aspects of payables flow is that of setting up payment dates. Frequently, it becomes very important to take advantage of any discounts ofered by a vendor. The invoice should be set up to reflect this. Most small businesses

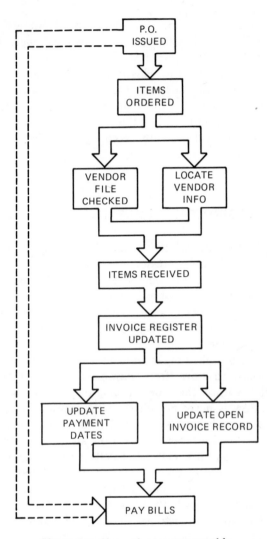

Figure 9-1 Flow of accounts payable

follow a policy of paying the bill as soon as it arrives rather than setting up specific payment dates. Unfortunately, not all businesses can operate in this manner, due to cash flow difficulties, nor is it always good practice to pay invoices in this manner.

Oftentimes, when an invoice does not offer any special discounts or payment incentives, it is best to book the invoice as a liability and set up a payment date either for the whole or a part, whichever gives you the greatest cash flow advantage. Remember, it is best to keep your cash in the bank as long as you can to get the most use out of it. This axiom holds true only for invoices with no discounts and for companies that are solid enough to do business in this manner. Companies that have a shaky payment record will find it difficult to get any credit, and when they do, it will probably be conditional—based on strict payment dates.

9.5 MANAGING THE CASH FLOW

In Chapter Eight, cash flow was discussed in terms of managing accounts receivable, stressing the importance of making sure bills are collected. For bills that you owe—payables—the management of cash is just as important. As mentioned earlier, this is directly related to how well the receivables function is working. If cash is not coming in, it is very difficult for cash to go out to pay bills.

Cash flow is looked on as an inward flow (from receivables) and an outward flow (from payables). It is management's responsibility to set the proper timing of payments so that the outward flow is never greater than the inward flow; the one should never get behind the other. The ideal situation is to have the inward flow lead the outward flow all the time. In a situation such as this, sufficient cash usually exists to pay all current liabilities as well as to take advantage of all offered discounts.

Handy tricks such as mailing bills on Fridays to get the advantage of keeping money in the bank over the weekend, or getting collectibles onto your customer's desk on Mondays will help increase cash flow. Mailing payments late in the afternoon to pick up an extra day also helps in cash management. One method that works well for high-volume sales and purchases is to set up a specific day each week or month to pay bills, and to keep the cash in an interest account until it is needed. Your bank can automatically move a preset or authorized amount into the checking accounts. This technique can mean a significant amount of extra cash due to interest, and is recommended by a number of accountants and banking institutions.

9.6 THE AUDIT PROCEDURE

Auditing of payables is extremely important since it controls cash flow. The auditing procedure consists of checking each payable against the original purchase order, checking the ordered goods to ensure that they are correct and in good shape, and checking for undershipments. Total items, cost per unit, and extensions must be checked and terms and discounts noted. Payment dates are set up and should be checked each day to see if any payable is ready for payment on that date. Specifically, once the account clerk has the payable, it is his or her responsibility to make sure that the correct accounts are debited and credited and the purchase and payment booked in the appropriate journal.

Surprisingly enough, the payables and receivables functions of the accounting system are very similar in actual function, and both deal with invoices. The only difference is that the invoices are going in opposite directions for payment.

For the specific files, the accountant is using vendor files instead of customer files while working with the payables function. Essentially, the information is the same and requires the same type of maintenance that receivables do. The same thought processes and tasks that applied to the receivables function apply to the payables function. The two are so close in design and function that they complement each other in the actual operation of the business.

9.7 PROCEDURES

The procedures for using the accounts payable package of this accounting system are very easy, especially if you have already read Chapters Five through Seven. Like the previous functions, everything is driven off the SYSTEM MENU and other internal menus. This makes it possible to conserve system memory and thus get the best possible use out of your computer.

9.8 SYSTEM MENU

The SYSTEM MENU should be displayed on the system terminal. To use the accounts payable function, the number 3 must be entered and RETURN depressed. This display is shown in Example 9-1. When this is done, the system will respond by displaying the PAYABLES MENU. This menu provides eight options to handle the payables function. What is very important to note at this point is that each time a new function of the accounting package has been introduced, a different method of data handling and more features have been added. So far in the accounting package, the payables offer the most extensive options.

The next several pages are designed to provide a complete examination of the payables package as it would work in a live situation. However, before getting into the running procedure, some of the error facilities must be covered.

```
        SYSTEM MENU

  ENTER SELECTION AND DEPRESS RETURN

      INVENTORY CONTROL           (1)
      BILLING/ACCOUNTS RECEIVABLE (2)
      ACCOUNTS PAYABLE            (3)
      GENERAL LEDGER              (4)
      PLANNING                    (5)
      DEPOSIT                     (6)
      UTILITY                     (7)

  SELECTION ?   3
```

Example 9-1

9.9 PAYABLES ERROR HANDLING

All through the accounting package, a great deal of time and code have been devoted to checking for operator errors. As you progress through this section, each error will be presented, with some minor exceptions. These exceptions are related to the menus, in which any entry other than those allowed will cause a redisplay of the menu.

The HELP option is built into the payables package and, if applicable, will give a redisplay of allowable options or inputs when entered. If help is not available, the system will indicate this by displaying the message **HELP NOT AVAILABLE**. Careful attention to the procedures in this book will lessen the need for help in using the system.

9.10   REPORTS

Reports are extremely important to any part of an accounting system, and payables are no exception. From the menu (Example 9-2), you can see that a fair number exist, from all the accounts to specific brekdowns. Each report in this system is presented as it would appear on a 64-character-wide display, although many systems will produce hardcopy. Each item will be explained as the report is displayed in the procedures. An Account Listing report is shown in Table 9-1.

```
PAYABLES MENU

LIST ACCOUNTS ON PRINTER               (1)
LIST CURRENT ACCOUNTS                  (2)
PRINT HISTORY OF ALL ACCOUNTS          (3)
PRINT ACCOUNTS NEEDING PAYMENT         (4)
PRINT HISTORY OF SELECTED ACCOUNTS     (5)
UPDATE OR ENTER NEW BILLS              (6)
DELETE ACCOUNT                         (7)
PAY BILL                               (8)

SELECTION ?   1
```

Example 9-2

Table 9-1
Account Listing for 8/24/78

LAST UPDATE WRITTEN ON 8/01/78

DATE DUE	PAYMENT	TOTAL	ACCOUNT #	INVOICE #	VENDOR NAME
8/31/78	24.90	24.90	178643	000800	ABC TOOLS
8/31/78	100.00	175.00	147300	000801	VERTOX

Same detail for all accounts in the data base.

9.11 PAYABLES MENU

When option number 1 is chosen, the system begins checking the storage device for information related to accounts, such as the existence of accounts and any dates related to the accounts, and prints them on the system hardcopy device. Should the system be unable to locate any accounts in the data base, it will give the response shown in Example 9-3. This will cause a redisplay of the PAYABLES MENU.

```
NO ACCOUNTS ON FILE

DEPRESS RETURN TO CONTINUE ?
```

Example 9-3

9.12   LIST CURRENT ACCOUNTS

Option number 2 will give you either the following: NO CURRENT ACCOUNTS ON FILE or the display shown in Example 9-4. The same detail is shown for each vendor record and invoice.

```
CURRENT ACCOUNTS FOR 8/24/79
VENDOR NAME   UNITED PLASTERING

DUE DATE    INTEREST    DATE PAID    CHECK #    INVOICE #
PAYMENT     BALANCE     AMT PAID
8/28/79     0000.00     8/26/79      1428       176380
125.00      0000.00     125.00
```

Example 9-4

9.13   PRINT HISTORY OF ACCOUNTS

Option number 3 allows you to print a history of all accounts, while option number 5 lets you select specific accounts. Selecting histories for specific accounts requires an input of the desired account number. It is necessary that the account number be entered correctly. If the account number is less than six numeric characters long, the system will respond with the error message: ACCOUNT NUMBER TOO SMALL and redisplay the input question. If the account number is greater than six digits, the system will respond with the error message: ACCOUNT NUMBER TOO BIG and redisplay the input question. When an account number meeting the input criteria is entered, the system will begin to look for the desired account number. If it is not found, the system will display the message: ACCOUNT # NOT ON FILE and redisplay the input question. When a valid number is entered and the system finds the correct information, it will print the information regarding that account on the hardcopy device. This display is shown in Example 9-5.

```
HISTORY RECORDS

ACCOUNT    176483
VENDOR     000803

DATE DUE    INTEREST    DATE PAID    CHECK #    INVOICE #
PAYMENT     BALANCE     AMT PAID
8/24/79      3.00       8/22/79      1496       686322
  75.00      28.00        75.00
```

Example 9-5

9.14   PRINT ACCOUNTS NEEDING PAYMENT

Option number 4 will give you a list of those payments you should make today (see Example 9-6).

Options 1 through 5, which have been printed so far, are the reports used by management to determine what is happening in the payables function of the bookkeeping department. With the exception of option 5, which requires the entry of a specific account number, these reports are auto-generated. As you have probably noticed, there are dates associated with the reports. These dates are taken from the data base for the records, and

```
ACCOUNTS NEEDING PAYMENT
ACCOUNT LISTING ON 082479
LAST FILE UPDATE WRITTEN ON 080179

DATE DUE  PAYMENT  TOTAL   ACCOUNT #  INVOICE #  VENDOR NAME
082479    25.00    100.00  000001     176483     ABC TOOL
082479    36.75    286.00  000002     187200     ABCA
082479    10.00     40.00  000003     972999     UNITED EGGS

TOTAL OF PAYMENT DUE  71.75
```

Example 9-6

from the data entered at the beginning of the system startup. This date becomes part of the inventory control, accounts receivable, and accounts payable packages and needs to be entered only once.

The final options in the payables package are designed for inputting and changing data. Accounts are set up to be deleted and cross checks are made with the operator to make sure the record should be deleted. When an account is deleted from the payables data base, a flag is set to keep it from showing up under bills to be paid. When the data base is passed through file maintenance in the UTILITY program, the account will be removed from the working data base and kept as an archive item. This is done so that complete audit trails are kept for tax purposes.

9.15 UPDATE OR ENTER NEW BILLS

To update or enter new billing, option number 6 is chosen. The system responds by asking for an account number. Should the account number entered be less than six characters or greater than six characters, the system will respond with an error message, ACCOUNT NUMBER TOO SMALL or ACCOUNT NUMBER TOO BIG, and will redisplay the input question.

When a valid number is entered, the system first looks to see if the number exists. If it does, the system assumes you will be updating an existing record and inputs will be handled as such. However, if the number does not exist, the system handles the inputs as new billing data and will place them in the logical order in the data base. The system does offer another option, that of entering nothing to the account number question. When this happens, the system immediately takes the last account number in the data base, increments it by one, and goes through the input loop.

For all practical purposes, building a data base item and updating one look exactly the same to the operator. When all the information is entered, the system displays the input information for a validation check to make sure that the item is being correctly input.

Should the redisplayed information contain an error, the system will recycle through the entire input cycle. This technique is sloppy and takes time, but it is effective for ensuring good data bases. If the operator decides that the items built in this section are correct, the system will then begin an automatic rewrite of the data base out to tape. This display is shown in Example 9-7.

The following is supplied as a reminder of the format to be used. Please cross check this with Example 9-7.

- ACCOUNT NAME—can be up to 15 characters
- DATE PAYMENT DUE—MM,DD,YY—six characters, mandatory
- TOTAL AMT DUE MAX ?—must be all numeric
- PAYMENT AMT DUE MAX ?—must be all numeric
- INTEREST ?—must be all numeric and in this form: #.##
- DATE BILL RCVD ?—MM,DD,YY again
- INVOICE # ?—six characters, mandatory

9.16   DELETE ACCOUNTS

To delete an account, select option number 7 from the PAYABLES MENU. Input the correct account number and when the computer asks if the information is correct, type in Y. Then type Y in answer to OK TO DELETE ? (see Example 9-8).

```
UPDATE OR ENTER NEW BILLS

NEW ACCOUNT #  249768
ACCOUNT NAME ?  DILITHIUM PRESS
DATE PAYMENT DUE MM,DD,YY ?  09,01,79
TOTAL AMT DUE MAX ?  214.68
PAYMENT AMT DUE MAX ?  21.47
INTEREST ?  8.75
DATE BILL RCVD ?  08,01,79
INVOICE # ?  004302
```

Example 9-7

```
DELETE ACCT

ACCT #  176438
ACCT NAME  JACKSON COOKS
TOTAL BAL  0000.00
ACCT OK (Y/N) ?  Y

****ACCOUNT DELETED--UPDATING TAPE****
```

Example 9-8

9.17 PAYBILL

The PAYBILL section makes it possible either to pay selected bills or, by entering a carriage return for the account number, to pay all bills that have a payment date the same as the date you are working in.

Should the account number entry be used as shown, the system will respond by asking and displaying the following:

- ACCOUNT #
- PAYMENT AMOUNT—the amount expected to be paid on the bill is displayed.
- DUE ON—this is the date payment is expected.
- TOTAL AMOUNT OF INVOICE—this is what the current invoice is worth.

The system will then ask if you want to pay this specific invoice. If so, the system will continue through the payment loop. If not, the system cycles to the next invoice and starts the pattern over. To pay a specific invoice, the system will ask:

- AMOUNT TO BE PAID
- CHECK NUMBER—this is the number of the check you will actually use.

Once this is done, the system will then cycle to the next invoice in the account record or, if finished, either display the input question for account number or automatically go to the next bill. This display is shown in Example 9-9.

There is an additional feature in the PAYBILL section. It will generate all bills to be paid and update them without operator intervention. This requires that the number 999777 be entered. This signals the system that all bills due are to be paid on the date you are working in. When this option is chosen, the system asks for the first check number to be used, since it assumes that your check book is in sequence. As the system is run, all open items are paid against a specific check and the detail is printed on the hardcopy device. Actual checks must be hand-generated and given to the vendors. This feature is handled as a special subroutine and should only be considered if you are convinced of the accuracy of your data base.

```
PAYBILL

INPUT ACCOUNT NUMBER ?   176001
PAYMENT AMOUNT   262.00
DUE ON   090679
TOTAL AMT OF INVOICE   562.00
AMOUNT TO BE PAID ?   262.00
CHECK # ?   011380

INPUT ACCOUNT NUMBER ?
```

Example 9-9

9.18   UTILITY

Throughout this accounting system, the UTILITY function has been called upon to update records and to take care of sorting and cleaning up records. This is called housekeeping. The UTILITY function is also available for the payables system. Its operation is completely transparent, with only minor displays of what is needed from the operator.

The UTILITY function in the payables package removes deleted records from the data base and writes them to the archive portion of the tape, sorting the accounts by due date and account number. It prepares the totals in a special buffer that will be used by the General Ledger package for summary reports. Once the UTILITY is started, it will not require any operator assistance in the MECA tape environment. For systems using audio cassettes, the system will prompt when the operator must switch or rewind a tape.

9.19   ERROR RESPONSES

The error responses used in this package were not shown in as much definition as those in Chapters Six and Seven. However, most of the error messages generated by this package are the same as the messages used by those subsystems. Nothing really new was added.

9.20   SYSTEM SUMMARY

Payables are the second most important function of accounting for small businesses. If payables are not correctly handled, a company can quickly find itself in difficulty with its vendors without really knowing what happened. More importantly, by correctly maintaining the payables function, cash flow trends and cash handling can be made easier to track and to manage properly.

Automated or manual accounting systems should be designed to provide the manager with as much information regarding the auditing and actual state of payables as is humanly possible. By becoming familiar with this automated system, you, as a user, should be able to modify it to meet your specific needs or, even better, be able to communicate your very specific needs to the small computer industry.

To restate, the design of this system is that of a bare bones package that provides certain capabilities within specific environments.

Chapter Ten

FIFTH KEY SYSTEM: GENERAL LEDGER

This is probably the most important chapter in the book. Here a complete discussion of accounting practices, audit trails and system integration is provided. The procedure portion provides the necessary instructions to build a chart of accounts, post journal entries, and develop financial statements.

10.1   REVIEW OF THE ACCOUNTING METHOD

This book began with an introduction to computers and accounting methods. You should now be familiar with the concepts of inventory control, accounts receivable and accounts payable. You should also have increased your understanding of the definition of accounting to include the recording, classifying, summarizing, and reporting of business transactions in a meaningful manner.

The concept of the general ledger can now be introduced. To fully appreciate the general ledger concept and the tie-in with the inventory control, accounts receivable and accounts payable packages, we must do some backtracking.

10.2   ACCOUNTING RECORDS

Investigation by historians and accountants alike has shown that double-entry bookkeeping has been practiced for centuries. Double-entry bookkeeping is the most logical method known for keeping track of a company's assets and liabilities and the transactions that affect them. The company accountant is charged with analyzing this data on a day-to-day basis and determining its effects on the total operation of the company. Analyzing the records and making determinations are the primary functions of bookkeeping.

All accounting can be described in terms of increasing or decreasing assets and equities. The problem is that information may be inadequate, and trends cannot be properly ascertained without other information from periodic worksheets containing the records of expenses and revenues on a daily, weekly, and monthly basis. These records are used to create the more permanent or summary information in the master balance sheet.

The system that uses these intermediate and final worksheets for analysis also involves a complex system of journals, ledgers, documents, and computer readouts, plus a host of other information that is logged, cross checked, and rechecked for accuracy. Although the system uses hundreds of forms, saves thousands of records, sales slips, POs and memo records, it is relatively simple and boils down to one simple fact: every debit must be offset by a credit to achieve a balance. In short, double-entry bookkeeping is simply a matter of cross checking.

10.3 SOME IMPORTANT CONCEPTS

A business can be thought of as an entity unto itself, regardless of who the owners are or will be. In turn, all the records are thought to be part of the entity and do not reflect the status of the owners.

Businesses that have been around for a while and have good financial backing are going concerns. A going concern uses the accrual basis of periodic income, and some method must be established to show the difference between corporate capital and actual income. This is done so that, if it becomes necessary at any time, the going concern concept can be abandoned and full disclosures made of current assets, equities, and total liabilities.

It is important to determine what type of financial entity a company will be, as well as the costs that it incurs. The costs must always be part of the accounting system and should reflect exactly what an item or service cost at the time it was bought. This will result in correct tracking of actual expenses rather than those inflated by markups.

Regardless of how the company is set up legally or the exact mechanics of the bookkeeping system, the accountant must determine and measure the net income of the business. Since the net income reflects management decisions, proper accounting becomes quite significant, since it can pinpoint bad judgment on the part of management.

The general process of business accounting and the general ledger are represented in Figure 10-1. From the figure, it can be seen that all business activity is summarized, categorized, and then analyzed to produce meaningful information for management. The summary data and input for analysis come from the multitude of reports and income statements that are generated by the accounting system. Figure 10-1 must be kept in mind while you are developing an understanding of the general ledger. The idea of information flow is one of the most important concepts in this chapter, especially in relation to the mini-type ledger described in the procedure section.

10.4 GENERAL LEDGER

Figure 10-1 shows the general flow of information through the accounting system. It also gives an idea of the hierarchy of

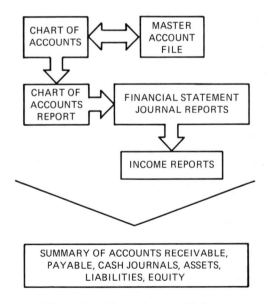

Figure 10-1 Flow of general ledger

journals, ledgers, and other worksheets involved. From the information contained in these documents, income statements, balance sheets and the net worth of the company are determined. Thus, the bottom line becomes a reality.

Throughout this book, the impact of decision making on the profit-loss picture of a company has been emphasized. It is the function of the information analyzed in the general ledger to describe the results of the decisions and to help make other decisions. The general ledger can be called a management information system (MIS). The MIS provides accounting data in terms of profit and loss. Unfortunately, it may not provide it until it is too late for management to improve the situation, a point to which we will return.

A system of accounts is established to facilitate the use of the information coming from the accounting system. These accounts must be classified in some manner. The account classifications are based on the income and balance sheets and are designed to have meaning in relation to them.

The income statement is concerned with:

- Revenue Accounts
- Expense Accounts
- Recurring Gain and Loss Accounts
- Interest Accounts
- Income Tax Accounts
- Income Distribution Accounts

while the balance sheet looks at:

- Liability Accounts
- Contributed Capital (that's capital put in by you)
- Retained Earning Accounts
- Adjustment Accounts

If you are familiar with accounting methods and systems, you realize that income statements and balance sheets may be concerned with other areas, but the ones mentioned here are the ones used in our model. They are adequate for most small businesses.

10.5   CHART OF ACCOUNTS

There is probably not an accounting book anywhere that does not use a subheading "Chart of Accounts" when describing the general ledger. The reason for this is simple. The accounts must be given numbers to reflect the type of account and possibly the status of the account, major or minor. This is done to set up the ledger in a meaningful way and to make the accountant's job of analyzing the business easier.

Ideally, the chart of accounts should be constructed so as to take into account possible future expansion. If this is done correctly, additional accounts can be added later. The chart of accounts is represented by numbers and names given to those numbers. The simplest system has the following structure, which is designed to be expanded upon.

- Asset accounts begin with 1 or 100 or 1000 depending on the bookkeeper setting up the system.
- Liability accounts are similarly numbered beginning with a 2, 200, or 2000.
- Equity accounts are normally numbered beginning with a 3.
- Operating expense accounts are represented with a 4 and miscellaneous accounts with a 5 or 6 depending on whether additional classifications are added.

Some accounting systems have account numbers in which each digit represents a certain attribute of the account. In this book, only the first digit will represent a particular attribute, although it is possible to redefine the account numbering system in any manner desired.

Since accountants use several terms to mean the same thing, this book will use terms such as "profit and loss statement" and "income statement" interchangeably, since they refer to the same thing. It is not the purpose of this book to engage in semantics; we suggest that you contact the American Accountants Association for any booklets they may have on older or newer accounting terminology. The terms used are not really important in any case—the results of an accounting system are the important thing.

10.6   HANDLING THE GENERAL LEDGER

The general ledger is a summary of all the results of doing business and is used by the accountant to analyze what is happening and to develop meaningful reports.

The system being described is double entry, that is, debits equal credits. This means that every transaction entered into the system should have an equal number of debits and credits. At some time during the month these entries are checked and a report called the Trial Balance is produced. If the debits equal the credits, the books are in balance and everything was entered correctly. If an error exists and something was not entered to the correct account, the debits and credits will be out of balance.

More specifically, a trial balance will be generated from whatever information is on hand in your business. First, check your asset accounts—cash assets, inventory assets, and any equipment that is part of the asset picture. Next, determine the status of the payables; then do the same with capital accounts. Once you have all this information, arrange it in the most meaningful form for your purpose, such as:

TRIAL BALANCE

	Debit	Credit
Cash	100	
Inventory	100	
Accounts Payable		100
Rent		100
	200	200

Although this example is extremely simple, it does describe the basic method of setting up a trial balance in a manual system. Should the balance figures be unequal, it would be necessary for the accountant to work backwards with the ledger sheets to find out where an improper entry was made. In the system described in this book, if a debit or a credit causes an out-of-balance condition, it will be identified immediately and action can be taken to correct it.

10.7   THE GENERAL JOURNAL AND POSTING

One of the primary journals used in accounting systems is the general journal. This journal is a record of all daily transactions along with specific references to the exact accounts affected. Normally the account reference is not entered until the transaction is actually posted to the account and cross reference made to the general journal page number. Keeping track of daily transactions can become very cumbersome and creates a major potential for error.

The general journal serves the purpose of supplying an immediate daily summary and makes it possible to post to the exact accounts at a later time—possibly on the close of books at the end of the month.

For automated systems, the act of updating the general journal ideally causes the necessary accounts to be updated with the posted information. Only the most up-to-date information is available because the system will not retain or accept outdated information. As a result of this, a trial balance can be generated with a fair amount of ease.

There can be any number of journals and subjournals to cover the actual operation of a business. These journals may be cash sales, credit sales, labor journals for contract labor, and any journal that best suits your needs. The journals and ledger systems are what the general ledger is all about; it is therefore necessary, if the system is to work properly, to make sure that you provide yourself with an adequate bookkeeping system.

The special journals are important since they reduce the amount of detailed recording in smaller journals. The journal detail can be handled by the person actually doing the job. The special journals also provide better control of the operation and make it easier to keep track of cash and purchase order requests.

Good examples of special journals are the accounts payable and receivable journals. In these subsystems, the accounts are set up to be handled in order of account number. This differs from the chart of accounts. Using subsidiary ledgers makes it possible to use only the most important data for analysis in the general ledger system.

This system uses the sales journal, which records sales to an account in which sales are handled as a debit to accounts receivable and as a credit to sales. Cash sales are handled in a cash sales journal. A purchase journal is set up to keep track of all purchases, including general needs and inventory.

10.8   REPORTS

The general ledger portion of the accounting system develops management reports. The system used in this book gives several types of reports.

The account distribution report is used to keep track of actual transactions within the accounting system. This report is important regardless of whether the system is manual or automated.

The general ledger report is a summation of all transactions and postings during a given period. It uses the general journal as part of its makeup. Its detail will be discussed in the procedure portion of this chapter.

The other reports are accounts receivable and accounts payable ledgers, cash disbursement journal, cash receipts journal, and purchasing report. In actual operation, the reports generated by the accounts receivable and accounts payable packages are used as part of the entire accounting analysis and tracking system.

10.9   AUDIT TRAILS

One of the most important functions of accounting is tracking information for tax purposes. The journals, subjournals, ledgers, and subledgers keep track of the audit trail data by cross referencing to each transaction by day, account, or invoice number. The actual document, such as a sales slip, must be kept on hand for future reference in case of an audit.

10.10   CLOSING PROCEDURES

Closing the books in a meaningful manner is just as important as keeping them up to date on a regular basis. Most business accounting records are kept on an accrual basis. This means that revenue is recognized when earned and expenses matched against revenue. Using the accrual method means that, at all times, revenue must keep in step with expenses and that both are related directly to the operating month. Each month the system starts over, even though receivables and payables may carry over into the next month.

Adjusting entries are made to cover the recorded data to ensure that the balances will be correct. This is done by transferring amounts from one account to another and by making the appropriate adjustments related to normal depreciation, expenses, or cash still outstanding. This process also produces year-to-date data. This is done so that each revenue and expense account falls to zero and shows up as such in a summary account. All accounts should equal zero at the end of each year and the start of the next.

When analyzing the accounting records and setting up the reports, you must remember that in all cases assets will equal liabilities plus capital, and debits and credits must always be equal. When these situations exist, the books are in balance unless fake entries were made to achieve a balance.

Each item debited or credited must be tracked and shown in the journals. Usually, an automated system takes advantage of the reports, the generation speed of the computer, and the audit trail capacity of the manual journals. For large-scale computer systems, the journals are all kept in the system. The system shown in this book provides a sound basis for an automated general ledger and holds a fairly large amount of data.

To put the concepts of this chapter into perspective, the exercises in Tables 10-1 and 10-2 are provided for figuring your personal balances and net worth. The exercises not only provide you with valuable information; they show you how the system works. Although these exercises are for personal income and net worth, the principles are the same. In a business system, additional items can be put in to further break down the actual income statement to make it even more meaningful.

10.11 THE STRUCTURE OF THIS GENERAL LEDGER

The general ledger package contained in this book provides a method of keeping a general journal and updating it on a daily basis. The chart of accounts can be rebuilt as necessary.

The system also provides reports on the trial balance and profit and loss statement. The chart of accounts can be printed along with the general journal entries and daily posting summary. The financial reports include the income statement, balance sheet, and monthly summaries of all transactions that

Table 10-1
Income and Expense Statement

INCOME		FIXED EXPENSES	
Gross Salary	$_____	Rent or Mortgage Payments	$_____
Deductions	− $_____	Income Taxes	$_____
Take Home Pay	$_____	Property Taxes	$_____
Other Income	$_____	Installment Payment	$_____
Total Income	$_____	Insurance	$_____
		Contributions/Dues	$_____
		Total Fixed Expenses	$_____
VARIABLE EXPENSES			
Utilities	$_____	TOTAL EXPENSES	
Medical	$_____	Fixed	$_____
Maintenance	$_____	Variable	$_____
Food	$_____	*Total*	$_____
Education	$_____		
Charge Accounts	$_____		
Total Variable Expenses	$_____		

TOTAL INCOME $_____ − LESS EXPENSES _____ = _____

have been posted. Table 10-3 is a list of all the available functions found in the general ledger function.

10.12 PROCEDURES

The general ledger package to be described in the following pages is designed to present a new method of data base management. It was first described in an article by Peter Reece in the August 1978 issue of *Interface Age Magazine* and prompted the redesign of this general ledger package.

Even though the package uses a technique different from that used in the previous chapters, it still uses the SYSTEM MENU to call the general ledger function and an internal menu for the

Table 10-2
Balance Sheet

ASSETS		LIABILITIES	
Cash	$_____	Accounts Payable	$_____
Cash Value of Insurance	$_____	Notes Payable	$_____
Notes or Accounts Receivable	$_____	Taxes	$_____
Autos	$_____	Loans	$_____
Real Estate	$_____	Liabilities	$_____
Pensions	$_____	*Total Liabilities*	$_____
Furnishings, Equipment, Other Assets	$_____		
Total Assets	$_____		
		NET WORTH	
		Assets	$_____
		Less Liabilities	– $_____
		Net Worth	$_____

different functions within the package. As with other sub-systems, this is done to maximize the use of memory and to make the system useful on a variety of machines.

10.13 SYSTEM MENU

The SYSTEM MENU shown in Example 10-1 has been used several times now and should be familiar to you. To work with the general ledger package, the SYSTEM MENU should be displayed on your CRT screen or printed on your teletype. Select option number 4 and depress RETURN. The system will respond with the first part of the general ledger package, the GENERAL LEDGER MENU (see Example 10-2).

Because a new technique of data handling is used in this chapter, the rest of the procedure portion will be a series of CRT type displays and sets of tables to explain what has happened in a particular section. This description is primarily for the functions of building the chart of accounts and establishing

Table 10-3
General Ledger Functions and Reports

FUNCTIONS

Build Chart of Accounts
Update General Journal
Update Cash Receipts Journal
Update Credit Sales Journal
Make Posting to Appropriate Accounts
Establish up to Three Additional Journals

REPORTS

List General Ledger Master Account File
List Chart of Accounts
Print General Journal
Print Cash Receipts Journal
Print Credit Sales Journal
Print Daily Posting
Print Trial Balance
Print Income or Profit Loss Statement

```
SYSTEM MENU

INVENTORY CONTROL            (1)
BILLING/ACCOUNTS RECEIVABLE  (2)
ACCOUNTS PAYABLE             (3)
GENERAL LEDGER               (4)
PLANNING                     (5)
DEPOSIT                      (6)
UTILITY                      (7)

SELECTION ?   4
```

Example 10-1

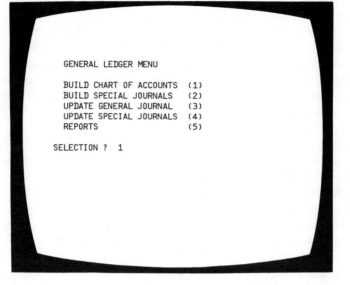

```
GENERAL LEDGER MENU

BUILD CHART OF ACCOUNTS   (1)
BUILD SPECIAL JOURNALS    (2)
UPDATE GENERAL JOURNAL    (3)
UPDATE SPECIAL JOURNALS   (4)
REPORTS                   (5)

SELECTION ?   1
```

Example 10-2

the journals. The reports are straightforward and are called on a one-by-one basis for a special menu designed to generate specific reports.

It is extremely important for you to follow these procedures closely since they resemble telling the machine what to do in a sentence form or a programming style. The tables in this chapter and in Appendix A will assist you in the use of the general ledger function.

10.14   THE CHART OF ACCOUNTS

The building of the chart of accounts will be something you do once and then leave alone. Start from the display shown in Example 10-2, except: SELECTION ? 1. Even though the chart will be built only once, it remains on the GENERAL LEDGER MENU and the associated code remains intact on the system tape. It should be pointed out that if the function is used, it destroys the existing chart of accounts data base.

Before you establish the chart of accounts, it is assumed that you have some understanding of a chart of accounts and that you have decided what your accounts will be called and how many will exist. Once these points are established the system can be run to build the chart.

Because the chart of accounts is used by the ledger package to direct the balancing of the books, it is important that it be built carefully so that information will be handled correctly within the system. Therefore, before you use this portion of the package it is important to sit down and pre-establish your chart of accounts so that the system can be used efficiently during the time you are building the accounts.

The chart of accounts, as mentioned before, is made up of asset accounts, liability accounts, equity accounts, income accounts, and expense accounts. Within each of these major account headings are subheadings for current, fixed, other, non-current, capital and sales accounts. Since the system has no idea how many accounts you have and the type of definition you want to use, it is necessary for you to tell it what you are doing.

The worksheet in Table 10-4 should be used to develop your accounts. Ideally, you will leave gaps between the account numbers in a manual system, and this automated system is designed to do the same thing as the process of developing the chart of accounts takes place.

The worksheet in Table 10-4 is designed to be similar to the questions the program will be asking you as the accounts are being built. You will notice that you have the option of either letting the system automatically number the accounts based on the information provided by you or entering the account number yourself as you go along. It is suggested that the following format be used:

- Asset accounts start with 1
- Liability accounts start with 2
- Equity accounts start with 3
- Income accounts start with 4
- Expense accounts start with 5

Since, during the initial design of this package, it was decided to use six-digit account numbers for nearly all features, the same holds true for the chart of accounts. When the automatic numbering system is used, the accounts will actually appear as: 001100. We suggest that this feature be used; otherwise you will have to exercise a great deal of care to ensure that the numbering is consistent.

Table 10-4
Chart of Accounts Worksheet

Enter type of accounts (Asset, Liability, Equity, Income, Expense) _____

How many of these accounts do you have?   _____

Will account numbering be automatic (Y/N)?   _____

If manual, what is the first account number?   _____

Write down each of your accounts that fits the category; if in manual mode for account numbers, write the account number in the column titled # for number; if you plan to use the automatic numbering function, leave this area blank; the system will generate the account numbers.

#	Account Description	Last Credit	Last Debit

Errors will occur if less than or more than six digits are entered for the account number. The system will reply with the error message: ACCOUNT NUMBER IS LESS THAN 6 DIGITS or ACCOUNT NUMBER IS GREATER THAN 6 DIGITS and the input cycle will again request the account number.

After the entire chart of accounts is built, the system will print the entire list to the hardcopy device for verification. Depressing RETURN at this point causes the system to save the entered information as a sort of scratch file. This is done to save time and to avoid wasting time if something goes wrong. RETURN also causes the system to cycle through to start developing definition to each account as taken from the worksheet provided.

As each account type is built, the system will save the information before starting the next heading. Once all the information is entered and the chart of accounts is built, the system prints the chart of accounts and, on receiving approval from you, sets up the general journal.

Examples 10-3 through 10-10 will show you how to set up a chart of accounts using this system.

From this point on, all inputs to the general ledger package will be made under the data base management system with the exception of requesting the reports and asking for utility.

10.15 ESTABLISHING THE JOURNALS

The general journal, the journal used to keep track of all the daily transactions, is automatically part of the system and does not require any input from the operator for its creation. The special journals must be defined to the system to meet specific needs. For this system, as many journals can be established as are needed, but three were chosen here as an arbitrary example. The journals and all entries to the journals are set up in the same fashion, which makes the operation almost transparent to the user.

Special ledgers are not addressed in this package; therefore, an accounts payable or receivable subsidiary ledger is not part

```
ENTER TYPE OF ACCOUNTS ?   ASSET
```

Example 10-3

```
ENTER TYPE OF ACCOUNTS ?  ASSET
ENTER TOTAL NUMBER OF ASSET ACCOUNTS ?  10
```

Example 10-4: The system uses the input for type of account to generate this question. The number input is used by the computer to set up the inquiry for the next set of questions.

```
ENTER TYPE OF ACCOUNTS ?  ASSET
ENTER TOTAL NUMBER OF ASSET ACCOUNTS ?  10
WILL NUMBERING BE MANUAL (1) OR AUTO (2) ?  2
```

Example 10-5

```
YOU HAVE 10 ASSET ACCOUNTS.
ARE THERE ANY SUBHEADINGS (Y/N) ? Y
```

Example 10-6

```
YOU HAVE 10 ASSET ACCOUNTS
ARE THERE ANY SUBHEADINGS (Y/N) ?   Y
HOW MANY SUBHEADINGS ?   3
```

Example 10-7

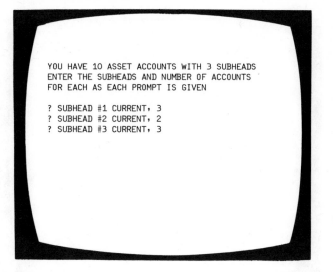

```
YOU HAVE 10 ASSET ACCOUNTS WITH 3 SUBHEADS
ENTER THE SUBHEADS AND NUMBER OF ACCOUNTS
FOR EACH AS EACH PROMPT IS GIVEN

? SUBHEAD #1 CURRENT, 3
? SUBHEAD #2 CURRENT, 2
? SUBHEAD #3 CURRENT, 3
```

Example 10-8: The system will prompt to the end of total subheads, then recycle back to the start of the account building cycle shown in Example 10-3. This takes place until all account heads and an @ are entered. Be sure to enter a comma as shown.

```
YOU HAVE:

    10 ASSET ACCTS
    15 LIABILITY ACCTS
     8 EQUITY ACCTS
    17 INCOME ACCTS
    17 EXPENSE ACCTS

IF THIS PRELIMINARY DATA IS CORRECT DEPRESS
RETURN TO CONTINUE ?
```

Example 10-9: The process continues until you have listed the total number of accounts and you get the response shown here.

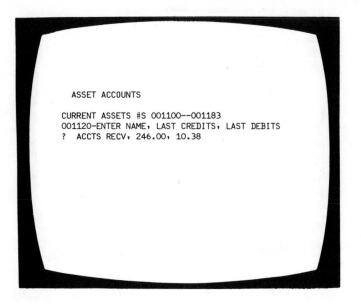

```
ASSET ACCOUNTS

CURRENT ASSETS #S 001100--001183
001120-ENTER NAME, LAST CREDITS, LAST DEBITS
?  ACCTS RECV, 246.00, 10.38
```

Example 10-10: This last display shows you how each account is
established. This cycle continues through the
entire chart of accounts.

From this point on, all inputs to the general
ledger package will be made under the data base
management system with the exception of requesting the reports and asking for utility.

of the general ledger subsystem. However, all the reports and information available from these packages are used in the general
ledger function. For totally integrated systems, the updating
from these packages to the general ledger is automatic.

Table 10-5 presents the acceptable inputs to the Data Base
Management System (DMBS) to make the next several screen
displays understandable as they describe the operation of the
rest of this package. As each function is presented, combina-
tions of words are entered to perform a specific function or to
look at a specific record.

This set of displays starts with the GENERAL LEDGER
MENU in Example 10-11 and takes you through the PRINT instruction for the profit and loss statement, as shown in Example
10-42. The printout for this statement is shown in Table 10-6.

Table 10-5
Inputs to Data Base Management System

Acceptable Input	Purpose	Acceptable Input	Purpose
+ (plus)	used by parser	IS MORE THAN	used by parser
− (minus)	used by parser	IS NOT	used by parser
999	end command word	IS THERE	used by parser
(less than)	used by parser	ISN'T	used by parser
(greater than)	used by parser	JOURNAL # OR NAME	used for P&L
A	used by parser	LESS	used by parser
ADD	used by parser	LOOK	used by parser
ADMINISTRATION	used for P&L	LOSS	used for P&L
ADVERTISING	used for P&L	MAKE	used by parser
AVAILABLE	used by parser	MATCH	used by parser
BE	used by parser	MINUS	used by parser
BEFORE	used by parser	MOUNT	command word
BEGINNING	used for P&L	NET	used by parser
CAN	used by parser	NOT	used by parser
CAN THERE	used by parser	OFFICE	used for P&L
CLOSE	command word	OPEN	command word
COST	used for P&L	OPERATING	used for P&L
CREATE	command word	OTHER	used for P&L
CREDIT	command word	PLUS	used for P&L
DEBIT	command word	PROFIT	used for P&L
DELETE	command word	PROMOTION	used for P&L
DELIVERY	used for P&L	PURCHASES	used for P&L
DEPRECIATION	used for P&L	POT	command word
DIVIDENDS	used for P&L	REMOVE	command word
ENDING	used for P&L	REVENUES	used for P&L
EQUIPMENT	used for P&L	REWIND	used for P&L
ET	command word for end	SALARIES	used for P&L
EXPENSES	used for P&L	SALES	used for P&L
FEDERAL	used for P&L	SEARCH	command word
FIND	command word	SHOULD	used by parser
FOR	used by parser	SHOULD HAVE	used by parser
GENERAL	used for P&L	SHOULD HAVE HAD	used by parser
GET	command word	STATE	used for P&L
GOODS	used for P&L	TAXES	used for P&L
GROSS	used for P&L	TRANSPORTATION-IN	used for P&L
HAD	used by parser	UNLOAD	command word
IN	used by parser	WAS	used by parser
INCOME	used for P&L	WASN'T	used by parser
INTEREST	used for P&L	WHO'S	used by parser
INVENTORY	used for P&L	WHOSE	used by parser
IS IT POSSIBLE	used by parser	WILL BE	used by parser
IS LESS THAN	used by parser	YET	used by parser

```
GENERAL LEDGER MENU

BUILD CHART OF ACCOUNTS   (1)
BUILD SPECIAL JOURNALS    (2)
UPDATE GENERAL JOURNALS   (3)
UPDATE SPECIAL JOURNALS   (4)
REPORTS                   (5)

SELECTION ?   2
```

Example 10-11

```
SPECIAL JOURNALS

READY ?   CREATE
```

Example 10-12

```
        SPECIAL JOURNALS

    READY ? CREATE
    TYPE ET WHEN DONE
```

Example 10-13: After you type in CREATE and depress RETURN, the system will respond as shown.

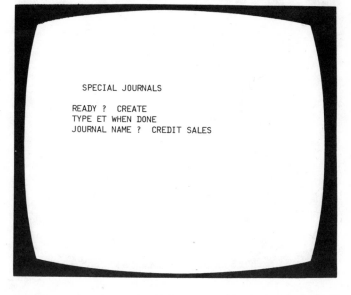

```
        SPECIAL JOURNALS

    READY ?  CREATE
    TYPE ET WHEN DONE
    JOURNAL NAME ?  CREDIT SALES
```

Example 10-14

```
SPECIAL JOURNALS

READY ?   CREATE
TYPE ET WHEN DONE
JOURNAL NAME ?  CREDIT SALES
BALANCE ?   0.00
```

Example 10-15

```
SPECIAL JOURNALS

READY ?   CREATE
TYPE ET WHEN DONE
JOURNAL NAME?   CREDIT SALES
BALANCE ?   0.00
CREDIT, DEBIT ?   0.00, 0.00
```

Example 10-16: At this point DBMS will recycle. This will allow you to build additional journals. It gives the journal number each time.

```
        SPECIAL JOURNALS

        READY ?  CREATE
        TYPE ET WHEN DONE
        JOURNAL #2  CREDIT SALES
        JOURNAL #3 NAME ?  ET
```

Example 10-17: The ET (end transaction) response means you are finished. The alternative is to continue building journals. Up to ten are allowed, with the general journal being counted as number one.

```
        READY ?   LIST JOURNALS
```

Example 10-18: This function will list all available journals.

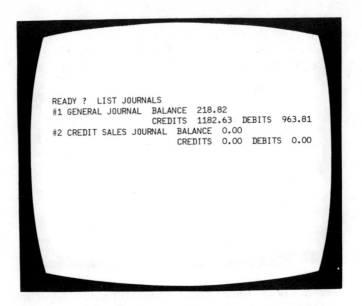

```
READY ? LIST JOURNALS
#1 GENERAL JOURNAL  BALANCE  218.82
                   CREDITS  1182.63  DEBITS  963.81
#2 CREDIT SALES JOURNAL  BALANCE  0.00
                        CREDITS  0.00  DEBITS  0.00
```

Example 10-19: The balance reflects the difference between debits and credits.

```
GENERAL LEDGER MENU

BUILD CHART OF ACCOUNTS   (1)
BUILD SPECIAL JOURNALS    (2)
UPDATE GENERAL JOURNALS   (3)
UPDATE SPECIAL JOURNALS   (4)
REPORTS                   (5)

SELECTION ?  3
```

Example 10-20

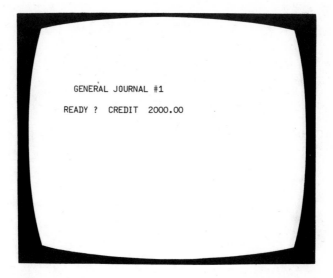

```
GENERAL JOURNAL #1

READY ?   CREDIT   2000.00
```

Example 10-21: The system will answer with another READY
and will continue doing so until 999 or ET is
entered. By entering either of these you direct
the system to return to the GENERAL
LEDGER MENU.

```
GENERAL LEDGER MENU

BUILD CHART OF ACCOUNTS   (1)
BUILD SPECIAL JOURNALS    (2)
UPDATE GENERAL JOURNALS   (3)
UPDATE SPECIAL JOURNALS   (4)
REPORTS                   (5)

SELECTION ?   4
```

Example 10-22

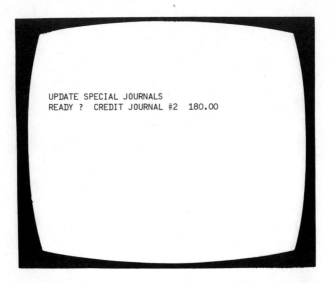

```
UPDATE SPECIAL JOURNALS
READY ?  CREDIT JOURNAL #2  180.00
```

Example 10-23: Entries to any journal can be verified by typing
in **VERIFY**. The system will print the entire
journal on the screen. The system will respond
with another **READY** and will continue doing
so until **999** or **ET** is entered.

```
GENERAL LEDGER MENU

BUILD CHART OF ACCOUNTS   (1)
BUILD SPECIAL JOURNALS    (2)
UPDATE GENERAL JOURNALS   (3)
UPDATE SPECIAL JOURNAL    (4)
REPORTS                   (5)

SELECTION ?   5
```

Example 10-24

```
REPORTS

MASTER ACCOUNT FILE     (1)
CHART OF ACCOUNTS       (2)
GENERAL JOURNAL         (3)
CASH RECEIPTS JOURNAL   (4)
DAILY POSTING           (5)
TRIAL BALANCE           (6)
PROFIT AND LOSS         (7)

SELECTION ?   1
```

Example 10-25

```
     MASTER ACCOUNTS FILE
     ACCT #   NAME              BALANCE
 1   100001   DILITHIUM PRESS   276.00
 2   100002   CARL WARREN       477.48
 3   100003   MERL MILLER       826.04
 4   100004   ROBOTICS PRESS    429.05
 5   101001   H LUKOFF          472.26
 6   101002   N WINKLESS        679.38
 7   210020   P H MILLER        486.30
 8   210021   JEFF MORTON       381.50
 9   210023   BASIC PROGRAMS    770.22
10   210024   MATRIX PUBLISH    190.90
11   210025   I A MAGAZINE      217.10
DEPRESS RETURN TO CONTINUE?
```

Example 10-26

```
REPORTS

MASTER ACCOUNT FILE    (1)
CHART OF ACCOUNTS      (2)
GENERAL JOURNAL        (3)
CASH RECEIPTS JOURNAL  (4)
DAILY POSTING          (5)
TRIAL BALANCE          (6)
PROFIT AND LOSS        (7)

SELECTION ?   2
```

Example 10-27

```
CHART OF ACCOUNTS

ASSET
001100  CASH
001120  ACCTS RECEIVABLE
LIABILITY
002100  ACCTS PAYABLE
002120  NOTES PAYABLE
EQUITY
003100  CAPITAL ACCT
003120  DRAWING ACCT
```

Example 10-28

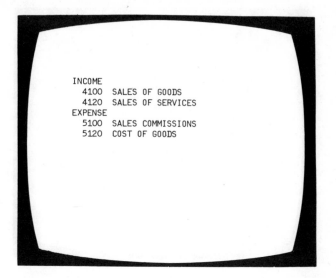

```
INCOME
  4100   SALES OF GOODS
  4120   SALES OF SERVICES
EXPENSE
  5100   SALES COMMISSIONS
  5120   COST OF GOODS
```

Example 10-29: Each account is listed by type, account number and name. The CRT will display up to 12 lines; depressing RETURN displays more. All are printed on the hardcopy device.

```
REPORTS

MASTER ACCOUNT FILE     (1)
CHART OF ACCOUNTS       (2)
GENERAL JOURNAL         (3)
CASH RECEIPTS JOURNAL   (4)
DAILY POSTING           (5)
TRIAL BALANCE           (6)
PROFIT AND LOSS         (7)

SELECTION ?   3
```

Example 10-30

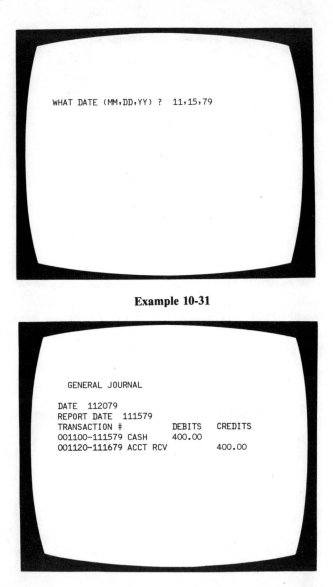

```
WHAT DATE (MM,DD,YY) ?   11,15,79
```

Example 10-31

```
GENERAL JOURNAL

DATE   112079
REPORT DATE   111579
TRANSACTION #           DEBITS    CREDITS
001100-111579 CASH      400.00
001120-111679 ACCT RCV            400.00
```

Example 10-32: The first date shown (112079) is the system date. It is in this form: MMDDYY. The same detail is offered for each transaction. The numbers 001100 and 001120 are account numbers. The dates 111579 and 111679 are the dates the transactions were entered. Only the transactions on or after the requested date are displayed.

```
        REPORTS

        MASTER ACCOUNT FILE    (1)
        CHART OF ACCOUNTS      (2)
        GENERAL JOURNAL        (3)
        CASH RECEIPTS JOURNAL  (4)
        DAILY POSTING          (5)
        TRIAL BALANCE          (6)
        PROFIT AND LOSS        (7)

     SELECTION ?   4
```

Example 10-33

```
        CASH RECEIPTS JOURNAL

     DATE      ACCT CREDITED    CASH-DB    A/R-CR
     110279    C D WARREN       160.25     160.25
     110279    SALES            400.00

               TOTALS           560.25     160.25
```

Example 10-34: Totals will reflect a balanced or out-of-balance condition.

```
REPORTS

MASTER ACCOUNT FILE    (1)
CHART OF ACCOUNTS      (2)
GENERAL JOURNAL        (3)
CASH RECEIPTS JOURNAL  (4)
DAILY POSTING          (5)
TRIAL BALANCE          (6)
PROFIT AND LOSS        (7)

SELECTION ?   5
```

Example 10-35

```
DAILY POSTING

DATE   071779
DESCRIPTION    POST/REF    DEBIT     CREDIT
CASH           001100      200.00
ACCT RCV       001120                200.00
```

Example 10-36: Notice that the cash account (001100) is debited and the accounts receivable account (001120) is credited. The lists shown here represent information as of the date shown.

```
REPORTS

MASTER ACCOUNT FILE    (1)
CHART OF ACCOUNTS      (2)
GENERAL JOURNAL        (3)
CASH RECEIPTS JOURNAL  (4)
DAILY POSTING          (5)
TRIAL BALANCE          (6)
PROFIT AND LOSS        (7)

SELECTION ?  6
```

Example 10-37

```
ENTER DATE (MM,DD,YY) ?  O9,11,79
```

Example 10-38

```
TRIAL BALANCE   DATE  091179

DESCRIPTION      DEBIT      CREDIT
CASH            1000.00
SUPPLIES          50.00
ACCTS PAYABLE               1350.00
RENT             300.00

TOTALS          1350.00     1350.00
```

Example 10-39

```
REPORTS

MASTER ACCOUNT FILE    (1)
CHART OF ACCOUNTS      (2)
GENERAL JOURNAL        (3)
CASH RECEIPTS JOURNAL  (4)
DAILY POSTING          (5)
TRIAL BALANCE          (6)
PROFIT AND LOSS        (7)

SELECTION ?   7
```

Example 10-40

```
READY ?  CREATE
TYPE ET TO QUIT

ITEM ?  SALES REVENUE M
ITEM ?  GROSS SALES
ITEM ?  NET SALES
ITEM ?  COST OF GOODS SOLD M
ITEM ?  BEGINNING INVENTORY
ITEM ?  PURCHASES
ITEM ?  GROSS PROFIT ON SALES M
```

Example 10-41: M tells the DMBS that the entry is a major heading. To see the profit and loss statement, you can request the desired headings and subheadings as you require. Appendix A shows what is available and what is required to change this function.

```
READY ?  PRINT PROFIT AND LOSS
```

Example 10-42: Based on the information entered under **CREATE**, the profit and loss statement will be printed. Table 10-6 is an example of what can be produced.

Table 10-6
Income Statement

```
DATE:  12/18/77

                    AMW ENTERPRISES INCOME STATEMENT

SALES REVENUE
    GROSS SALES------------------------------------------          $700,000
    LESS: SALES RTNS AND ALLOWANCES-----------       $15,300
          CASH DISCOUNTS ON SALES-----------         $12,400       $27,700
    NET SALES---------------------------------------------      ** $672,300 **
COST OF GOODS SOLD
    BEGINNING INVENTORY--------------------------     $58,700
    PURCHASES----------                 $400,000

    LESS: PURCSE RTNS AND ALLOWANCES-----    $12,100
    NET PURCHASES----------                  $387,900
    TRANSPORTATION-IN-----------             $43,200  $431,100
    GOODS AVAILABLE FOR SALE-----------               $489,800
    LESS: ENDING INVENTORY----------                  $45,600
    COST OF GOODS SOLD------------------------------------------$444,200
GROSS PROFIT ON SALES--------------------------------------------$228,100
OPERATING EXPENSES
    SELLING EXPENSES
        SALES SALARIES AND COMMISSIONS      $30,000
        SALES TRAVEL----------              $15,000
        ADVERTISING AND PROMOTION           $28,000
        DELIVERY EXPENSE----------          $7,000
        OTHER SELLING EXPENSES-----------   $5,000    $85,000
    GENERAL AND ADMINISTRATIVE EXPENSES
        ADMINISTRATIVE SALARIES----------   $32,000
        INSURANCE----------                 $8,000
        DEPRECIATION OF OFFICE EQIPMENT     $3,000
        OTHER ADMINISTRATIVE EXPENSES       $12,000   $55,000
    TOTAL OPERATING EXPENSES---------------------------          $140,000
OPERATING INCOME-------------------------------------------       $88,100
OTHER REVENUES
    INTEREST----------                      $7,000
    DIVIDENDS----------                     $3,000    $10,000
OTHER EXPENSES
    INTEREST EXPENSE----------------------------      $2,100      $7,900
NET INCOME BEFORE TAXES-------------------------                  $96,000
FEDERAL AND STATE INCOME TAXES-----------                         $50,000
NET INCOME-------------------------------------------             46,000
                                                                 ======
```

10.16 UTILITY

The utility function of the general ledger is the same as for the other packages and is designed to require only minimum operator intervention. Utility for the general ledger does all the account updating and record checking. No special sorts are performed for this function.

10.17 ERROR RESPONSES

Because the general ledger package is different in design concept from that used earlier in this book, Table 10-7 is provided with a list of error responses and their meanings.

Table 10-7
General Ledger Error Responses

ERROR RESPONSE	MEANING	OPERATOR RESPONSE
ENTER COMMAND	An attempt was made to enter either non-command word or non-recognizable word	Enter correct command—See Table 10-5 or Systems Manual
NO EXISTING FILE	Attempt made to locate a file not in the database	Ask for new file name
NO EXISTING RECORD	Attempt made to locate a record within a file that is non-existent	Re-enter record request or all to display all record names
NO SUCH JOURNAL	Attempt to view a non-existing journal	Re-enter or all journals for a list of all valid journal names and numbers
UNABLE TO DELETE	Attempt made to delete a non-existing file or record	Re-enter request
INCQT ACCOUNT	Attempt made to either credit a debit account or debit a credit account	Re-enter or all accounts for listing of all account types
FILE FULL	Response when accessing a full file (no more room on storage device)	Last notation on file points next disk or tape
ILLEGAL COMMAND	Displayed when an attempt is made to rewind, overlay or cause a rewrite while in an update mode	Enter a return system will respond with either a "?" or the next request
DON'T UNDERSTAND	Operator has entered an absolute meaningless request	Re-enter or type list-system displays all valid inputs
UNABLE TO MATCH	Request was made to find a match of some non-existent item in the data base	Re-try
NOT FINISHED	Attempt made to terminate a session before all fields satisfied in a given record	Enter return and continue entering data or enter 999 or et to terminate

ALL OTHER ERRORS MAY BE FOUND IN
THE CTBL SYSTEMS MANUAL(S)

10.18 SUMMARY

The general ledger is the most important accounting tool the small businessman has. With the general ledger and associated journals, you can correctly track the day-to-day functions of your business. It is this subsystem that provides answers related to profit and loss conditions and the data needed to make intelligent decisions.

As you become familiar with the system, you will find that it is adaptable to disk, tape, paper tape, and disk tape environments. Depending on the capabilities of the machine and available storage, the system can be used to handle a great deal of information.

The most important aspect of the system is that it provides you with timely information, assuming that the information was entered on time and correctly.

This subsystem ends the actual accounting package. Chapter Eleven describes a planning package and deposit package that may be used to enhance business operations.

Chapter Eleven

SUPPORT PACKAGES

This chapter presents the planning and deposit applications, which are designed to enhance the accounting package and provide you with even greater benefits from the microcomputer. The planning package provides a method of comparing current and past financial data and of making projections based on fluctuations and financial history. The deposit program makes it possible to automate the cash drawer and to develop a cash receipts ledger.

11.1   INTRODUCTION

There are two functions in the support packages: planning and deposit. The planning package uses current and historical information to project what might happen over a period of time. The deposit package is used to automate the cash register. This system makes it easy to reconcile the cash drawer and prepare the deposit slip. The information derived from it can be saved or used in any manner desired, but its primary purpose is to make a deposit slip.

11.2   PLANNING

One reason companies fail is a lack of information and the resulting lack of accurate planning. The planning package presented in this chapter is based on the logic of projecting what will happen if current trends continue. Trends are important in any business. With the help of automated planning that uses information from the rest of the accounting system, you can make realistic management decisions.

The planning package is a management tool used to make projections by analyzing historical information in relation to current data. Planning is based on sales accounts, income accounts, revenue and expense accounts. You have the choice of using the information by percentage, fixed amount, or any other criteria that you establish for each type of account. Figure 11-1 shows the general flow of the planning package. Notice that actual bottom line figures are compared with planned balances. Of course, this comparison has meaning only after the first fiscal period of operation.

The planning package is driven off the SYSTEM MENU, which sets up the PLANNING MENU and the specific options available. The Planning Report is the only report generated. It is

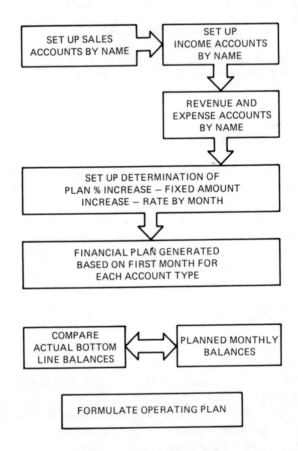

Figure 11-1 Flow of planning

based on the data you input. A sample report is shown in Table 11-1.

Table 11-1
Planning Report

PLANNING REPORT FOR 09/07/78   BASED ON 9% GROWTH RATE

	JAN	FEB	MAR	APR	MAY	JUN	JUL	AUG	SEP	OCT	NOV	DEC	JAN
SALES REPORTS													
GROSS SALES	10000	10900	11881	12950	14115	15386	16771	18280	19925	21718	23673	25804	28126
SALES RTN	1100	1199	1306	1424	1552	1692	1844	2010	2191	2389	2604	2838	3093
NET SALES	8900	9701	10575	11526	12563	13694	14927	16270	17734	19329	21069	22966	25033
INCOME ACCTS													
ACCTS RECV	25000	27250	29702	32375	35289	38465	41927	45700	49814	54297	59184	64510	70316
RENTALS	200	218	237	259	282	307	335	365	398	434	473	516	562
REV/EXP ACCT													
INTEREST	4000	4360	4752	5180	5646	6154	6708	7312	7970	8687	9459	10321	11250
DIVIDENDS	200	218	237	259	282	307	335	365	398	434	473	516	562
GEN EXPENSES	1000	10900	11881	12950	14115	15386	16771	18280	19925	21218	23673	25804	28126

From this example report, you can see that the percentage option calculates a straight growth pattern and does not take in account your innate abilities to second guess what will happen over a given period of time. This option report is useful however for establishing goals snd should be used as such.

In this chapter, we will treat examples in the same manner as in Chapter Ten. We will give you a series of screens to follow. The first display is the SYSTEM MENU, shown in Example 11-1.

Regardless of which option is chosen in Example 11-2, the system will react as if there are 13 months in a year. The current month is taken as the starting point and is called 1; the system will calculate for the next 12 months, including the starting month, as well as the same month one year later.

The fixed percentage option (A) allows you to enter a fixed percentage and uses this percentage for all calculations. Only one entry is required at this point and all examples will be based on this option.

The fixed increase option (B) asks for a fixed dollar amount of growth. The system will use this amount to calculate the plan. Option C allows you to choose specific dollar amounts for each month. It requires an entry for each month for the categories displayed.

For option A, the system will ask only for starting dollar amounts for the categories listed. The same is true of option B. However, for option C the system will need both the starting dollar amount and the planned dollar growth. To avoid difficulty with this option the system prompts for the inputs. These displays are shown in Examples 11-9 through 11-14.

```
SYSTEM MENU

ENTER SELECTION AND DEPRESS RETURN

    INVENTORY CONTROL              (1)
    BILLING/ACCOUNTS RECEIVABLE    (2)
    ACCOUNTS PAYABLE               (3)
    GENERAL LEDGER                 (4)
    PLANNING                       (5)
    DEPOSIT                        (6)
    UTILITY                        (7)

SELECTION ?   5
```

Example 11-1

```
    PLANNING

THIS PLANNING PACKAGE ALLOWS YOU TO MAKE PROJECTIONS
BASED ON MONTH ONE.  YOU CAN HAVE THE PROJECTION BY:

  (A)   FIXED PERCENTAGE OF THE FIRST MONTH
  (B)   FIXED AMOUNT INCREASE OFF FIRST MONTH
  (C)   INDIVIDUAL INCREASE BY FIXED AMOUNT
        OR PERCENTAGE-ENTERED FOR EACH MONTH

DEPRESS RETURN TO CONTINUE ?
```

Example 11-2

```
THE PLANNING SYSTEM WILL CALCULATE EXPECTED GROWTH
BASED ON THE OPTION CHOSEN FOR THESE AREAS:

  SALES ACCOUNTS
  INCOME ACCOUNTS
  REVENUE AND EXPENSE ACCOUNTS

OVER THE NEXT SEVERAL SCREENS YOU WILL BE ASKED
A NUMBER OF QUESTIONS-AT THE END ALL INPUTS

DEPRESS RETURN TO CONTINUE ?
```

Example 11-3

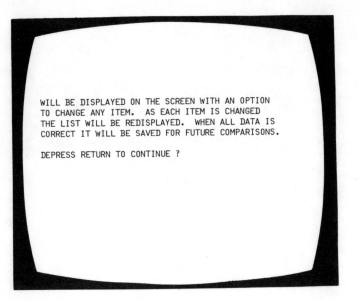

WILL BE DISPLAYED ON THE SCREEN WITH AN OPTION
TO CHANGE ANY ITEM. AS EACH ITEM IS CHANGED
THE LIST WILL BE REDISPLAYED. WHEN ALL DATA IS
CORRECT IT WILL BE SAVED FOR FUTURE COMPARISONS.

DEPRESS RETURN TO CONTINUE ?

Example 11-4

IS OLD PLAN TO BE UPDATED (Y/N) ?   Y

Example 11-5

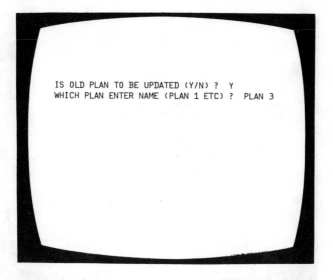

```
IS OLD PLAN TO BE UPDATED (Y/N) ?   Y
WHICH PLAN ENTER NAME (PLAN 1 ETC) ?   PLAN 3
```

Example 11-6: This option is given so that previous plans can be updated quickly by speeding up the process of getting to a specific input routine.

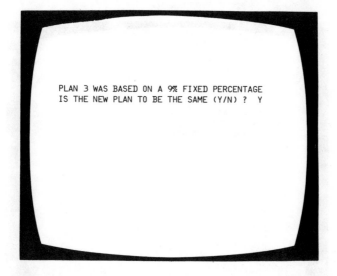

```
PLAN 3 WAS BASED ON A 9% FIXED PERCENTAGE
IS THE NEW PLAN TO BE THE SAME (Y/N) ?   Y
```

Example 11-7: If you enter N at this point, the system will provide you with a list of options, ask for the starting month, and cycle through the inputs needed for calculation based on your chosen option.

```
IS OLD PLAN TO BE UPDATED (Y/N) ?   N
ENTER PLAN NAME (PLAN 1 ETC) ?   PLAN 1
WHAT IS STARTING MONTH ?   JAN
MAKE SELECTION AND DEPRESS RETURN

   (A)   FIXED PERCENTAGE
   (B)   FIXED INCREASE
   (C)   INCREASE BY MONTH

SELECTION ?   A
```

Example 11-8: If this is your first plan, the system will react in the manner shown.

```
WHAT IS PERCENTAGE ?   9
HOW MANY SALES ACCOUNTS ?   3
HOW MANY INCOME ACCOUNTS ?   2
HOW MANY REVENUE AND EXPENSE ACCOUNTS ?   3
```

Example 11-9

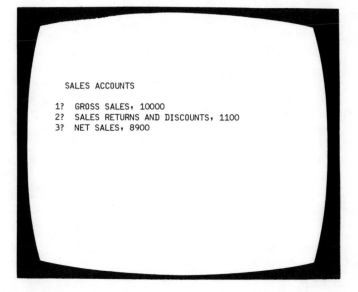

```
    SALES ACCOUNTS

1?  GROSS SALES, 10000
2?  SALES RETURNS AND DISCOUNTS, 1100
3?  NET SALES, 8900
```

Example 11-10: Note that commas must be entered to separate
the fields.

```
    INCOME ACCOUNTS

1?  ACCOUNTS RECEIVABLE, 25000
2?  RENTALS, 9000
```

Example 11-11

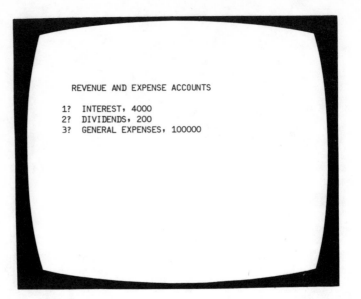

```
REVENUE AND EXPENSE ACCOUNTS

1?  INTEREST, 4000
2?  DIVIDENDS, 200
3?  GENERAL EXPENSES, 100000
```

Example 11-12

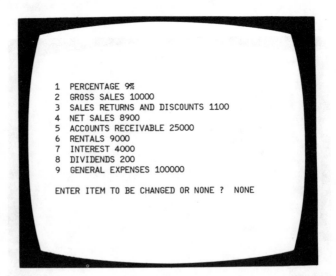

```
1   PERCENTAGE 9%
2   GROSS SALES 10000
3   SALES RETURNS AND DISCOUNTS 1100
4   NET SALES 8900
5   ACCOUNTS RECEIVABLE 25000
6   RENTALS 9000
7   INTEREST 4000
8   DIVIDENDS 200
9   GENERAL EXPENSES 100000

ENTER ITEM TO BE CHANGED OR NONE ?  NONE
```

Example 11-13: If you need to change an item, you must enter the name of the item. The old item will be displayed with an input prompt. This is your signal to enter the new information.

PLAN NOW BEING SAVED

Example 11-14: Once the data is saved, the report will be printed on the hardcopy device and the SYSTEM MENU will be displayed.

11.3 DEPOSIT

The deposit function in this accounting package is as simple as the planning package. It serves one purpose, to automate the cash drawer. Figure 11-2 represents the general flow of the deposit system. Although the deposit function is not integrated with the rest of the accounting system, this is fairly easy to do if you use linked disks and tapes. It provides complete tracking of daily operations.

Figure 11-2 shows that the system handles cash, checks and money orders. At the end of the day the drawer is reconciled and the deposit memo shown in Table 11-2 is created by the system. Although audit trail features for automatic cross referencing are not built into the software, the possibility for them to be maintained does exist. Audit trails for the deposit function are kept by saving copies of sales and credit slips and attaching them to the file copy of the deposit memo.

The deposit package is driven off the SYSTEM MENU, which puts you directly into the deposit function. There is no

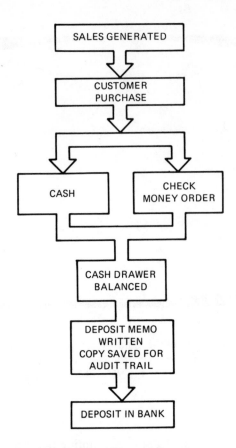

Figure 11-2 Flow of deposit

deposit menu. All functions are interactive and begin by displaying the date, which was entered when the system was initialized for the day from the system executive routines.

As with the planning package, only one report is generated. The deposit package, as shown by the procedures, is simple and straightforward. All functions such as error codes are covered in Appendix A. The displays for the deposit function start with the SYSTEM MENU (Example 11-15) and end with Example 11-17.

11.4 SUMMARY

The planning and deposit systems are available to enhance the system, but omitting them will not affect the operation of the accounting package in general. They are provided as examples of other functions that can be used in a business environment

Table 11-2

DEPOSIT MEMO

DATE 050779

MAKER	AMOUNT
MIRGHANBARI	74.00
WILLIAMS	51.00
ANGELO	80.00
DAVIES	50.00
SMITH/GF	237.00
BILLETER/MS L	25.50
VOSMIH	50.00
SILVERMAN	39.00
BELL	25.50
MAMMEN/LESLIE	64.80
WALLACE	25.00
JACKSON	20.00
TOTAL CHECKS	
AND MONEY ORDERS	741.80
TOTAL CURRENCY	1000.00
TOTAL DEPOSIT	1741.80

---

but are usually left out.

This is as far as we go. We hope that you will use the system presented in this book to build a more sophisticated accounting system. You should find that the applications presented here are readily adaptable to other systems, both tape and disk. All files and records built in these accounting packages use sequential files, but will work in a random system with the use of the proper code—which, incidentally, has not been provided here.[1]

How you use a computer is, of course, your decision, but we hope you will remember that it is a tool just like any other piece of equipment. If you spend some time learning a little BASIC programming, you will greatly enhance your computer's value.

Throughout this book we have emphasized that this is a "bare bones" package. We hope you will use it as a starting point to define your own unique system and that it helps improve your bottom line.

---

[1]There is one exception to this, the CTBL TRS-80 version. This package uses both sequential and random files.

```
        SYSTEM MENU

ENTER SELECTION AND DEPRESS RETURN

    INVENTORY CONTROL              (1)
    BILLING/ACCOUNTS RECEIVABLE    (2)
    ACCOUNTS PAYABLE               (3)
    GENERAL LEDGER                 (4)
    PLANNING                       (5)
    DEPOSIT                        (6)
    UTILITY                        (7)

SELECTION ?  6
```

Example 11-15

```
ENTER DATE (12,21,77) ?  05,07,79
ENTER STARTING DRAWER TOTAL ? 100
ITEM, MAKER, AMOUNT ?
```

Example 11-16: The system prompts continually as checks and
money orders are entered. When an ET is
entered, it asks for the final drawer count.

FINAL DRAWER COUNT ?   236.18

Example 11-17: When the system asks for the final drawer
count, enter the total amount of cash in the
drawer, including the starting amount, and
depress RETURN. The system will now
generate the deposit slip twice and return to the
SYSTEM MENU.

Appendix A

GENERAL FUNCTIONS

A.1 INTRODUCTION

The purpose of this appendix is to enhance the chapters that preceded it. In Section A.2 you will find flow charts for the SYSTEM MENU, inventory control and billing/accounts receivable packages. These flow charts are representative of the basic structure of the entire CTBL package. The same logic is used throughout the package.

Section A.3 describes tape saving techniques. These techniques are used in BASIC to save data (information) on magnetic tape.

R.H. Distler developed special function routines for interfacing TDL/XITAN software to the MECA tape system. These routines are covered in Section A.4.

We hope that between the information found in the preceding chapters and the additional descriptions found in this appendix, you will have a sufficient understanding of accounting and automation principles to develop a working system of your own.

A.2 FLOW CHARTS

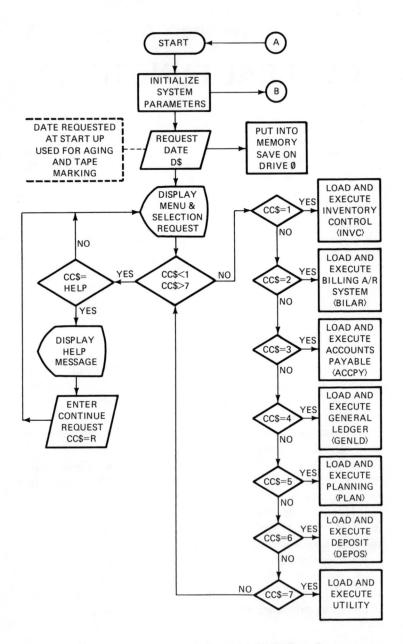

Figure A-1 Flowchart for SYSTEM MENU Exec Program

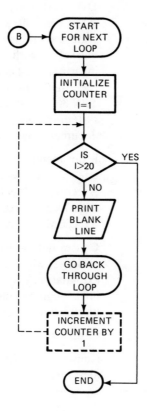

Figure A-2 Flowchart for Clear Screen
CTBL-1 System

Table A-1
System Menu Inputs

Acceptable Input	Purpose
10/17/79 (MM/DD/YY) or 101779 (Date can be delimited by slashes (/), spaces, or no delimiter.	MM = Month entry DD = Day entry YY = Year entry Date used to age accounts and mark files with transaction information. Date required at each day's startup. In case of TRS-80 software, date entered at system initialization and used for document marking.
1, 2, 3, 4, 5, 6, 7	From menu—causes selection of one to seven system functions. An entry of less than 1 or greater than 7 causes redisplay of SYSTEM MENU.
HELP or HE or H	Causes default to HELP message, which is a short explanation of SYSTEM MENU. HELP can be entered at any point, date or selection.
CR Carriage Return	Causes redisplay of system menu.
R	Causes return from HELP message.

Table A-2
System Menu Variables

Variable	Purpose
CC$	Holds value of menu request string.
D$	Holds date input.
D/$	Holds converted date value without delimiters.
D	Holds decimal value of date input to be poked into memory and saved on drive zero.
I	Counter for next loop; used for screen clear.

Table A-3
System Menu Errors

Error Response	Meaning	Operator Response
REDISPLAY DATE INPUT	Date input was greater than 8 or less than 6 characters.	Re-enter date either as 10/12/78 or 101278 or HELP.
REDISPLAY SYSTEM MENU	Selection less than 1 or greater than 7.	Enter 1-7 for specific option or HELP.
See BASIC manual for system errors.		
HELP message	Explains purpose of menu.	Enter R to return to start sequence.

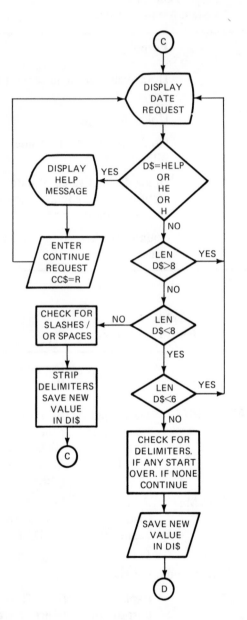
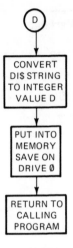

Figure A-3 Flowchart for SYSTEM MENU Exec Data Subroutine

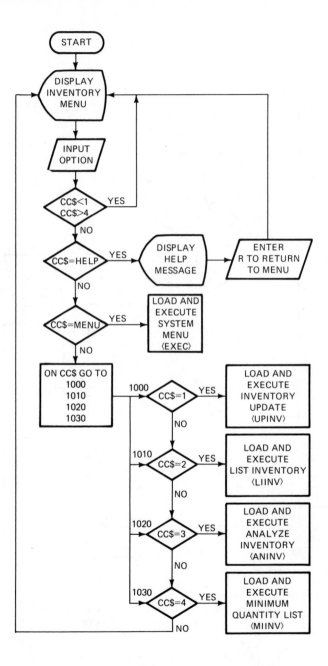

Figure A-4 Flowchart for Inventory Menu

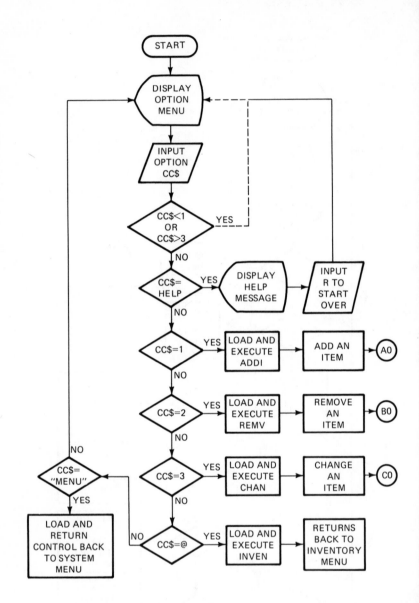

Figure A-5 Flowchart for Update Inventory
CTBL-INVEN UPDATE

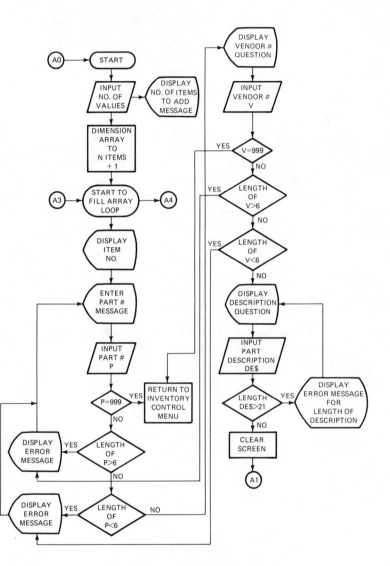

Figure A-6.1 Flowchart for Add Item to Inventory
CTBL-INVEN UPDATE

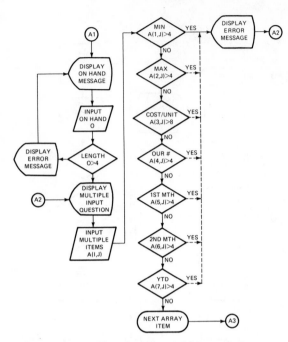

Figure A-6.2 Flowchart for Add Item to Inventory
CTBL-INVEN UPDATE

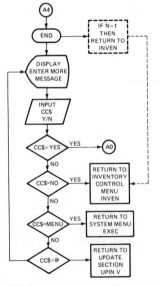

Figure A-6.3 Flowchart for Add Item to Inventory
CTBL-INVEN UPDATE

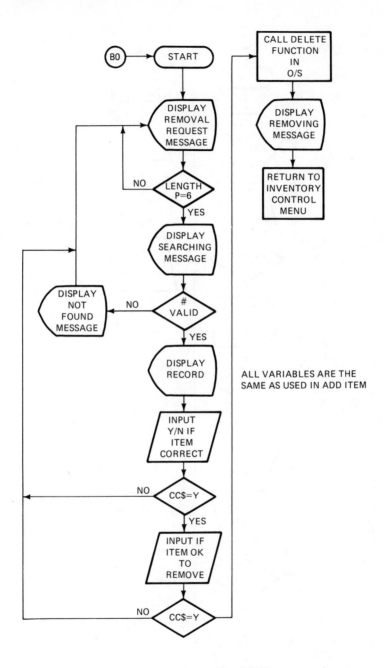

Figure A-7 Flowchart for Remove Item from Inventory
CTBL-INVEN UPDATE

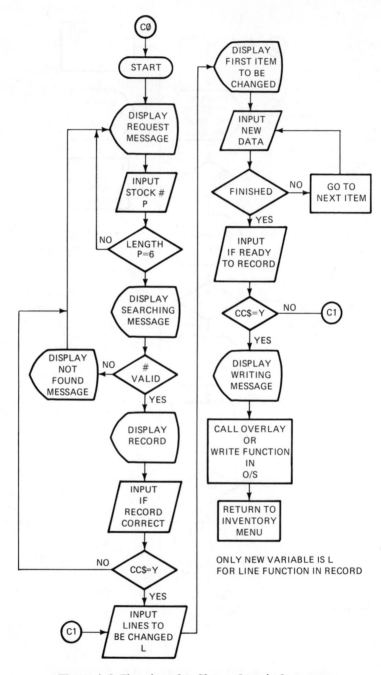

Figure A-8 Flowchart for Change Item in Inventory
CTBL-INVEN UPDATE

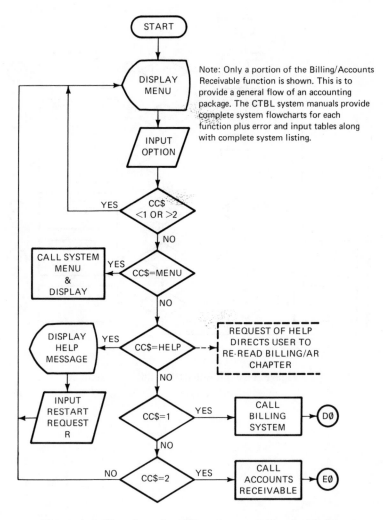

START

DISPLAY MENU

Note: Only a portion of the Billing/Accounts Receivable function is shown. This is to provide a general flow of an accounting package. The CTBL system manuals provide complete system flowcharts for each function plus error and input tables along with complete system listing.

INPUT OPTION

CC\$ <1 OR >2 — YES

NO

CALL SYSTEM MENU & DISPLAY ← YES — **CC\$=MENU**

NO

DISPLAY HELP MESSAGE ← YES — **CC\$=HELP** ----- **REQUEST OF HELP DIRECTS USER TO RE-READ BILLING/AR CHAPTER**

NO

INPUT RESTART REQUEST R

CC\$=1 — YES — **CALL BILLING SYSTEM** → **DØ**

NO

CC\$=2 — YES — **CALL ACCOUNTS RECEIVABLE** → **EØ**

NO

Figure A-9 Flowchart for Billing Accounts Receivable Menu ACCRC

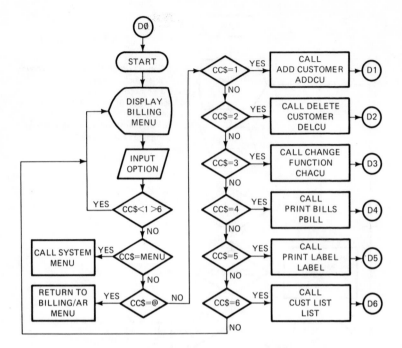

Figure A-10 Flowchart for Billing System
BILL

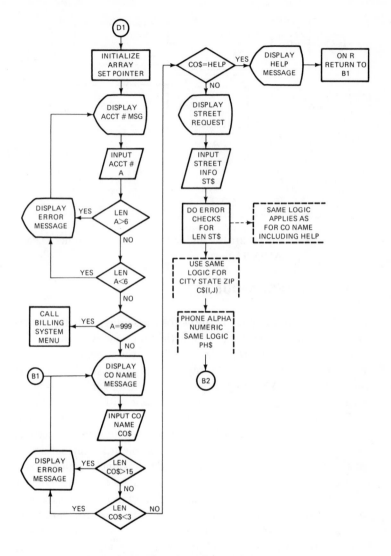

Figure A-11 Flowchart for Add Customer
ADDCU

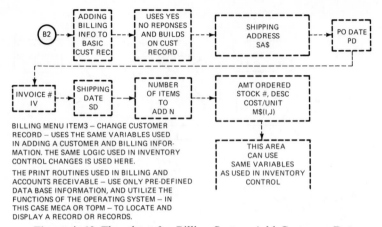

BILLING MENU ITEM3 – CHANGE CUSTOMER
RECORD – USES THE SAME VARIABLES USED
IN ADDING A CUSTOMER AND BILLING INFOR-
MATION. THE SAME LOGIC USED IN INVENTORY
CONTROL CHANGES IS USED HERE.

THE PRINT ROUTINES USED IN BILLING AND
ACCOUNTS RECEIVABLE – USE ONLY PRE-DEFINED
DATA BASE INFORMATION, AND UTILIZE THE
FUNCTIONS OF THE OPERATING SYSTEM – IN
THIS CASE MECA OR TOPM – TO LOCATE AND
DISPLAY A RECORD OR RECORDS.

Figure A-12 Flowchart for Billing System Add Customer Data
ADDCU

A.3 TAPE TECHNIQUES

BASIC is not designed to allow for the saving of strings on external media, paper tape, magnetic tape, or even disk. This
function is usually taken care of by the operating system
associated with the mass storage device being used. For users
with TDL/XITAN setups, the system allows for the saving of
string and numeric data on magnetic tape with relative ease.

The reason for the flexibility in the TDL/XITAN software is
the function called SWITCH, which allows the user to switch
ports around as needed. Thus, for example, the console device
or the list device can become the reader or punch, which means
that a print statement will cause an output to the system device
for saving data. The reverse is also true; an input causes a query
of the reader port and the input statements look for data from
the tape as if it were the console.

Using this type of format requires a very good understanding
of your system and exactly where the ports are defined. Also required is an understanding of how to format output so that it
can be recognized as data or some other type of information.
The problem with this system is that it is slow even when used
with TOPM, and care must be taken with the format of the
records within the files.

Microsoft BASIC, which is supplied with MECA, offers this
same capability but uses a directive called CONSOLE. The
problem is that the operating system must be patched to use

your I/O, as described in the MECA manual. Once this is done the technique can be used.

This method of saving data is efficient in terms of saving but inefficient when reading. However, efficiency is only relative to what the user expects from the system. As a result, it is not unusual to find several methods of saving information in one system that does not use the operating system to take care of this basic function.

Another method used to save information on tape is to place it in upper memory at a known location, then direct the system to save it on tape. Two programs—the saving character program and VARPTR—are commonly used to perform this function.

The last method demonstrated in this appendix is the conversion of data from a string array and back again, since BASIC allows for the saving of numeric arrays and not string arrays. This function is not new and has been used as a saving technique for several years. Many references to it can be found in the technical literature. However, the important point is that it is a unique technique that uses the very basic functions of microcomputer structure and BASIC to function. This conversion technique is prone to error and time-consuming.

All the functions listed so far are inefficient as far as time is concerned, but when related to a slow-moving medium—tape—they are very fast. What is nice about this technique is that it does not require any special handling of the ports, the SAVE and LOAD functions work as they should, and the actual function is transparent to the user.

The technique, as mentioned, works by determining the length of the string to be saved, setting up a numeric array in which to save the data, then cycling through the string array, character by character, adding the results to the numeric array. The number 256 is the highest number of possible configurations in an 8-bit byte, and is therefore used to convert the ASCII value of a character to a numeric value, which allows for the packing of the data into a tighter array.

SAVING BY CHARACTERS

```
10 REM THIS PROGRAM DEMONSTRATES ONE METHOD
20 REM USED TO STORE DATA IN MEMORY FOR
30 REM FOR FUPOSES OF THIS PROGRAM A
40 REM PROGRAM STATEMENT IS USED.
```

```
50 REM
60 REM FOR PRACTICAL APPLICATIONS, THIS
70 REM METHOD CAN BE USED BY UTILIZING A
80 REM VARIABLE AND POKING INTO UNUSED
        MEMORY.
90 REM
100 S$ = "THIS IS THE TEST STATEMENT"
110 REM ASSUME A SYSTEM WITH 24000 WORDS
        OF MEMORY
120 Y = 22000 + LEN (S$)
130 REM NOTICE THAT 2K ARE RESERVED AS
        UNDECLARED
140 REM MEMORY.  ANY AMOUNT MAY BE USED
        DEPENDING
150 REM UPON THE SYSTEM AND THE LOCATION
160 REM OF ANY OPERATING SYSTEMS.
170 FOR X = 0 TO LEN (S$)-1:REM '-1'
        COMPENSATES FOR THE
180 REM ZERO IN THE ARRAY
190 REM
200 REM Z IS USED AS THE VARIABLE TO HOLD
210 REM THE VALUES OF THE CONVERTED STRING
220 REM EACH TIME THE LOOP CYCLES.  THE
230 REM LOOP WORKS LEFT TO RIGHT AND EACH
240 REM TIME DEFINES THE ASCII EQUIVALENT
250 REM OF THE NEXT CHARACTER.  THE + 1
        COMPENSATES FOR THE ZERO ( 0 )
        CELL IN THE ARRAY.
260 Z = ASC (MID$(S$,X+1))
270 REM
280 REM NOW THE ASCII EQUIVALENT OF THE
290 REM WORD LENGTH OF EACH CHARACTER IS
300 REM PLACED INTO MEMORY BEGINNING
        AT THE 22K MARK.
310 POKE X + 22000,Z
320 REM
330 REM NOW CALL THE NEXT CHARACTER AND
        KEEP GOING
340 NEXT X
350 PRINT "DATA FROM 22000 TO "; Y ;
    "LOCATIONS"
360 END


DATA FROM 22000 TO   22026 LOCATIONS
```

CONVERTING TO NUMERIC ARRAYS

```
10 REM CONVERTING A STRING A$ INTO A
20 REM 16 INTEGER ARRAY T THEN BACK
30 REM TO THE STRING A$
40 REM NOTICE EACH FUNCTION IS HANDLED AS
       A SUBROUTINE
50 L = LEN (A$)
60 I=1 : K=1
70 T(K) = ASC (MID$(A$,I,1))
80 I=I+1
90 IF I > L THEN T(K+1) = 0
100 RETURN
110 T(K) = T(K)+256 *ASC(MID$(A$,I,1))
120 I = I +1
130 K = K + 1
140 IF I < = L THEN 70
150 T(K) = 0
160 REM CONVERT T BACK TO A$
170 A$ = "": REM SET TO NULL STRING
180 FOR J = 1 TO 16
190 L = INT (T(J)/256)
200 R = T(J)-256*L
210 IF R =0 THEN RETURN
220 A$ = A$ + CHR$(R)
230 IF L = 0 THEN RETURN
240 A$ = A$ + CHAR$(L)
250 NEXT J
260 RETURN
270 END
```

VARPTR FUNCTION

```
10 REM DEMONSTRATION PROGRAM FOR STRING
20 REM SAVES COURTESY MECA APP NOTE 130
30 REM FROM MECA USERS MANUAL. TO USE YOU
40 REM MUST BE FAMILIAR WITH MECA
       PROCEDURES AND BASIC.
50 REM
60 DIM PR(24,50)
70 PRINT:PRINT:PRINT "TYPE END TO QUIT
   STORING DATA":PRINT:PRINT
80 INPUT"TYPE A STRING OF <= 24
   CHARACTERS";IN$
```

```
90 IF LEFT$(IN$,3)="END"THEN 130
100 INPUT"WHICH HOLE (1-24) SHOULD I PUT
    IT IN";IQ
110 GOSUB 480
120 GOTO 80
130 PRINT:PRINT:PRINT"NOW I'LL SAVE THE
    ARRAY":PRINT:PRINT
140 CSAVE "*PR TEST0"
150 PRINT:PRINT:PRINT"NOW I'LL RELAOD THE
    ARRAY":PRINT:PRINT
160 PRINT:PRINT:PRINT"TYPE ZERO TO
    QUIT":PRINT:PRINT
170 PRINT:INPUT"WHICH STRING WOULD YOU
    LIKE TO SEE (1-24)";IQ
180 IF IQ=0 THEN END
190 GOSUB 230
200 PRINT:PRINT:IN$
210 GOTO 170
220 END
230 REM ----------------------------------------------------
240 REM
250 REM ROUTINE TO GET STRING FROM AN ARRAY
260 REM      PR=TWO DIMENSIONAL ARRAY
270 REM      IQ=POINTER TO SECOND DIMENSION
280 REM      IN$=STRING TO BE RETURNED
290 REM
300 REM----------------------------------------------------
310 REM
320 REM
330 IN$=" "
340 L=0
350 J=0
360 P=VARPTR(PR(0,IQ)):REM FUNCTION TO
    FIND ADDRESS OF FIRST BYTE
370 FOR J= 0 TO 23
380 L = PEEK (P + J)
390 IF L = 0 THEN RETURN
400 IN$ = IN$ + CHR$(L)
410 NEXT J
420 RETURN
430 REM ----------------------------------------------------
440 REM
450 REM END OF ROUTINE
460 REM
470 REM ----------------------------------------------------
```

```
480 REM  -----------------------------------------------------------------
490 REM
500 REM ROUTINE TO PUT STRING IN AN ARRAY
510 REM      PR=TWO DIMENSIONAL ARRAY
520 REM      IQ=POINTER TO SECOND DIMENSION
530 REM      IN$=STRING TO BE STORED
540 REM
550 REM  -----------------------------------------------------------------
560 REM
570 REM
580 K=LEN(IN$)
590 IF K= 0 THEN RETURN
600 L =0
610 J = 0
620 P = VARPTR (PR(0,IQ))
630 FOR J=0 TO 23
640 IF K>0 THEN 670
650 POKE P + J,0
660 GOTO 690
670 POKE P+J,ASC(RIGHT$(IN$,K))
680 K = K - 1
690 NEXT J
700 RETURN
710 REM  -----------------------------------------------------------------
720 REM
730 REM END OF ROUTINE
740 REM
750 REM  -----------------------------------------------------------------
```

A.4 SPECIAL ROUTINES

TOPM

TOPM is a program designed to sit at the top end of user memory and is 913 decimal bytes long. Systems using the TDL/XITAN monitor must take into account the fact that the Zapple monitor uses the upper end of memory for stack operations and care must be taken not to put TOPM in that area. To determine where to assemble TOPM, find the last byte location of user memory, subtract 913 from that point, and use that location as the assembly point for the program.

TOPM can be assembled for any point in memory but is most effective when used at the top end of memory. Since it is not the purpose of this appendix to delve into the art of assembly programming, it is suggested that if you are not familiar with this type of programming, do not attempt to work with this program. We have provided no instructions on how to edit or assemble the program—only the source code.

You will notice that at the top of TOPM are vectors to specific functions within the program. Also, notice that these functions correspond to the functions found in Zapple, which makes the patching of TDL/XITAN software easy, since all vectors are found at the front of the TDL/XITAN programs. TOPM, although shown here for use with BASIC, is designed to be used with all TDL/XITAN software. The vectors in the programs are changed to point to TOPM rather than Zapple.

TOPM is a passive program in that you do not jump or go to it directly. Your software uses it as a monitor program to control the MECA Alpha tape system. It is important to remember that to use TOPM, the TDL/XITAN software must be patched to point to the correct vectors (see FIXB).

TOPM works by making drive zero of the tape system the reader, and drive one the punch. For all practical purposes, the use of TOPM is transparent to you; all BASIC functions work the same with one exception: Control X (CTRL X) now causes the TOPM buffer to unload completely instead of jumping back to Zapple.

Using TOPM is simple. The program is loaded, and the patched version of BASIC is loaded. The command structure is now different, so that MECA tapes must be removed from the system and TOPM tapes substituted. A LOAD command, in BASIC, will cause drive zero to activate and look for the named program; when it is found, the console bell will ring and loading will occur.

Saving or punching a tape is the same, except that drive one becomes the active drive. What this means is that all new information is always on drive one and that to read it, it must be transferred to drive zero.

To avoid confusion in the process, you must forget that the MECA O/S exists when using the TOPM system and TDL/XITAN software. The best rule of thumb to use is that all the functions described in the TDL/XITAN manuals regarding tape apply to TOPM. The functions of using the buffered tape routines in Zapple only apply to using the SMB cassette system and should not be used except when using the program COPYM.

Points to remember:

1. When using TOPM, MECA becomes a high-speed reader punch. Drive zero is the reader and drive one the punch.
2. TOPM is a monitor program; therefore, the user should forget Zapple and MECA when using this system.
3. TOPM is transparent to the user; only the software, such as BASIC, needs to be patched to point to TOPM.
4. TOPM is a bare bones package to provide reader punch capability; files cannot be named or directories displayed.

```
1;001 * PROG "$TOPM"
1;002 * VERSION 3.1
1;003 *
1;004 *
1;005 * MICROPROCESSR
1;006 * Z80 (TDL SOFTWARE)
1;007 *
1;008 *
1;009 *
1;010 * PROGRAM FOR "TDL" TO USE
1;011 * MECA "ALPHA-1" AS A CONTROLLED
1;012 * READER AND PUNCH
1;013 *
1;014 *
1;015 * WRITTEN BY R.H.DISTLER JR
1;016 * WRITTEN BY R.H.DISTLER JR
1;017 * 01-17-79
1;018 *
1;019 * IN MECA ASSEMBLER FORMAT
1;020 *
1;021 *
1;022 * DRIVE#0 IS READER
1;023 * DRIVE#1 IS PUNCH
1;024 *
1;025 *
1;026 * REF
1;027 * TDL USER'S MANUAL
1;028 * TDL MONITOR MANUAL
1;029 * MECA MANUAL
1;030 *
1;031 * NOTES:
1;032 * THIS PROGRAM IS USED TO RUN YOUR I/O
1;033 * DEVICES FOR TDL,AND IS FIXED
1;034 * AT CO,CI,LO,AND TAPE I/O
1;035 *
1;036 * SET "REG0"=RESTART ADDRESS OF TDL
```

```
1;037 *
1;038 * SET "MEMAX"=TOP OF RAM FOR TDL.
1;039 *
1;040 * PUT AS MUCH RAM AS YOU CAN IN YOUR
1;041 * TAPE I/O
          BUFFERS(RBUFF-ERBUF/WBUFF-EWBUF)
1;042 *
1;043 * TIMING IS SLOW FOR THE "ALPHA-1"
1;044 * SO YOU CAN SEE THINGS GOING ON
1;045 *
1;046 * DON'T FORGET TO PATCH YOUR VECTORS
          IN TDL
1;047 *
1;048 * AFTER A "SAVE" OR "ASAVE" USE
1;049 * "(CONTROL)X" OR "X ESC ESC"
1;050 * TO EMPTY THE WRITE BUFFER ON TAPE
1;051 *
1;052 *    EQUATES
1;053 *    MORE DOWN THE LINE
1;054 *
1;055 ZERO EQU 0
1;056 MAX EQU ZERO
1;057 PSW EQU M
1;058 SP EQU M
1;059 BELL EQU 7
1;060 *
1;061 * TDL RESTART ADDRESS
1;062 *
1;063 REGO EQU 007DH
1;064 *
1;065 *
1;066 *
1;067 * TOP OF RAM FOR TDL
1;068 *
1;069 MEMAX EQU 9FFFH
1;070 *
1;071 *
1;072 *
1;073 *
1;074 * FLAG ID
1;075 *
1;076 * #0 USED IN TI FOR 1ST CALL FROM TDL
1;077 * #1 INITIATE DR#0 (READ)
1;078 * #2 INITIATE DR#1 (WRITE)
1;079 * #3
```

```
1;080 * #4
1;081 * #5
1;082 * #6
1;083 * #7
1;084 *
1;085 *
1;086 * FLAG BYTE IS STORED IN RAM AT
        "FLAGS"
1;087 *
1;088 *
1;089 BEGIN EQU $
1;090 *
1;091 * VECTORS FOR "TDL" TO GET INTO THIS
        PROG
1;092 *
1;093   JMP $ DUMMY
1;094   JMP CI CONSOLE INPUT
1;095   JMP TI FROM TAPE BUFFER
1;096   JMP CO CONSOLE OUTPUT
1;097   JMP TO TO TAPE BUFFER
1;098   JMP LO LIST OUTPUT
1;099   JMP CSTS CONSOLE STATUS
1;100   JMP IOCHK I/O CHECK
1;101   JMP IOSET I/O SET
1;102   JMP MEMCK MEMORY LIMIT CHECK
1;103   JMP RESTART EMPTY BUFFER ON TAPE
1;104 *
1;105 * YOUR CONSOLE INPUT
1;106 CI IN 0
1;107   ANI 01H TEST BIT #0
1;108   JZ CI
1;109   IN 1
1;110   RET
1;111 *
1;112 * YOUR CONSOLE OUTPUT
1;113 CO IN 0
1;114   ANI 80H TEST BIT #7
1;115   JZ CO
1;116   MOV A,C
1;117   OUT 1
1;118   RET
1;119 *
1;120 * YOUR LIST (PRINTER) OUTPUT
1;121 LO IN 2
1;122   ANI 82H TEST BIT #7,1
```

```
1;123    JNZ LO
1;124    MOV A,C
1;125    OUT 3
1;126    RET
1;127 *
1;128 CSTS IN O
1;129 * LOOK TO SEE IF CONSOLE HAS
             CHARACTER
1;130 * WAITING "A" REG=FF HEX IF YES/OO
             IF NO
1;131    ANI 01H TEST BIT #O
1;132    MVI A,OFFH
1;133    RNZ
1;134    CMA
1;135    RET
1;136 *
1;137 IOCHK MVI A,OA9H
1;138 * I/O CONFIGURATION IS FIXED
1;139    RET
1;140 *
1;141 IOSET MOV A,C
1;142 * THIS MONITOR HAS NO I/O SET AND
1;143 * IS FIXED AT CO,CI,LO
1;144    RET
1;145 *
1;146 MEMCK PUSH H
1;147 * LOAD H/L WITH HIGHEST RAM ADDRS
1;148 * THAT TDL CAN USE
1;149    LXI H,MEMAX
1;150    MOV A,L
1;151    MOV B,H
1;152    POP H
1;153    RET
1;154 *
1;155 RESTART JMP KALL
1;156 *
1;157 *
1;158 *
1;159 * DRIVE COMMAND
1;160 STOPX EQU 080H
1;161 FASTX EQU 081H
1;162 REWDX EQU 082H
1;163 PLAYX EQU 083H
1;164 WRITX EQU 004H
1;165 ERASX EQU 084H
```

```
1;166 *
1;167 *
1;168 * OUTPUT PORTS OF ALPHA-1
1;169 OUT1 EQU 0FCH
1;170 OUT2 EQU 0FDH
1;171 *
1;172 *
1;173 * INPUT PORTS OF ALPHA-1
1;174 IN1 EQU 0FCH
1;175 IN2 EQU 0FDH
1;176 IN3 EQU 0FEH
1;177 *
1;178 *
1;179 * EXECUTION DRIVE SELECT
1;180 EXCT0 EQU 008H
1;181 EXCT1 EQU 010H
1;182 *
1;183 * READ DRIVE SELECT
1;184 RDS0 EQU 000H
1;185 RDS1 EQU 002H
1;186 *
1;187 * LOCATION PULSE SELECT
1;188 PULS0 EQU 002H
1;189 PULS1 EQU 004H
1;190 *
1;191 * BUSY BIT SELECT
1;192 BUSY0 EQU 008H
1;193 BUSY1 EQU 010H
1;194 *
1;195 *
1;196 * DRIVE COMMANDER
1;197 *    REG H = EXECT BIT
1;198 *XXXXXXXXXXXXXXXXXXXXXXXXXXXXXX
1;199 *
1;200 STOP MVI A,STOPX RESET DRIVE
1;201   CALL DOIT
1;202 WAIT MVI D,126 SET TIMER FOR
1;203   MVI E,ZERO    400MS
1;204   JMP TIMER
1;205 *
1;206 *
1;207 PLAY MVI A,PLAYX
1;208   CALL DOIT
1;209   MVI D,79 SET TIMER FOR
1;210   MVI E,63  250 MS
```

```
1;211   JMP TIMER GET HEAD UP
1;212 *
1;213 *
1;214 FAST MVI A,FASTX SET FAST FORWARD
      MODE
1;215   JMP DOIT
1;216 *
1;217 *
1;218 SWM CALL PLAY
1;219   MVI A,WRITX SET WRITE MODE
1;220   JMP DOIT
1;221 *
1;222 ERASE MVI A,ERASX SET ERASE MODE
1;223   CALL DOIT
1;224   IN IN3 GET STATUS
1;225   ANI 20H TEST WRITE MODE
1;226   JNZ EOK
1;227   CALL STOP
1;228   STC SET ERROR FLAG
1;229   RET
1;230 EOK JMP PLAY START ERASING
1;231 *
1;232 *
1;233 *
1;234 REWD CALL STOP
1;235   MVI A,REWDX REWIND DRIVE
1;236   CALL DOIT
1;237 RWD1 IN IN2 GET BUSY BIT
1;238   ANA B TEST
1;239   JNZ RWD1 STILL BUSY
1;240   JMP STOP
1;241 *
1;242 *
1;243 * OUTPUT COMMAND TO DRIVE
1;244 *
1;245 DOIT OUT OUT1
1;246   ORA H SET EXECUTION BIT
1;247   OUT OUT1
1;248   MVI D,2 SET TIMER
1;249   MVI E,79  1 MS
1;250   CALL TIMER
2;001   XRA H ZERO EXECUTION BIT
2;002   OUT OUT1
2;003   MVI D,2 SET TIMER
2;004   MVI E,79  1 MS
2;005   JMP TIMER
```

```
2;006  *XXXXXXXXXXXXXXXXXXXXXXXXXXXXXX
2;007  *
2;008  *
2;009  *
2;010  * TIME AT 2MHZ =
2;011  * ((D-2) X 3200)
2;012  * + ((E-1) X 12.5) + 32
2;013  *
2;014  TIMER DCR D BUMP OUTSIDE LOOP
2;015    RZ IF ZERO RETURN
2;016  TIME DCR E BUMP INSIDE LOOP
2;017    JZ TIMER IF ZERO,GOTO OUTSIDE LOOP
2;018    JMP TIME ELSE,CONTINUE INSIDE
2;019  *
2;020  *
2;021  * COUNT PULSES TILL D=0
2;022  *      MASK IN C
2;023  *
2;024  PULSE IN IN2 GET STATUS
2;025    ANA C TEST
2;026    JZ PULSE JUMP TILL POS
2;027    DCR D BUMP COUNTER
2;028    RZ
2;029  PUL1 IN IN2 GET STATUS
2;030    ANA C TEST
2;031    JNZ PUL1 STILL POS
2;032    JMP PULSE GET NEXT ONE
2;033  *
2;034  *
2;035  * THIS IS USED TO GET
2;036  * LAST BIT ON TAPE
2;037  *
2;038  LAST CALL LASTX
2;039    CALL LASTX
2;040    JMP STOP
2;041  LASTX IN IN2 GET STATUS
2;042    ANI 20H WRITE CLOCK ZERO ?
2;043    JNZ LASTX
2;044  LAST1 IN IN2 GET STATUS
2;045    ANI 20H IS WRITE CLOCK POS ?
2;046    JZ LAST1
2;047    RET
2;048  *
2;049  *
2;050  ****************************
2;051  *
```

```
2;052 *
2;053 * WRITE A BYTE FROM C TO TAPE ON
            DRIVE #1
2;054 * IF DRIVE IS NOT BUSY IT
2;055 * WILL START IT
2;056 *
2;057 WRT1 IN IN2
2;058   ANI BUSY1 TEST BUSY BIT
2;059   CZ HEAD START DRIVE UP
2;060   RC IS ERROR
2;061 WRITE IN IN3 GET STATUS
2;062   ANI 20H TEST WRITE MODE
2;063   JNZ WOK
2;064   CALL STOP
2;065   STC SET ERROR FLAG
2;066   RET
2;067 *
2;068 WOK MVI D,08H SET BIT COUNTER
2;069 WO IN IN2 GET STATUS
2;070   ANI 20H IS WRITE CLOCK ZERO ?
2;071   JNZ WO NO
2;072 W1 IN IN2 GET STATUS
2;073   ANI 20H IS WRITE CLOCK ONE ?
2;074   JZ W1 NO
2;075 *
2;076   MOV A,C PUT BYTE GOING OUT IN A
2;077   RLC PUT NEXT BIT OUT IN #0
2;078   MOV C,A SAVE REMAING BITS IN C
2;079   ANI 01H ZERO ALL BITS BUT #0
2;080 *
2;081 * BITS #1&2 ARE ZERO AND SET
2;082 * READ DRIVE SELECT NOT=DRIVE #1
2;083 *
2;084   OUT OUT2 OUTPUT BIT TO DRIVE
2;085 *
2;086   DCR D BUMP BIT COUNTER DOWN (1)
2;087   JNZ WO MORE BITS TO GO OUT
2;088 *
2;089 *
2;090 * AFTER LAST BYTE CALL "LAST"
2;091 * TO GET ALL 8 BITS ON TAPE
2;092 *
2;093 *
2;094   ORA A RESET ERROR FLAG
2;095   RET DONE
```

```
2;096 *
2;097 *
2;098 ********************************
2;099 *
2;100 *
2;101 * PUT ON HEADER
2;102 *
2;103 *
2;104 * PUT OUT 20 PULSES
2;105 * OF CLEAN TAPE
2;106 *
2;107 *
2;108 * THEN A SYNC BURST
2;109 *
2;110 *
2;111 * THEN YOUR DATA
2;112 *
2;113 *
2;114 *
2;115 HEAD PUSH H
2;116   PUSH B
2;117   LDA FLAGS
2;118   ANI 4 TEST BIT #2
2;119   CZ INIT1 INITIATE DRIVE #1
2;120   JC SYNCE IS ERROR
2;121   MVI H,EXCT1
2;122   MVI B,BUSY1
2;123   MVI C,PULS1
2;124   CALL ERASE
2;125   JC SYNCE IS ERROR
2;126   MVI D,20 SET NUMBER
2;127   CALL PULSE
2;128   MVI A,ZERO
2;129   OUT OUT1 LET GO OF THE WRITE CLOCK
2;130 *
2;131 *
2;132 * PUT ON SYNC BURST
2;133 * OUTPUT 4 "00"
2;134 * THEN   1 "01"
2;135 * FOR SYNC BURST
2;136 *
2;137 *
2;138 SYNC LXI B,0400H SET BYTE COUNTER/C=0
2;139 SYNC1 CALL WRITE
2;140   JC SYNCE IS ERROR
```

```
2;141   DCR B BUMP COUNTER DOWM (1)
2;142   JNZ SYNC1 MORE ZEROS TO GO
2;143   INR C BUMP TO = "01"
2;144   CALL WRITE OUTPUT IT
2;145 *
2;146 * NOW THATS DONE YOU CAN OUTPUT
2;147 * DATA TO THE TAPE, WHICH IS IN
2;148 * WRITE MODE AND MOVING.
2;149 *
2;150 * CALL "LAST" AFTER LAST BYTE
2;151 * TO GET ALL OF IT ON TAPE
2;152 *
2;153 *
2;154 SYNCE POP B
2;155   POP H
2;156   RET
2;157 *
2;158 *
2;159 * UNLOAD WRITE BUFFER TO TAPE
2;160 *
2;161 UBUF PUSH D
2;162   LXI B,0855H OUTPUT START MARK
2;163 U1 CALL WRT1 PUT IT ON TAPE
2;164   JC UBUFE IS ERROR
2;165   DCR B
2;166   JNZ U1 MORE TO GO
2;167 ***** NOTE: B IS ZERO NOW
2;168 *
2;169 U2 POP D
2;170   MOV A,E NOW TEST HL VS. DE
2;171   SUB L
2;172   MOV A,D
2;173   SBB H
2;174   PUSH D
2;175   JC U3 ALL OUT
2;176 *
2;177   MOV C,M GET MENORY BYTE
2;178   CALL WRITE PUT IT ON TAPE
2;179   JC UBUFE IS ERROR
2;180   INX H BUMP THE ADDRS
2;181   DCR B TEST FOR 256 BYTES OUT
2;182   CZ U5 IF YES GO PUT OUT RE-SYNC
        BYTES
2;183   JMP U2
2;184 *
2;185 * PUT ON END OF FILE MARK
```

```
2;186 *
2;187 **********************************
2;188 *
2;189 * END OF FILE MARKER IS
2;190 * 16 55'S THEN 8 AA'S
2;191 *
2;192 U3 MVI E,16
2;193 U4 MVI C,55H
2;194    CALL UX
2;195    JNZ U4
2;196    MVI E,8
2;197 U8 MVI C,0AAH
2;198    CALL UX
2;199    JNZ U8
2;200    JMP U7 THATS THE END OF TAPE RECORD
2;201 **********************************
2;202 UX CALL WRITE PUT IT ON TAPE
2;203    JC UBUFE IS ERROR
2;204    DCR B TEST FOR 256 BYTES OUT
2;205    CZ U5 IF YES GO PUT OUT RE-SYNC
          BYTES
2;206    JC UBUFE IS ERROR
2;207    DCR E
2;208    RET
2;209 U7 PUSH H
2;210    MVI H,EXCT1
2;211    CALL LAST
2;212    ORA A RESET ERROR FLAG
2;213    POP H
2;214 UBUFE POP D
2;215    RET    ALL DUMPED OUT OR ERROR
2;216 *
2;217 U5 LXI B,0500H OUTPUT 5 "00" FOR
          RE-SYNC
2;218 U6 CALL WRITE
2;219    RC IS ERROR
2;220    DCR B BUMP COUNTER
2;221    JNZ U6
2;222    RET
2;223 *
2;224 *
2;225 * LOAD READ BUFFER FROM TAPE
2;226 *
2;227 LBUF MVI B,8 FIND 8 55'S IN A ROW
2;228 L1 CALL READO GET BYTE OFF TAPE
2;229    JC STOPO RETURN ON ERROR
```

```
2;230   CPI 55H START OF FILE TAG?
2;231   JNZ LBUF NOPE
2;232   DCR B
2;233   JNZ L1
2;234   ***** NOTE: B IS ZERO NOW
2;235   CALL R1
2;236   JC STOPO RETURN ON ERROR
2;237   MOV M,A FIRST REAL DATA BYTE
2;238   MVI A,BELL TELL YOU GOT IT
2;239   OUT 1
2;240 L2 INX H
2;241   CALL R1
2;242   JC STOPO RETURN ON ERROR
2;243   CPI 55H
2;244   JZ ELO POSSIBLE END OF FILE MARKER
2;245   MOV M,A
2;246   JMP L2
2;247   ELO MVI E,1 INITIALIZE COUNT OF
        "55'S"
2;248 EL1 CALL R1
2;249   JC STOPO RETURN ON ERROR
2;250   CPI 55H
3;001   JNZ EL2
3;002   INR E BUMP "55'S" COUNT
3;003   MOV A,E
3;004   CPI 16 FOUND MARKER YET?
3;005   *****************************
3;006   *
3;007   * SET JUMP ADDRESS TO
3;008   * "ENDL" FOR OLD TAPES
3;009   *
3;010   JZ EL3   MAYBE
3;011   JMP EL1
3;012 EL2 MVI M,55H
3;013   INX H
3;014   DCR E
3;015   JNZ EL2
3;016   MOV M,A REAL BYTE
3;017   JMP L2 NEXT DATA BYTE
3;018 EL3 CALL R1
3;019   JC STOPO RETURN ON ERROR
3;020   CPI 0AAH
3;021   JZ ENDL THATS THE END
3;022   MVI M,55H
3;023   INX H
3;024   JMP EL3
```

```
3;025 *
3;026 ENDL ORA A NO ERROR
3;027 STOP0 PUSH H
3;028   PUSH PSW
3;029   MVI H,EXCT0
3;030   CALL STOP
3;031   POP PSW
3;032   POP H
3;033   RET THATS IT
3;034 *
3;035 READO IN IN2
3;036   ANI BUSY0 TEST BUSY BIT
3;037   CZ RG0 START DRIVE
3;038   INR B THIS OFFSET DCR B AFTER "R1"
3;039 R1 IN IN2 GET STATUS
3;040 ***** NOTE: ANI ZEROS CARRY BIT
3;041   ANI 040H IS READ DATA READY ?
3;042   JNZ R2 YEP
3;043   IN IN2 NO
3;044   ANI BUSY0 TEST BUSY BIT
3;045   JNZ R1 STILL BUSY
3;046   STC SET ERROR FLAG
3;047   RET RETURN WITH ERROR
3;048 R2 IN IN1 GET DATA BYTE
3;049   DCR B BUMP COUNTER
3;050   JZ R3
3;051   RET
3;052 *
3;053 RGO PUSH H START DRIVE #0 TO READ
3;054   PUSH D
3;055   PUSH B
3;056   LDA FLAGS
3;057   ANI 2 TEST BIT#1
3;058   CZ INIT0  INITIATE DR #0
3;059   MVI H,EXCT0
3;060   MVI B,BUSY0
3;061   MVI C,PULS0
3;062   CALL PLAY
3;063   MVI A,RDS0
3;064   OUT OUT2 READ DRIVE SELECT
3;065   POP B
3;066   POP D
3;067   POP H
3;068   RET
3;069 * TEST CHECK SUM
3;070 R3 PUSH PSW SAVE DATA
```

```
3;071   MVI B,10 GET FIVE "00"
3;072 R4 CALL R1
3;073   JC AIRO IS ERROR
3;074   ANA A SET FLAGS REG
3;075   JNZ AIRO MUST BE ZERO
3;076   DCR B BUMP COUNTER
3;077   JNZ R4 FIVE ON THE FLOOR
3;078   POP PSW GET DATA
3;079   ORA A RESET ERROR FLAG
3;080   RET
3;081 *
3;082 AIRO POP PSW GET DATA
3;083   STC SET ERROR FLAG
3;084   RET
3;085 *
3;086 *
3;087 ***********************************
3;088 *
3;089 * THINGS FOR TDL I/O TAPE
3;090 *
3;091 *
3;092 *
3;093 * OUTPUTS WRITE BUFFER FROM START
3;094 * TO POINTER ON DR#1
3;095 *    RESETS POINTER
3;096 *
3;097 KALL PUSH H ON OLD STACK
3;098   LXI H,ZERO
3;099   DAD SP SAVE OLD STACK
3;100   LXI SP,STACK+1 NEW ADDRS
3;101   PUSH H OLD STACK ADDRS
3;102   PUSH D
3;103   PUSH B
3;104   ORA A INSURE CARRY CLEAR
3;105   PUSH PSW
3;106 *
3;107   LHLD POITW
3;108   LXI D,WBUFF
3;109   MOV A,E
3;110   CMP L
3;111   JNZ K1
3;112   MOV A,D
3;113   CMP H
3;114   JZ K2 BUFFER EMPTY
3;115 *
```

```
3;116 K1 LHLD POITW
3;117    DCX H
3;118    XCHG
3;119    LXI H,WBUFF
3;120    SHLD POITW RESET POINTER
3;121    CALL UBUF PUT BUFFER ON TAPE
3;122    CC TIOE CALL IF ERROR
3;123 K2 SUB A RESET FLAGS
3;124    STA FLAGS
3;125    POP PSW
3;126    POP B
3;127    POP D
3;128    POP H
3;129    SPHL RESET OLD STACK ADDRS
3;130    POP H OFF OLD STACK
3;131    JMP REGO BACK INTO TDL LAND
3;132 *
3;133 *
3;134 *
3;135 *
3;136 * INITIATE DR #0
3;137 INITO MVI H,EXCTO
3;138    MVI B,BUSYO
3;139    MVI C,PULSO
3;140    CALL REWD
3;141    CALL FAST
3;142    MVI D,MAX
3;143    CALL PULSE GET OFF OF LEADER
3;144    MVI D,150
3;145    CALL PULSE
3;146    LDA FLAGS
3;147    ORI 2 SET BIT#1
3;148    STA FLAGS
3;149    CALL STOP
3;150    RET
3;151 *
3;152 * INITIATE DR #1
3;153 INIT1 MVI H,EXCT1
3;154    MVI B,BUSY1
3;155    MVI C,PULS1
3;156    CALL REWD
3;157    CALL ERASE
3;158    RC IS ERROR
3;159    MVI D,MAX
3;160    CALL PULSE
```

```
3;161   CALL PULSE
3;162   LDA FLAGS
3;163   ORI 4 SET BIT#2
3;164   STA FLAGS
3;165   RET
3;166   *
3;167   *
3;168   *
3;169   * LOADS READ BUFFER FROM TAPE DR#0
3;170   * ON 1ST CALL FROM TDL,WHEN ALL
3;171   * DATA IN BUFFER IS USED, IT REFILLS
3;172   * BUFFER AS NEEDED FROM DR#0
3;173   * DATA TO TDL IN A
3;174   *
3;175   TI PUSH H ON OLD STACK
3;176   LXI H,ZERO
3;177   DAD SP SAVE OLD STACK ADDRS
3;178   LXI SP,STACK+1 NEW ADDRS
3;179   PUSH H OLD STACK ADDRS
3;180   PUSH D
3;181   PUSH B
3;182   ORA A INSURE CARRY CLEAR
3;183   PUSH PSW
3;184   *
3;185   LDA FLAGS
3;186   ANI 1 TEST BIT#0
3;187   CZ TI4 IF NOT SET AND FILL BUFFER
3;188   JC TI2 IF ERROR
3;189   TI1 LHLD POITR PICK UP POINTER
3;190   MOV C,M GET RAM BYTE
3;191   INX H
3;192   SHLD POITR REPLACE POINTER
3;193   XCHG
3;194   LHLD ERBUX
3;195   XCHG
3;196   MOV A,E TEST END OF BUFFER
3;197   SUB L
3;198   MOV A,D
3;199   SBB H
3;200   JNC TI3 MORE DATA YET
3;201   CALL TI4 REFILL BUFFER
3;202   TI2 CC TIOE CALL IF ERROR
3;203   TI3 POP PSW
3;204   MOV A,C
3;205   POP B
```

```
3;206    POP D
3;207    POP H
3;208    SPHL RESET OLD STACK ADDRS
3;209    POP H OFF OLD STACK
3;210    RET
3;211 *
3;212 TI4 LDA FLAGS
3;213    ORI 1 SET BIT #0
3;214    STA FLAGS
3;215    LXI H,RBUFF
3;216    SHLD POITR RESET POINTER
3;217    CALL LBUF FILL BUFFER
3;218    DCX H
3;219    SHLD ERBUX SET END OF BUFFER
3;220    RET
3;221 *
3;222 *
3;223 TIOE POP D SAVE RETURN ADDRS
3;224    LXI H,EM
3;225 EMO MOV C,M
3;226    CALL CO
3;227    ORA A SET PSW
3;228    JM EMD DONE IF BIT#7=1
3;229    INX H
3;230    JMP EMO
3;231 EMD POP PSW
3;232    STC SET ERROR
3;233    PUSH PSW
3;234    XCHG GET RETURN ADDRS
3;235    PCHL RETURN
3;236 *
3;237 * ERROR MESSAGE
3;238 EM DB ODH CR
3;239    DB OAH LF
3;240    DB 'T'
3;241    DB 'A'
3;242    DB 'P'
3;243    DB 'E'
3;244    DB ' '
3;245    DB 'E'
3;246    DB 'R'
3;247    DB 'R'
3;248    DB 'O'
3;249    DB 'R'
3;250    DB ODH CR
```

```
4;001   DB 8AH LF BIT#7 SET
4;002 *
4;003 *
4;004 * LOADS WRITE BUFFER FROM TDL, WHEN
4;005 * BUFFER IS FULL ITS EMPTYED ON
4;006 * TAPE DR#1 THEN REFILLED
4;007 * AS NEEDED FROM TDL
4;008 *
4;009 * DATA IS PASSED IN C FROM TDL
4;010 * ON RETURN TO TDL IT IS IN A AND C
4;011 *
4;012 *
4;013 *
4;014 TO PUSH H ON OLD STACK
4;015   LXI H,ZERO
4;016   DAD SP SAVE OLD STACK
4;017   LXI SP,STACK+1 NEW ADDRS
4;018   PUSH H OLD STACK ADDRS
4;019   PUSH D
4;020   PUSH B
4;021   ORA A INSURE CARRY CLEAR
4;022   PUSH PSW
4;023 *
4;024   LHLD POITW PICK UP POINTER
4;025   MOV M,C STORE BYTE IN RAM
4;026   MOV A,C
4;027   CMP M
4;028   JZ TOK
4;029   STC SET ERROR FLAG
4;030   JMP TOE
4;031 TOK INX H
4;032   SHLD POITW REPLACE POINTER
4;033   XCHG
4;034   LHLD EWBUX
4;035   XCHG H/L=POITW     D/E=EWBUX
4;036   MOV A,E TEST END OF BUFFER
4;037   SUB L
4;038   MOV A,D
4;039   SBB H
4;040   JNC TO1 MORE ROOM YET
4;041   LXI D,WBUFF
4;042   DCX H END OF DATA
4;043   XCHG H/L=START     D/E=END
```

```
4;044   SHLD POITW RESET POINTER
4;045   CALL UBUF UNLOAD BUFFER
4;046 TOE CC TIOE CALL IF ERROR
4;047 *
4;048 TO1 POP PSW
4;049   POP B
4;050   POP D
4;051   POP H
4;052   SPHL RESET OLD STACK ADDRS
4;053   POP H OFF OLD STACK
4;054   MOV A,C IN A FOR TDL
4;055   RET
4;056 *
4;057 * PROG STORAGE AREA MUST BE IN RAM
4;058 *
4;059 FLAGS DB ZERO
4;060 *
4;061 POITR DW RBUFF
4;062 POITW DW WBUFF
4;063 ERBUX DW ERBUF
4;064 EWBUX DW EWBUF
4;065 *
4;066 *
4;067 * BUFFERS AND STACK MUST BE IN RAM
4;068 *
4;069 *
4;070 * START OF READ BUFFER
4;071 RBUFF NOP
4;072 ERBUF EQU RBUFF+061EH
4;073 *
4;074 *
4;075 *
4;076 * START OF WRITE BUFFER
4;077 WBUFF EQU ERBUF+1
4;078 EWBUF EQU WBUFF+061EH
4;079 *
4;080 *
4;081 *
4;082 *
4;083 STACK EQU BEGIN
4;084 *
4;085   END
```

FIXB

FIXB is a special program to take care of fixing TDL/XITAN BASIC so that it points to TOPM. The program as shown assumes that TOPM was set up for a 32K system beginning at 07A55 HEX.

FIXB is used by, first, loading any version of TDL/XITAN BASIC so that it begins at 0300 HEX. Then, loading FIXB will cause an overlay on BASIC to point to the vectors of TOPM. This function is done before initializing BASIC, and the new version of BASIC should be saved with the patches. Usually, it is saved under MECA.

The only point that needs to be changed in FIXB is the TOPM equate; this must equal exactly the point at which TOPM is located. FIXB is 29 decimal bytes long and should be saved on MECA as part of your new system software. As you become more familiar with using specialized programs such as TOPM and FIXB, you will find that you can perform overlays for auto-patching user and commercial software.

```
1;001 * PROG "FIXB"
1;002 * 01-26-79
1;003 * RHD
1;004 * FOR VER 3.1 OF TOPM
1;005 * USED TO SET I/O VECTORS IN TDL
1;006 * BASIC LOADED AT 300 HEX WITH THE
1;007 * ADDRS TO "TOPM" PROG.
1;008 *
1;009 *
1;010 * SET TOPM TO EQU THE 1ST ADDRS IN
          "TOPM"
1;011 * SET BASIC TO EQU THE 1ST VECTOR IN
          "BASIC"
1;012 *
1;013 *
1;014 TOPM EQU 0B000H
1;015 BASIC EQU 309H
1;016 *
1;017   ORG BASIC
1;018   JMP TOPM+3
1;019   JMP TOPM+6
1;020   JMP TOPM+9
1;021   JMP TOPM+12
1;022   JMP TOPM+15
```

```
1ï023   JMP   TOPM+18
1ï024   JMP   TOPM+21
1ï025   JMP   TOPM+24
1ï026   JMP   TOPM+27
1ï027   JMP   TOPM+30
1ï028 *
1ï029   END
```

COPYM

Readers who have developed programs in TDL/XITAN BASIC using the ordinary cassette system will want to be able to convert these tapes from TDL format to MECA/TOPM format without re-keying all the information. Users who make use of CTBL and later convert to a MECA system will also want to take advantage of the system as quickly as possible. Therefore, COPYM was developed to provide the ability to copy TDL formatted tapes to MECA/TOPM tapes.

The COPYM program uses both TOPM and Zapple to perform the copy function and requires that the primary cassette system, the one used in the TDL/XITAN environment, is controlled (see the TDL manual for information on setting up a controlled reader punch).

The following procedures are followed to use the COPYM program.

1. Load TOPM.
2. Load COPYM; use 3000 HEX.
3. Reset to Zapple.
4. Make sure the tape you want to copy from is in the reader cassette and a fresh cassette is in drive one of the MECA drive.

For the next few steps, it is assumed that you are familar with the Zapple monitor and its functions as they relate to using the cassette system.

5. Set the reader equal to U—user-defined routine points to buffered cassette routines.
6. Turn cassette on and type in K.C.O.F.; this turns cassette motors off.

7. Type in k.c.o.i.; this turns the cassette on, loads the first buffer of TDL cassette buffer, and returns to Zapple.
8. Type G3000; this jumps to COPYM. The TDL monitor will now turn on and continue to read the primary tape. As the tape is being read, the contents of the tape will be displayed in HEX on the console. When COPYM determines from TOPM that the TOPM buffer is full, the primary cassette motor will stop and the contents will be written to drive one of the MECA system. This will continue until a HEX 1A (end of file marker) is detected. When this happens and more data exists on the tape, the process must be started over by exiting to Zapple and beginning at step 6.

```
1#001  * PROG "COPYM"
1#002  * 08-23-78 1130
1#003  * THIS IS A SHORT PROGRAM TO
1#004  * COPY TDL TAPES TO MECA
1#005  * TAPES
1#006  START CALL 0F006H
1#007   JC ENDT
1#008   MOV C,A
1#009   CALL 06009H VECTOR TO TOPM
1#010   CALL 0F58FH HEX OUT
1#011   CALL 0F488H SPACE OVER
1#012   JMP START
1#013  ENDT CALL 0601BH EMPTY BUFFER
1#014   JMP 0F00OH RESTART TDL
1#015   END
```

TMFIX

TMFIX is an overlay program that is used with the MECA operating system. As delivered, the MECA O/S is set up to communicate through only one assigned port, usually the CRT. For owners of systems with multiple ports, such as XITAN, it is desirable to be able to use the full power of the system. TMFIX causes an overlay of the O/S and points to the Zapple functions of console in, console out, and console status. When this overlay is made, you can change the console status in Zapple, and MECA will follow.

To use this program:

1. Boot the MECA system.
2. Load the operating system applicable to your system from the MECA-supplied tapes.
3. Load TMFIX.
4. Save the patched O/S either under a new name or with the overlay function.
5. Follow the procedures outlined in the MECA user's manual for making a boot tape of the operating system.

Important: Before attempting to use any of the programs described in this section, make sure that you are familiar with the MECA system and the Zapple monitor.

```
1;001 * PROG "TMFIX"
1;002 * BY RHD
1;003 * 08-07-78
1;004 * USED TO PATCH TDL I/O
1;005 * ON THE "SMB-2"
1;006 * TO THE MECA OS
1;007 *
1;008 *
1;009 *     EQUATES
1;010 CR EQU ODH
1;011 LF EQU OAH
1;012 ESC EQU 1BH
1;013 PSW EQU M
1;014 *
1;015 *
1;016 * 1ST BYTE OF YOUR MECA OS
1;017 OS EQU 0000H
1;018 *
1;019 * THINGS IN TDL
1;020 * DON'T FORGET THE H (HEX)
1;021 *
1;022 * CONSOLE INPUT
1;023 CI EQU OF003H
1;024 *
1;025 * CONSOLE OUTPUT
1;026 CO EQU OF009H
1;027 *
1;028 * CONSOLE STATUS
1;029 CSTS EQU OF012H
1;030 *
1;031 * SET "OS" TO = 1ST BYTE OF YOUR
          MECA OS
```

```
1;032 * ADDRESS AS LOADED TO WORK ON
1;033 * NOT THE RUN TIME ADDRESS
1;034 * THEY CAN BE THE SAME IF YOU LIKE
1;035 * DON'T FORGET THE H (HEX)
1;036 *
1;037 *
1;038 * TO USE THIS PROG. LOAD YOUR MECA OS
1;039 * THEN LOAD THE OBJECT CODE OF THIS
1;040 * PROG. AS A OVERLAY ON MECA OS
1;041 * NOW SAVE YOUR NEW MECA OS
1;042 *
1;043 * YOUR MECA CONSOLE IS NOW SAME AS
1;044 * TDL AS YOU ASSIGN IT MECA WILL
1;045 * FOLLOW TO THE NEW DEVICE (CRT TO
        TTY ECT.)
1;046 *
1;047   ORG 06D0H+OS
1;048 WIN CALL CI INPUT A CHAR
1;049   PUSH PSW
1;050   CALL OUT
1;051   POP PSW
1;052   ORI 80H SET BIT#7
1;053   RET
1;054 ROOM MVI A,LF
1;055   JMP NOLF
1;056   ORG 06EBH+OS
1;057 OUT ANI 7FH KILL PAR. BIT
1;058   CPI LF
1;059   JNZ NOLF
1;060   MVI A,3CH <
1;061 NOLF PUSH B /C
1;062   MOV C,A
1;063   CALL CO OUTPUT CHAR
1;064   POP B /C
1;065   CPI CR
1;066   RNZ
1;067   JMP ROOM
1;068   ORG 0701H+OS
1;069 * NO TIME TO OUTPUT ON READ/WRITE
1;070   RET
1;071   ORG 0704H+OS
1;072 CRLF MVI A,CR
1;073   JMP OUT
1;074   ORG 070AH+OS
1;075 CHEKC CALL CSTS GET CONSOLE STATUS
```

```
1;076    INR A CSTS RET. W/FFFF IF WAITING
1;077    RNZ
1;078    CALL CI INPUT CHAR
1;079    CPI ESC IS IT ?
1;080    RET
1;081    END
```

Appendix B

INDEX TO HARDWARE AND SOFTWARE SUPPLIERS

B.1 HARDWARE

The following manufacturers and retailers supply either complete microcomputer systems or peripheral devices.

The A-Team Inc.
P.O. Box 719
Bloomfield, CO 80020
Attn: Sales Manager

AB ATEW
Box 125, S-642 00
Flen, Sweden
Telex: 641 20 ATEW S

Advanced Microcomputer Products
P.O. Box 17329
Santa Ana, CA 92713
(714) 968-3655

Alpha Digital Systems
Route 4, Box 171A
Boone, NC 28607
(704) 264-7946

Alpha Microsystems
17875-M Sky Park North
Irvine, CA 92714
(714) 957-1404

American Microsystems, Inc.
3800 Homestead Rd.
Santa Clara, CA 95051
(408) 246-0330

Anderson Jacobson
521 Charcot Avenue
San Jose, CA 95131
Attn: Bob Miller
(408) 263-8520

Andromeda Systems Inc.
14701 Arminta Street, Suite J
Panorama City, CA 91402
Attn: Les Lazar
(213) 781-6000

APF Electronics Inc.
444 Madison Avenue
New York, NY 10022
Attn: Neil Lipper
(212) 758-7550

Apple Computer, Inc.
10260 Bandley Drive
Cupertino, CA 95014
(408) 996-1010

Applied Systems Corp.
26401 Harper Ave.
St. Clair Shores, MI 48081
(313) 779-8700

Automated Computer Systems
2361 E. Foothill Blvd.
Pasadena, CA 91107
(213) 449-0616

AXIOM
5932 San Fernando Road
Glendale, CA 91202
Attn: Simon Harrison
(213) 245-9244

BASF Systems
Crosby Drive
Bedford, MA 01730
Attn: J.W. Ehrlich

Basic Business Systems, Inc.
1 Belmont Ave.
Bala Cynwood, PA 19004
(215) 839-6221

Bedford Computer Systems, Inc.
Three Preston Court
Bedford, MA 01730
(617) 275-0870

Beehive International
4910 Amelia Earhart Drive
Box 25668
Salt Lake City, UT 84125
Attn: Dave Zeiter
(801) 355-6000

Billing Computer Corporation
2000 E. Billing Avenue
Provo, UT 84601
Attn: National Sales Director
(801) 375-0000

Bowmar Instrument Corp.,
Commercial Products Division
8000 Bluffton Road
Fort Wayne, IN 46809
Attn: Tom Utley
(219) 493-4472

Braemar Computer Devices, Inc.
11950 Twelfth Avenue
South Burnsville, MN 55337
Attn: Richard Morris
(612) 890-5135

Byte, Inc.
930 West Maude St.
Sunnyvale, CA 94086
(408) 739-8000

CALCOMP California Computer
  Products, Inc.
1270 N. Kraemer
Anaheim, CA 92806
Attn: Carol Felton
(714) 632-5461

California Micro-Computer Corp.,
  Inc.
P.O. Box 3199
Chico, CA 95927
(916) 891-1420

CENTRONICS Data Computer
  Corporation
Hudson, NH 03051
Attn: Chuck Clemente
(603) 883-0111

C. ITOH Electronics, Inc.
5301 Beethoven Street
Los Angeles, CA 90025
Attn: Ken Hidaka
(213) 390-2668

CMC Marketing Corporation
5601 Bintliff, Suite 515
Houston, TX 77036
Attn: Bill Tatroe
(713) 783-8880

Commodore Business Machines, Inc.
901 California Ave.
Palo Alto, CA 94304
(415) 326-4000

Computall Corporation
2740 S. Harbor Boulevard, Suite "K"
Santa Ana, CA 92704
Attn: Al Whedon
(714) 754-7854

Computer Applications
3030 Bridgeway
Sausalito, CA 94965
Attn: Arthur Jopling
(415) 332-9401

Computer Enterprises
P.O. Box 71
Fayetteville, NY 13066
(315) 637-6208

Computer Hardware, Inc.
4111 North Freeway Boulevard
Sacramento, CA 95834
Attn: Rogert Lotz
(916) 929-2020

Computer Mart of New Jersey
501 Route 27
Iselin, NJ 08830
(201) 283-0600

Computer Mart of Pennsylvania
550 DeKalb Pike
King of Prussia, PA 19406
(215) 265-2580

Computer Power & Light, Inc.
12321 Ventura Blvd.
Studio City, CA 91604
(213) 760-0405

COMPUTER TEXTile
10960 Wilshire Boulevard, Suite 1504
Los Angeles, CA 90024
Attn: Sales Manager
(213) 477-2196

Computerware
830 First St.
Encinitas, CA 92024
(714) 436-3512

Computer Workshop
1776 E. Jefferson St.
Rockville MD 20852
(301) 468-0455

Computronics Engineering
7235 Hollywood Boulevard
Hollywood, CA 90046
Attn: J.B. Stanton
(213) 876-3326

Compu-Text
287 Wood Road
Braintree, MA 02184
Attn: Theodore Magida
(617) 848-1800

Control Logic, Inc.
9 Tech Circle
Natick, MA 01760
(617) 655-1170

Cramer Electronics
85 Wells Ave.
Newton, MA 02159
(617) 969-7700

Cromemco, Inc.
280 Bernardo Avenue
Mountain View, CA 94043
Attn: Alice Ahlgren
(415) 964-7400

CyberGrafix Advertising Design
20201 Staff Street
Canoga Park, CA 91306
Attn: Shela Clarke
(213) 341-0350

Cybersystem, Inc.
4306 Governors Dr.
Huntsville, AL 35805
(205) 837-2080

Daneva Control Pty. Ltd.
70 Bay Road
Sandringham, Victoria 3181, Australia
Attn: Stuart Wright
(03) 598-5622
Telex: DANEVA 34439

Data Access Systems, Inc.
100 Route 46
Mountain Lakes, NJ 07046
Attn: Sales Manager

Data General
Route 9
Westboro, MA 01581
Attn: Howard Steiner
(617) 366-8911, Ext. 4756 or 4752

Datamedia Corporation
7300 N. Crescent Boulevard
Pennsauken, NJ 08110
Attn: Robert Sullivan
(609) 665-2382

Data Printer Corporation
99 Middlesex Street
Malden, MA 02148
Attn: Nick Siedun
(617) 321-2400

Dataproduct Corporation
6219 Desota Avenue
Woodland Hills, CA 91305
Attn: Gerry Coulter
(213) 887-8465

Data Terminals and Communications
590 Division Street
Campbell, CA 95008
Attn: Bruce Brough
(415) 326-6141

Data World, Inc.
7541 Ravensridge Drive
St. Louis, MO 63119
Attn: Kenneth Taggart
(314) 961-2229

Deciter—Division of Jameburg
  Corporation
129 Flanders Road
Westboro, MA 01581
Attn: Bill Sanford
(617) 366-8334

Digital Electronics Corp.
415 Peterson St.
Oakland, CA 94601
(415) 532-2920

Digital Equipment Corp.
146 Main St.
Maynard, MA 01754
(617) 879-5111

The Digital Group
P.O. Box 6528
Denver, CO 80206
(303) 777-7133

Dynabyte
1005 Elwell Court
Palo Alto, CA 94303
Attn: Rick Mehrlich
(415) 965-1010

EBNEK, Inc.
522 South Broadway
Wichita, KS 67202
(316) 265-0131

ECD Corp.
196 Broadway
Cambridge, MA 02139
(617) 661-4400

Electronic Control Technology
P.O. Box 6
Union, NJ 07083
(201) 686-8080

E&L Instruments, Inc.
61 First Street
Derby, CT 06418
Attn: Sales Manager
(203) 735-8774

Electronic Memories & Magnetics
  Corp.
P.O. Box 36
Hawthorne, CA 90250
(213) 777-4070

Electronic Products Associates
1157 Vega St.
San Diego, CA 92110
(714) 276-8911

Electronic Tool Company
4736 West El Segundo Blvd.
Hawthorne, CA 90250
(213) 644-0113

ESMARK
507½ E. McKinley Highway
Mishawaka, IN 46544
Attn: Steve Toussaint
(219) 255-3035

EXIDY, Data Products Division
969 W. Maude Avenue
Sunnyvale, CA 94086
Attn: Paul Terrell
(408) 736-2110

Fairchild Microsystems Division
1725 Technology Dr.
San Jose, CA 95110
(408) 998-0123

Franklin Systems Corporation
733 Lakefield Road
Westlake Village, CA 91361
Attn: Frank Pters
(805) 497-7755

Futureworld
2514 University Drive
Durham, NC 27707
Attn: Giles L. Cloninger
(919) 489-7486

Galusha Corporation
12062 Valley View Street, Suite 220
Garden Grove, CA 92645
Attn: Sales Director

General Instrument Corporation
300 Shames Drive
Westbury, NY 11590
Attn: George Weiss
(516) 333-9500

Gentle Electric
130 Oxford Way
Santa Cruz, CA 95060
Attn: Carl Fravel

George Risk Industries, Inc.
GRI Plaza
Kimball, NE 69145
Attn: Robert Nickels
(308)235-4645

GSI Systems Corporation
223 Crescent Street
Waltham, MA 02154
Attn: Gerald Gershon
(617) 899-6698

HAL Communications Corp.
Box 365
807 E. Green St.
Urbana, IL 61801
(217) 367-7373

Heath Company
Benton Harbor, MI 49022
Attn: Virgil Bennett
(616) 982-3417

Hewlett-Packard Corp.
1507 Page Mill Road
Palo Alto, CA 94304
(415) 856-1501

IBM
1133 Westchester Ave.
White Plains, NY 10604
(914) 696-1900

IMSAI Manufacturing Corporation
14860 Wicks Boulevard
San Leandro, CA 94577
Attn: Walt Slater
(415) 483-2093

Infinite, Inc.
1924 Waverly Place
Melborne, FL 32901
(305) 724-1588

INFO 2000
20630 South Leapwood Avenue
Carson, CA 90746
Attn: Sales Manager
(213) 532-1702

Intel Corp.
3065 Bowers Ave.
Santa Clara, CA 95051
(408) 987-8080

Intelligent Systems Corp.
5965 Peachtree Corners East
Norcross, GA 30071
(404) 449-5961

Interact Electronics, Inc.
P.O. Box 8140
Ann Arbor, MI 48107
Attn: Michael Tucker
(313) 973-0120

The Interpring Group, Inc.
50 Hunt Street
Watertown, MA 02172
Attn: Sharon Rogolsky
(617) 926-1510

Intertec Data Systems Corporation
19530 Club House Road
Gaithersburg, MD 20760
Attn: Sales Manager
(301) 948-2400

International Data Systems, Inc.
400 N. Washington St., Suite 106
Falls Church, VA 22046
(703) 536-7373

International Microsystems, Inc.
11554 C Ave. DeWitt
Auburn, CA 95603
(916) 885-7262

Intersil, Inc.
10710 N. Tantau Ave.
Cupertino, CA 95014
(408) 996-5000

Keltron Corporation
225 Crescent Street
Waltham, MA 02154
Attn: Ted Chadurjian
(617) 894-0525

Lear Siegler, Inc.,
Data Products Division
714 N. Brookhurst
Anaheim, CA 92803
Attn: John Pagliaro
(714) 774-1010

Logical Machine Corporation
1294 Hammerwood Avenue
Sunnyvale, CA 94806
Attn: Steven Sester
(408) 744-1290

MarComm, Inc.
124 Tenth Street
Ramona, CA 92065
Attn: Sales Director
(714) 789-3833

Martin Research
3336 Commercial Ave.
Northbrook, IL 60062
(312) 498-5060

MECA
7026 O.W.S. Road
Yucca Valley, CA 97604
Attn: Nancy Millican
(714) 365-7686

Megatek Corporation
3931 Sorrento Boulevard
San Diego, CA 92121
Attn: Peter Shaw
(714) 455-5590

MicroAge
1425 W. 12th Place, Suite 101
Tempe, AZ 85281
Attn: W. Craig Tenney
(602) 967-1421

MICRODATA Corporation
17481 Red Hill Avenue
Irvine, CA 92714
Attn: Richard Yamaguchi
(714) 540-6730

Micropolis
7959 Deering Avenue
Canoga Park, CA 91304
Attn: Charles Ramsey
(213) 703-1121

Microproducts
1024 17th Street
Hermosa Beach, CA 90254
Attn: Sales Manager
(213) 374-1673

Micro V Corporation
17777 S.E. Main Street
Irvine, CA 92714
Attn: Art Shahan
(714) 957-1517

Microworld
1425 W. 12th Place
Tempe, AZ 85281
(602) 894-1193

Midwest Scientific Instruments
220 W. Cedar
Olathe, KS 66061
(913) 782-8027

Monolithic Systems Corp.
14 Inverness Dr. East
Englewood, CO 80110
(303) 770-7400

Morrow Computer & Electronic
  Design, Inc.
315 Wilhagan Road
Nashville, TN 37217
Attn: Sales Manager

MOS Technology, Inc.
Valley Forge Corporate Center
950 Rittenhouse Road
Norristown, PA 19403
(215) 666-7950

Mostek Corp.
1215 West Crosby Road
Carrollton, TX 75006
(214) 242-0444

Motorola Semiconductor Products
5005 E. McDowell Road
Phoenix, AZ 85008
Attn: Sales Manager
(602) 244-6900

M&R Enterprises
P.O. Box 1011
Sunnyvale, CA 94088
(408) 738-3772

MSI Data Corporation
340 Fischer Avenue
Costa Mesa, CA 92626
Attn: Richard Roper
(213) 393-0622

Multisonics, Inc.
6444 Sierra Court
P.O. Box 2295
Dublin, CA 94566
(415) 829-3300

National Semiconductor Corp.
2900 Semiconductor Dr.
Santa Clara, CA 95051
(408) 737-5000

The NewO Company
246 Walter Hays Drive
Palo Alto, CA 94303
Attn: Sid Owen

Nortek, Inc.
2432 N.W. Johnson Street
Portland, OR 97210
Attn: Sales Manager
(503) 226-3515

North Star Computers
2547 Ninth Street
Berkeley, CA 94702
Attn: T. Burt
(415) 549-0858

Noval, Inc.
7044 Convoy Court
San Diego, CA 92123
(714) 292-4643

Objective Design, Inc.
P.O. Box 20325
Tallahassee, FL 32304
Attn: Sales Director
(904) 224-5545

Ohio Scientific
1333 S. Chillicothe Rd.
Aurora, OH 44202
(216) 562-3101

Oliver Advanced Engineering, Inc.
676 W. Wilson Avenue
Glendale, CA 91203
Attn: Julie Griess
(213) 240-0080

Pacific Cyber/Metrix, Inc.
3120 Crow Canyon Rd.
San Ramon, CA 94583
(415) 837-5400

PCC/Pertec Division
9600 Irondale Avenue
Chatsworth, CA 91311
Attn: Carol hays
(213) 999-2020

Pertec Computer Corporation
Microsystems Division
21111 Erwin Street
Woodland Hills, CA 90049
Attn: Neil McElwee
(213) 999-2020

Plessey Microsystems
1641 Kaiser
Irvine, CA 92714
(714) 540-9931

PolyMorphic Systems
460 Ward Drive
Santa Barbara, CA 93111
Attn: Otto Janssen
(212) 986-6668

Princeton Electronic Products, Inc.
Department H, P.O. Box 101
North Brunswick, NJ 08920
Attn: Sales Manager
(201) 297-4448

PRINTRONIX
17421 Derian Avenue
P.O. Box 19559
Irvine, CA 92713
Attn: Mel Posin
(714) 549-8272

Process Computer Systems, Inc.
750 N. Maple Road
Saline, MI 48176
Attn: Tim Pellegrino
(313) 429-4971

Processor Technology
Box G
6200 Hollis St.
Emeryville, CA 94608
(415) 652-8080

Quay Corp.
P.O. Box 386
Freehold, NJ 07728
(201) 681-8700

Quodata Corp.
196 Trumbull St.
Hartford, CT 06130
(203) 728-6777

Radio Shack
Division of Tandy Corp.
205 N.W. 7th St.
Fort Worth, TX 76102
(817) 390-3583

Ramtek Corporation
585 North Mary Avenue
Sunnyvale, CA 94086
(408) 735-8400

RCA
New Holland Ave.
Lancaster, PA 17604
(717) 397-7661

RCA/Electro-Optics and Devices
Route 202
Somerville, NJ 08876
Attn: Walt Dennen
(201) 685-6423

R2E of America
3406 University Ave. S.E.
Minneapolis, MN 55414
Attn: Ronald Larsen
(216) 562-9908

Rockwell International
Electronic Devices Division
5310 Miraloma Avenue
P.O. Box 3669
Anaheim, CA 92803
Attn: Leo Scanlon
(714) 632-2321

Rondure Company
2522 Butler Street
Dallas, TX 75235
Attn: R. Shannon

S.D.S. Technical Devices, Ltd.
P.O. Box 1998
Winnipeg, Canada R3C 3R3
Attn: George Sagi
(204) 944-1448

Signetics Corp.
811 East Arques Ave.
P.O. Box 9052
Sunnyvale, CA 94086
(408) 739-7700

Silconics
525 Oakmead Parkway
P.O. Box 9025
Sunnyvale, CA 94086
Attn: Doug Vaughn
(408) 732-1650

Smoke Signal Broadcasting
6304 Yucca
Hollywood, CA 90028
Attn: Ed Martin
(213) 462-5652

Southwest Technical Products Corp.
219 West Rhapsody
San Antonio, TX 78216
(512) 344-0241

Space Byte Computer Corporation
6464 Sunset Boulevard
Los Angeles, CA 90028
Attn: Milt Hubatka
(213) 468-8085

Spectrum 8
7753 Densmore Ave.
Van Nuys, CA 91406
(213) 988-9700

Summagraphics Corporation
35 Brentwood Avenue
Fairfield, CT 06430
Attn: Morris Samit
(203) 384-1344

Sylvanhills Laboratory, Inc.
P.O. Box 646
Pittsburg, Kansas 66762
(316) 231-4440
Attn: Sharon Bell

Synertek Systems
2589 Scott Blvd.
Santa Clara, CA 95050
(408) 988-5689

System Computer and Interfaces
223 Crescent Street
Waltham, MA 02154
Attn: Edward Letscher
(617) 899-2359

Systems Engineering Enterprises
1749 Rockville Pike
Rockville, MD 20852
(301) 468-1822

Systems Research, Inc.
1650 Westwood Blvd., Suite 202
Los Angeles, CA 90024
(213) 475-0381

Tarbell Electronics
950 Doulen Place, Suite B
Carson, CA 90746
Attn: Don Tarbell
(213) 538-4251

Technical Systems Consultants, Inc.
Box 2574
W. Lafayette, IN 47906
(317) 742-7509

Technico, Inc.
9130 Red Branch Rd.
Columbia MD 21045
(301) 596-4100

Terak Corp.
14425 N. Scottsdale Rd., Suite 100
Scottsdale, AZ 85260
(602) 991-1580

TLF
P.O. Box 2298
Littleton, CO 80161
(303) 794-1634

Tranti Systems, Inc.
23 Republic Rd.
North Billerica, MA 01862
(617) 667-4146

Vector Graphic, Inc.
31364 Via Colinas
Westlake Village, CA 91361
Attn: Lori Harp
(213) 991-2302

Wang Laboratories, Inc.
20 South Ave.
Burlington, MA 01803
(617) 272-8550

Warner & Swasey Co.
30300 Solon Industrial Parkway
Solon, OH 44139
(216) 368-6100

Wave Mate
1015 W. 190th St.
Gardena, CA 90248
(213) 329-8941

Western Data Systems
3650 Charles St. #2
Santa Clara, CA 95050
(408) 988-0300

Wyle Laboratories
3200 Magruder Blvd.
Hampton, VA 23666
(804) 838-0122

XITAN, Inc.
P.O. Box 3087
1101-H State Road
Princeton, NJ 08540
Attn: Chris Rutkowski
(609) 921-0321

ZEDA Computer Systems
1662 W. 820 N.
Provo, UT 84601
Attn: Clair Smith
(801) 377-9948

ZILOG
10340 Bubb Road
Cupertino, CA 95014
Attn: Dave West
(408) 446-4666

B.2 SOFTWARE

This list of software suppliers covers manufacturers of both system and application software. Every attempt has been made to assemble the most complete list of software vendors possible. However, due to the lack of good software and professional suppliers, we suggest that you choose carefully when buying software.

If you want a complete list of software, including published software, we suggest you buy the *SSI Microcomputer Software Guide* from your local computer store, or direct from: Jim Schreier, 4327 East Grove Street, Phoenix, Arizona 85040.

Aaron Associates
P.O. Box 1720 A
Garden Grove, CA 92640
Attn: Bud Aaron
(714) 539-0735

Administrative Systems, Inc.
1642 South Parker Road, Suite 300
Denver, CO 80231
Attn: Edward Y. Gateley
(303) 755-9694

Alpha Data Systems
Box 267
Santa Barbara, CA 93102
(805) 682-5693

Billings Computer Corporation
2000 E. Billings Avenue
Provo, UT 84601
Attn: National Sales Director
(801) 375-0000

Business Computer Systems
216 Collier Drive
Springfield, IL 62704
Attn: Sales Manager
(217) 787-3448

Byte Shop of Westminster
14300 Beach Boulevard
Westminster, CA 92683
Attn: Marty Rezmer
(714) 894-9131

Command, Control and
  Communications Corporation
1823 West Lomita Boulevard
Lomita, CA 90717
Attn: Sales Manager
(213) 325-6883

COMPAL Computer Systems
12321 Ventura Boulevard
Studio City, CA
Attn: Irv Kalb
(213) 760-3345

Computer Components, Inc.
6791 Westminster Avenue
Westminster, CA
Attn: Steve Fish
(714) 898-2611

Computer One
#306 Kahala Office Tower
4211 Waialae Ave.
Honolulu, HI 96816
(808) 737-2933

The Computer Store
120 Cambridge Street
Burlington, MA 01803
Attn: R.F. Brown
(617) 272-8770

Computerware
830 First Street
Encinitas, CA 92024
Attn: Paul Searby
(714) 436-3512

Creative Polyware Unlimited
2805 East State Boulevard
Fort Wayne, IN 46805
Attn: Cindy Shull
(219) 484-7611

Cromemco, Inc.
280 Bernardo Avenue
Mountain View, CA 94043
Attn: Dr. Alice Ahlgren
(415) 964-7400

Dataware, Inc.
495 Delaware Street
Tonawanda, NY 14150
Attn: Sales Manager
(716) 695-1412

Demarco Shatz Corporation
952 Manhattan Beach Boulevard
Manhattan Beach, CA 90266
Attn: Mr. Shatz
(213) 545-4539

Diaspar Data Systems
P.O. Box 888
San Juan Capistrano, CA 92675
Attn: David Mitchell

Digital Research
P.O. Box 579
Pacific Grove, CA 93950
Attn: John R. Pierce
(408) 649-3896

dilithium Press
30 N.W. 23rd Place
Portland, OR 97210
Attn: Merl Miller
(503) 243-1158

Dymax
P.O. Box 310
Menlo Park, CA 94025
Attn: Laura Reininger
(415) 323-6117

EIDOS Systems Corporation
315 Wilhagan Road
Nashville, TN 37217
Attn: Sales Manager
(615) 385-0632

Engram Associates, Inc.
11601 Rodney Parham Rd.
Little Rock, AR 72212
(501) 227-8885

IMSAI Manufacturing Corporation
14860 Wicks Boulevard
San Leandro, CA 94577
Attn: Walt Slater
(415) 483-2093

The Interpring Group, Inc.
50 Hunt Street
Watertown, MA 02172
Attn: Sharon Rogolsky
(617) 926-1510

Lupfer & Long, Inc.
Box 135
Hanover, NH 03755
Attn: Sales Manager
(603) 643-4503

Magnemedia
17845 Sky Park Circle, Suite H
Irvine, CA 92714
(714) 549-9122

Michael Shrayer Software, Inc.
1253 Vista Superba Drive
Glendale, CA 91205
Attn: Phyllis Harris
(213) 956-1593

Microcomputer Business Systems
560 Bellwood Drive
Santa Clara, CA 95050
Attn: Dennis Wong
(408) 988-3059

Micro Dynamics, Inc.
3139 West 160 Street
Cleveland, OH 44111
Attn: N. Costanzo
(216) 228-6500

Micro Information Systems
158 Valparaiso
San Francisco, CA 94133
Attn: William F. Anderson
(415) 441-4597

Micromatics
P.O. Box 5710
Columbus, OH 43221
Attn: J.L. Comer
(614) 882-7396

Microsoft
300 San Mateo N.E.
Albuquerque, NM 87108
(505) 262-1486

Mission Control Computers
2008 Wilshire Boulevard
Santa Monica, CA
Attn: Alan Porter
(213) 829-5137

Musgrove Engineering
9547 Kindletree Drive
Houston, TX 77040
Attn: John Musgrove
(713) 466-3486

National Software Exchange
1000 Lake St. Louis Blvd., Suite 17
Lake St. Louis, MO 63367
Attn: John McCain
(314) 625-2400

Newtech Computer Systems, Inc.
230 Clinton Street
Brooklyn, NY 11201
Attn: Dorothy Siegel
(212) 625-6220

Osborne & Associates, Inc.
P.O. Box 2036
Dept. D4
Berkeley, CA 94702
(415) 548-2805

PRS—The Program of the Month
  Corporation
257 Central Park West
New York, NY 10024
Attn: Sales Manager
(212) 787-1526

Pertec Computer Corporation/
  Microsystems Division
21111 Erwin Street
Woodland Hills, CA 91367
Attn: Neil McElwee
(213) 999-2020

R & B Computer Systems
2916 N. 68th Street, #1
Scottsdale, AZ 85251
Attn: Charles Booth
(602) 949-7862

Scientific Research
P.O. Box 490099-B
Key Biscayne, FL 33149
(305) 361-1153

Softco Company
2952 N. Meade Avenue
Chicago, IL 60634
Attn: Thad Mack
(312) 778-3805

Softech
10756 Vanowen
North Hollywood, CA 91605
(213) 985-5763

Software Dynamics
2111 W. Crescent, Suite G
Anaheim, CA 92801
Attn: Ira D. Baxter
(714) 635-4760

Software Records
P.O. Box 8401-B
Universal City, CA 91608

Space Byte Computer Corporation
6464 Sunset Boulevard
Los Angeles, CA 90028
Attn: Milt Hubaka
(213) 468-8085

Structured Systems Group
5615 Kales Ave., Dept. B6
Oakland,, CA 94618
(415) 547-1567

Tarbell Electronics
950 Dovlen Place, Suite B
Carson, CA 90746
(213) 538-4521 or 538-2254

Technical Systems Consultants, Inc.
P.O. Box 2574
W. Lafayette, IN
Attn: Dan Vanada
(317) 423-5465

TJB Microsystems, Ltd.
10991 124th Street
Edmonton, Alberta, Canada T5M 0H9
Attn: Tom Forester

UPPER CASE Books
502 E. John Street
Champaign, IL 61820
Attn: Barbara Maggs
(217) 384-4382

Appendix C

MECA INITIALIZATION

Supplied courtesy of

MECA
7026 O.W.S. Road
Yucca Valley, CA 92284

C.1 BRINGING YOUR MECA OPERATING SYSTEM ON LINE

The Version 3.0 MECA Operating System is configured to allow it to be brought on line with a minimum of effort on the most popular systems.

You will need one of these systems:

1. MITS with a 2SI0 Card
2. IMSAI with a SI02 Card
3. Other S-100 Bus Systems with 3P + S type I/O interfacing.

Using the tape supplied, try the following Cold Start/ Bootstrap procedure. (Read the entire procedure before beginning.) Take careful note of the Recovery from a Bootstrap Failure Procedure.

The Bootstrap/Initialization Routine requires that you specify the I/O configuration by setting the senses switches. The following chart will help you with your machine.

If you have:	**Set switches on:**
IMSAI with SI02	Programmed Input 0 (A8)
MITS with a 2SI0	Sense Switch A9

Any other switch setting will trap your computer in the initialization routine. This allows you to "customize" the I/O for your machine (see Step 12 in the next section).

C.2 ALPHA-1 COLD START (BOOTSTRAP) PROCEDURE

Important: In the following Cold Start (Bootstrap) procedure, it is important that you be able to switch the power to the computer and the drive on and off at the same time. This is most easily accomplished if you have a switch-controlled extension cord. This cord should be available from most hardware stores. It will provide you with the convenience of one-switch power-on for your system.

1. Be sure that you double check the cables plugged into your drives.
2. Turn on power.
3. Install the tape on drive zero.
4. Reset the computer (Reset and Stop switches).
5. Press down on the External Clear switch (same as Reset). If tape is not rewound, it will begin to rewind.
6. Release Clear.
7. Press Run. Computer lights should be as follows:
   A. Wait light on.
   B. Run light on (IMSAI only).
   C. D0 light on (D1 through D7 off).
   D. Address Bus A15 through A10 on (A9 and A8 off; others do not matter).
8. When fully rewound, the drive will raise the head and enter Play mode.
9. In approximately 5 seconds (depending on how far out the Bootstrap has been written), the Interrupt Enable light will blink. This indicates that the system is performing correctly. If this does not happen, or if the Interrupt Enable light comes on and stays on, there is a problem. See Recovery from a Bootstrap Failure, Section D.3.

10. If your machine is performing normally, in approximately 6 seconds, the Wait light should go out and the drive will stop. For IMSAI and MITS, it will begin execution. For other I/O configurations, use the following procedure. For MITS or IMSAI with 2SI0, skip Steps 11 through 15.

    Note: If your computer does not have data switches, see the instructions in Section D.2.1.

11. Stop the computer.

12. Examine the following locations and modify them as instructed.

HEX Address	Present Contents (HEX)	Change to:
3005	0	Your Status Port address.
3006	1	Your Input Ready Bit (Mask) location.
3007	1	Your Data I/O Port.
3008	80	Your Output Ready Bit (Mask) location.
3009	CA (JZ)	C2 (JNZ) if your Ready Bits above have a Negative True Sense.
300A	0	The 1st initialization byte for your I/O Card. It will be output to the Status Port address.
300B	0	The 2nd initialization byte.

13. After Step 12 is done and checked, set the Address 3000 (HEX) in the Data switches and press Examine. (Address 3000 HEX = Address Switches A12 and A13 up, all others down.)

14. Now change the switches so that A8 and A9 are up, but all the rest are down.

15. Press Run.

16. Your Console Output Device should display the following Message:

    + + MECA OS VER. 3.0 + +
    OK—

    All of your drives should have rewound and the Directory for drive zero should have been read.

17. Before trying any other O.S. functions, you should make additional copies of your O.S. as follows:

You Type:	Computer Response:
LOAD BDMPR	Indicates File Name and Address Range. New prompt.
REWIND	Rewinds tape and new prompt.

At this point, remove the O.S. tape on drive zero and install a new uncommitted tape. Manually rewind it. Make sure the tape is unprotected.

NEWTAPE	It will go into write mode and erase approximately 20 seconds of tape, then rewind and write an empty directory on the front of the tape. Then it will display a new prompt.
UNLOAD	Green light blinks and new prompt.
EXEC 1B00 3000 3FFF 3000	It will write a Bootstrap copy of the 16K operating system on the front of the new tape. Then you will get a new prompt.

To generate additional system tapes, you should repeat this procedure from Step 17, REWIND Command.

If you are using the tapes just generated and you have a custom I/O configuration, you will get the Bootstrap and Go function if switches A8 and A9 are set on (up) before beginning the Bootstrap procedure.

C.2.1 Special Note for Users with Computers Which Do Not Have Data Switches

Make the following changes in Section D.2:

13. Change Memory Location 3020 HEX from C2 HEX to 21 HEX.
14. Begin Program Execution (jump to) 301C HEX.
15. None.

C.3   RECOVERY FROM A BOOTSTRAP FAILURE

There are many possible reasons for failure of the Bootstrap routine to execute successfully. A few are:

- The wrong tape is installed.
- The tape had an error (hard or soft).
- There is a hardware malfunction.

The proper procedure for recovering from a Bootstrap failure is as follows:

1. If Interrupt Enable is on, simply stop the drive manually.
2. If Interrupt Enable is not on, hold down on the drive manual stop switch (this should unload the Head) and turn off the computer power (or the main power if all the system components are switched together).
3. Turn the power back on and the Bootstrap may be retried.
4. In the event that there is no manual stop switch for the drive:
   A. If the drive is not moving tape, remove power from the computer and the drive (preferably simultaneously).
   B. If the drive is in Play mode and moving tape, wait until it is past the Bootstrap program (approximately 10 to 15 seconds) and remove power from both drive and computer.

When power is turned back on, the head should unload automatically. You can try the Bootstrap again.

C.4   MECA OPERATING SYSTEM OPERATION

After bringing up your system, the computer should give the normal O.S. prompt, OK—. This is your signal that it is in the command mode. If you do not see the prompt. the O.S. is not in command mode. At certain points during the O.S. execution, there are built-in pauses (mainly to assure that the display will not page off a T.V. monitor). At these pauses, it will be necessary for you to input something from the keyboard to signal it to continue (normally this should be a carriage return).

As a rule of thumb, when the computer stops with no prompt and you wish to continue, type a carriage return.

In addition, carriage returns with no other input (null line) are used by the support programs to return to the O.S. (EDITR, DEBUG).

The system abort command is an "escape" in the stand-alone O.S. and a "Control C" when operating under Extended BASIC. Hitting an abort character will cause the system to stop the present tape or listing operation. For tape operations, it will also report an **ERROR Q** message. *Remember,* you must type a carriage return after error messages are reported in order to return to command mode.

The backspace character for the stand-alone O.S. is the "line-feed." It will print a less than (<) sign or back up the cursor, depending upon the particular I/O configuration you have. Note, under Extended BASIC, it is the normally defined BASIC backspace character.

C.5   3.0 O.S. ORGANIZATION

The stand-alone O.S. will load into a 4K block of memory starting at relative zero. The following O.S. configurations are supplied on your tape to allow optimum system configuration.

O.S. Title	Memory Location
BOOTSTRAP	3000-3FFF
@24KOS	5000-5FFF
@32KOS	7000-7FFF
@40KOS	9000-9FFF
@48KOS*	A000-AFFF
@56KOS†	C000-CFFF

*This is actually a 44K O.S.
†This is actually a 52K O.S.

The 16K O.S. is supplied in Bootstrap form only. Systems of less than 16K are of very limited use in any applications which use an operating system, although a special O.S. could be designed for a particular application.

In general, it is best to locate your O.S. in the highest available memory.

Each O.S. Tape is organized as follows:

Tape Location	Contents
0-1024 Decimal	Bootstrap Region (Reserved)
1024- Decimal	Tape Directory
1380-? Decimal	First File

The tape directory is always stored at the same tape location. The standard directory size is 456 bytes (1C8 HEX), which allows for 50 file names. This may be easily expanded or contracted for special applications but any tape which is exchanged with other users should have the "standard" directory size.

The standard operating system is configured for a dual drive system and space is allotted for two directories (more than 2 drive operating systems should be ordered special).

In the following discussion, the high order HEX digit of the O.S. addresses is variable, based upon your O.S. location and is thus designated "x".

The drive zero directory will be read into memory by the O.S. and stored at x1C8 (HEX). The drive one directory will be stored at x000. *Note:* Before the drive one directory is read, x000-x10F contains the O.S. initialization routine. Therefore, after system initialization, *manual O.S. re-entry point is x390 (HEX).*

You should keep in mind at all times that there are two copies of a tape directory: the memory copy and the tape copy. The memory copy is updated during O.S. operation as required and is not always the same as the tape copy. They are only the same if no saves, overlays, deletes or tends have been done since the last directory read or record operation. Therefore, it is very important that you do not try to fool the system until you become very familiar with it.

The best method of avoiding trouble is:

1. Manually rewind tapes after they are installed (if the tape makes a funny noise, it is not installed properly).
2. Always issue an **UNLOAD** before removing a tape. (The exception to this is after an error on a **COPY** command. In this case, you should issue a **MOUNT** command before doing an unload.)

The remainder of the O.S. will be described in a MECA application note, and a source listing is available for a charge.

The message EH? means that the system cannot interpret your input line.

C.6   BRINGING UP OTHER MECA OPERATING SYSTEMS

The following procedure may be used to generate a Bootstrap tape of any other operating system included on your MECA tape.

To do the 24K operating system:

1. Bring up the normal 16KOS.
2. LOAD BDMPR :0.
3. LOAD @24KOS :0 5000.
4. Modify the initialization section at 5005-500B as you did for the 16KOS (not required for MITS and IMSAI with standard 2SIO cards).
5. Install a new tape on drive zero.
6. REWIND :0.
7. NEWTAPE :0.
8. EXEC 1B00 5000 5FFF 5000.

For the other operating systems, change Steps 3, 4 and 8 above according to the following table:

O.S.	Step 3, LOAD:	Step 4, MODIFY:	Step 8, EXEC:
32K	@32KOS :0 7000	7005-700B	1B00 7000 7FFF 7000
40K	@40KOS :0 9000	9005-900B	1B00 9000 9FFF 9000
48K	@48KOS :0 A000	A005-A00B	1B00 A000 AFFF A000
56K	@56KOS :0 C000	C005-C00B	1B00 C000 CFFF C000

Note: 48K is actually 44K O.S. and 56K is actually 52K O.S.

C.7   MECA OPERATING SYSTEM—VERSION 3.0 COMMAND DESCRIPTION

There are four data fields used to specify what functions the O.S. is to perform. These fields must occur in the order specified in the specific command description. Blanks are used to delimit the fields.

Command Field: This field specifies the drive/computer function to be performed. On the Version 3.0 O.S., two characters are sufficient to define the function, although at least four are recommended. The only default allowable for this field is the exclamation point (!) which specifies that the O.S. should repeat the immediately preceding command (manual retry). *Note:* Any keyboard entry at all will not allow use of this function. There is no maximum field length.

Name Field: The name field is a minimum of one non-blank character. The characters A-Z, 0-9, and all special characters are allowed. There is no maximum field length, but the O.S. will only use the *first five* characters.

Drive I.D. Field: This is a two-character field which must have a colon (:) as the first character and a number 0-3 as the second. It specifies which drive the operation is to be performed on.

Numeric Modifier Fields: These fields are always last sequential fields and are HEX numbers which normally represent memory addresses. The TEND command is an exception, in which this field specifies a tape location. In the EXEC command, three fields are used to set the machine registers.

In the O.S. command statement, several defaults are applied as follows:

A carriage return will force defaults of *all* fields which would normally follow.

A period (.) requests a default on the field which is expected at that point.

The defaults which apply will be discussed under the appropriate commands. In general: A name field will default to the last name specified to the O.S. and the drive I.D. field will default to the last specified drive.

There is no command field default other than the retry (!).

Command Form(s)	Function
LOAD fname : d addr LOAD fname :d LOAD fname LOAD . :d LOAD	This specifies that the requested file be loaded at the memory address specified. If the address is omitted, the file will load in the memory locations from which it was dumped.
LDGO fname :d LDGO . :d LDGO	This specifies that the requested file should be loaded and control transferred to the first byte.

SAVEQ fname :d aaaa bbbb SAVE fname :d . bbbb SAVE . :d aaaa SAVE . :d SAVE fname SAVE	This specifies that the memory locations from aaaa (HEX) to bbbb (HEX) are to be saved under the name specified. The Q will suppress the automatic directory recording function and allow for faster operation when the user becomes familiar with the system. If the address range is omitted, then the program assigns them as follows:

1. If a file has just been loaded, the default addresses are the memory locations just loaded. *Note:* This includes directory saves and loads.
2. If you have just returned from EDITR, the default addresses are that of the EDITOR source file.
3. If any assembly has just been completed, the default addresses are assigned the values where the machine code was stored.

OVERQ fname :d aaaa bbbb etc.	Analogous to the SAVE command except that, if the file name fname exists in the directory specified, an attempt will be made to overlay the file (use the same tape space). Obviously, this cannot be accomplished if the new file is considerably larger than the old file. The file may "grow" by approximately 1K bytes with the present O.S. If the file will not fit the space available, the O.S. will automatically put it at the end of the tape. If the file name does not exist, the O.S. will do a SAVE command.
REWIND :d REWIND	This is an O.S. and tape drive synchronization command. It rewinds the drive and sets the O.S. location pointer to zero. Use this command any time you have done manual operations to the drive or changed tapes without using the UNLOAD command.
UNLOAD :d UNLOAD	This command should normally be used before removing a tape from the drive. It will cause the directory to be written on tape if it has been flagged as changed.
MOUNT :d MOUNT	This command causes the directory to be read from the drive specified and flags the drive as available. This command will be executed automatically if another command needs the directory but the drive is flagged as "not mounted."

TEND :d aaaa
TEND . aaaa

This command sets the end of tape location pointer to the value aaaa. This parameter specifies where the next write operation is to begin. This command may be used to skip defective areas of tape or "reserve" large areas of tape for special functions. Beware of indiscriminate use of this command.

NEWTAPE :d
NEWTAPE

This command initializes a tape for use in the system. It erases approximately 20 seconds of tape and writes an empty directory. A rewind command *must* be issued prior to executing this command.

SHOW aaaa

This command will print the contents of the memory location aaaa (HEX) and aaaa + 1 formatted as an 8080 address or 16-bit number. Address aaaa + 1 is represented by the first two HEX digits and aaaa by the last two. This is basically a two-byte "peek."

EXEC aaaa hhll ddee bbcc
etc.

This command may be used to transfer control to the HEX address aaaa with the 8080 machine registers set as follows:
   H,L = hhll (HEX)
   D,E = ddee (HEX)
   B,C = bbcc (HEX)
This allows transfer to a machine language program from the O.S. All machine register designations are optional and will be filled with zeros or the value of the immediately preceding specified register, if unspecified:
   EXAMPLE: EXEC 3F00 12FD transfers control to 3F00 HEX with HL = DE = BC = 12FD HEX.

DIREC :d
DIREC

This requests a listing of the files on the drive specified. If there are more than 28 files, the system will pause after listing the first 28 and wait for input from the operator before continuing.

DELETE name1 :d
etc.

This will cause the file name specified to be dropped from the directory specified. If it is not in the directory, an **ERROR C** occurs. Nothing is done to the tape and the space occupied by the file is lost until a "data pack" operation is performed. Also, the new directory is not stored on the tape unless an **UNLOAD** is issued.

COPY :d1 :d2

This command allows the copying of programs and data files from drive to drive. Also, if d1 = d2, it performs a "data pack" operation in which all the dead files will be compressed out of the tape. The copy takes place from drive d1 to drive d2 and only the files listed in the "memory copy" of the directory for drive d1 are added to the tape on drive d2.

Note: Both drives should have been "mounted" prior to issuing this command.

Several uses of this command are illustrated below:

A. To copy all files from drive zero to a new tape on drive one.
   1. REWIND :0
   2. MOUNT
   3. REWIND :1
   4. NEWTAPE
   5. COPY :0 :1

B. To copy selected files from drive zero to drive one. After Step 2 above, delete the unwanted files from the directory on drive zero (*Note:* This *does not* delete them from the directory on tape), then continue with Step 3.

C. To add files to drive one, replace Step 4 by a MOUNT :1 command.

D. To compress out unused space on drive zero:
   1. REWIND :0
   2. LOAD the first file.
   3. DELETE it.
   4. SAVE it again on the tape. This puts it on the end of the tape.
   5. TEND :0 500
   6. COPY :0 :0

Important: If you do not set the TEND parameter, it will copy the files on the end of the tape. This has the useful function of backing up the data on the same tape if there is room.

Caution: Do not set the TEND parameter to anything except 500 unless you know what you are doing.

Note: Steps 2 through 4 above assure that drive-to-drive speed variations will not cause a data file overlap and loss of data. Of course, if you have a multiple-drive system, you should prefer to copy drive to drive, which also packs out the dead file space.

GLOSSARY

Account: Record of similar transactions under one heading in the ledger.

Account Balance: Difference between the sum of the debits and sum of the credits posted in an account.

Accounts Payable: Sum of the amounts owed to creditors.

Accounts Receivable: Sum of the amounts due from customers.

Accrual Basis: Method of record keeping and accounting in which all income earned and expenses incurred, prepaid or unpaid, are identified with specific periods of time.

Adjusting Entry: An entry made in the general ledger that corrects or brings an account up to date.

Array: Memory area of a specific size that holds information.

ASCII: American National Standard Code for Information Interchange. Used for information exchange between different equipments.

Asset: Any property which has monetary value.

Bad Debt: An uncollectible account receivable.

Balance Sheet: Statement of financial condition of a business at a certain date; shows assets, liabilities and capital.

BASIC: Beginners All-purpose Symbolic Instruction Code. A common computer programming language of which over 85 different versions currently exist.

Capital: Difference between the total assets and total liabilities of a business; also referred to as equity.

Cash Basis: Method of record keeping in which only cash received and cash paid out are recorded.

Chart of Accounts: List of accounts systematically arranged.

Closing Entries: Entries made at the end of a financial period to close temporary capital accounts and transfer net profit or loss to the capital or surplus account.

Closing the Ledger: Operation of closing all temporary capital accounts at the end of a financial period and transferring the net profit to capital or surplus accounts.

Collateral: Income or property used to guarantee the security of a debt.

CPU: Central Processing Unit. The brain of the computer—the part of the computer that does the work.

Deferred Expense: Expense incurred in one period but not used until a later period.

Deferred Income: Income received in one period but not earned until a later period.

Digital: For our purposes, means control by computer logic. For example, the turning on and off of a tape system, based on the function that is to take place within the computer program.

Disk System: Magnetic storage system that uses disk-shaped storage medium—similar in design to phonograph records.

Double Entry Bookkeeping: Recording each business transaction using a two-way, self-balancing entry.

Encumbered Asset: Property against which there is a lien or a claim.

Equity: Actual value of your financial interest in an asset.

Error Routine: Routine that checks to see if information is correct and, if not, elicits a response that prompts the operator to enter the correct information.

Fixed Expenses: Payments made at regular times for set amounts.

General Journal: Record of business transactions not recorded in special journals.

General Ledger: Record which summarizes all the transactions of the business.

Gross Profit: Excess of net sales over cost of goods sold.

Guarantor: Person who promises to pay someone else's debt if that person does not pay as promised.

Income: All taxable and untaxable money received for your own use.

Invoice: A document showing information on goods sold; quantity, price, description.

Journal: A book showing the first record of business transactions.

Lease: An agreement to pay for the right to use property for a set period of time.

Liability: The amount you owe others.

Liquidity: Ease of converting your assets to cash at market value.

Net Profit: Amount of money available after deducting expenses from total income.

Mass Storage: Large-capacity information storage device, such as magnetic tape, magnetic disk, paper tape.

Menu: Selection device in a computer program, used to display the different options available within the program. The menu is used to conserve memory in a computer system.

Net Worth: Sum of money left when market value of liabilities is deducted from assets.

Opening Entry: Entry made to record assets, liabilities, and capital.

Operating Expenses: Expenses incurred during the process of doing business.

Petty Cash Fund: Cash fund for minor expenses.

Physical Inventory: List of merchandise on hand.

Promissory Note: Written promise to pay money on demand or at fixed times.

RAM: Random Access Memory; memory device that holds information in the form of electrical pulses that can be changed. RAM can be written to, have information stored in it or read from it. The information can be looked at or modified.

ROM: Read Only Memory; a memory device that has a pre-written program burned electrically into it. This device can only be read from and not written into.

Secured Debt: A debt with property as collateral.

Sort: A data processing feature primary to business applications; it puts information in logical sequences. For example, it can put vendor numbers in numeric order.

Subsidiary Ledger: Supporting ledger made up of a group of similar accounts, the total of which agrees with the controlling account in the general ledger.

Tape Systems: Refers to magnetic tape systems—either 9-track high-density big-system devices or audio-quality cassette tape systems used with microcomputer-based systems.

Trial Balance: List of account balances in the general ledger. Its purpose is to prove accuracy of postings to the ledger and establish a summary of data for financial statements.

Unsecured Debt: One for which the lender does not require collateral as security to assure repayment.

Variable Expenses: Regular expenses, such as utilities, whose amounts may fluctuate.

Working Memory: Memory allocated to the user by virtue of program design; it gathers the data being put in. A major portion of processing or computing is performed in working memory.

Worksheet: Analysis sheet which collects and classifies the data used for preparing financial statements.

INDEX

DATE